W9-BIY-193

MAIN CURRENTS IN CUMULATIVE CAUSATION

Main Currents in Cumulative Causation

The Dynamics of Growth and Development

Phillip Toner

HD
75
.T66
1999

First published in Great Britain 1999 by
MACMILLAN PRESS LTD
Houndmills, Basingstoke, Hampshire RG21 6XS and London
Companies and representatives throughout the world

A catalogue record for this book is available from the British Library.

ISBN 0–333–74688–0

First published in the United States of America 1999 by
ST. MARTIN'S PRESS, INC.,
Scholarly and Reference Division,
175 Fifth Avenue, New York, N.Y. 10010

ISBN 0–312–22051–0

Library of Congress Cataloging-in-Publication Data
Toner, Phillip, 1955–
Main currents in cumulative causation : the dynamics of growth and
development / Phillip Toner.
p. cm.
Includes bibliographical references and index.
ISBN 0–312–22051–0 (cloth)
1. Economic development.   2. Statics and dynamics (Social
sciences)   3. Classical school of economics.   I. Title.
HD75.T66   1999
338.9—dc21   98–42211
                                                              CIP

This book is printed on paper suitable for recycling and made from fully managed and
sustained forest sources.

10   9   8   7   6   5   4   3   2   1
08   07   06   05   04   03   02   01   00   99

Printed and bound in Great Britain by
Antony Rowe Ltd, Chippenham, Wiltshire

Contents

List of Figures

Preface

The purpose of this book is to critically examine the logical structure of the concept of circular and cumulative causation and the evolution of this structure over time. The study demonstrates that a coherent model of growth and development has evolved over the past seventy years founded on the concept of circular and cumulative causation (CC). Further, it is argued that the proponents of this theory constitute a distinct and coherent school within the discipline of growth and development studies. This study identifies the central propositions of this theory, establishes its boundaries and critically evaluates the principal contributions of its chief proponents.

The analysis begins by placing the development of the concept of CC in the context of the cost controversy of the 1920s and 1930s, when the validity of Alfred Marshall's partial equilibrium methodology and his concept of internal and external economies and increasing returns were widely defended and contested. Allyn Young's contribution to this controversy in his famous 1928 paper was the foundation for subsequent development of CC theory. The book examines such subsequent development of the theory in the work of leading figures in this school, including Paul N. Rosenstein-Rodan, Ragnar Nurkse, Albert O. Hirschman, Gunnar Myrdal, Lauchlin Currie, and Nicholas Kaldor. Substantial reference is also made to a number of leading academics who greatly clarified the key concepts used by the leading figures or participated in debates occurring within the school. They include Tibor Scitovsky, J. Marcus Fleming, J. Meade, E.J. Mishan, Hollis Chenery, Heinz Arndt, John Sheahan, and Paul Streeten. The study concludes with a brief critical overview of important contemporary writers in this tradition, including A.P. Thirlwall, J.S.L. McCombie and John Cornwall.

The study is warranted for a number of reasons. There is virtually a complete absence in standard references on the history of economic thought, growth theory, or development economics to circular and cumulative causation or any group or school with whom the concept could be associated. The study seeks to fill this lacuna in the literature. The study also has important implications for the current revival of interest in the notion of external economies and increasing returns, especially as represented by endogenous growth theory and certain studies of economic development in Northeast Asia.

One of the key conclusions of this study is that a number of important ideas on the growth process and methods for its analysis from early contributors to the CC doctrine have been lost in the doctrine's subsequent development.

Accordingly, it is argued that the contemporary CC research programme could greatly benefit by a rehabilitation of these earlier ideas and methods.

One of the potential dangers in studies of this type is the tendency to impose an order or system on what may be considered by others to be genuinely unrelated or at least highly divergent traditions. A corollary difficulty arises in presuming an author's knowledge and particular understanding of their contemporaries or the work of earlier authors in their tradition. Some may view this latter difficulty as applying for example to my criticisms of Kaldor and his commentators for failing to adequately identify the very considerable contribution of Myrdal to the CC tradition. It is left to the reader to determine how far this study is prey to or evades these dangers.

Finally, while the authors examined here did cite one another's work to varying degrees, this study is *not* proposing that they viewed themselves or others as part of a self-conscious school of economic thought. Rather, the argument advanced here is the more modest proposal that they constitute a definite school of thought because they employed a distinct intellectual apparatus – that is, the concept of circular and cumulative causation.

Acknowledgements

This study arose out of some fifteen years' experience in industry policy with state and Federal Governments. Over that time I had the privilege of working for several years with Colin Edwards, who not only introduced me to the pleasures of Nicholas Kaldor and Hollis Chenery but demonstrated how their theory of economic growth could be successfully applied in economic policy.

Professor Rodney Jensen of Queensland University provided several papers on his notion of 'fundamental economic structure' or the systematic similarities in input–output structures with different market sizes. Professor Robert Dixon from the University of Melbourne encouraged me to seek a publisher for my work on cumulative causation. He also introduced me to the work of Dr Lauchlin Currie and his biographer Dr Roger J. Sandilands. This was a serendipitous introduction for a number of reasons. Currie's name is altogether absent in other accounts of the cumulative causation doctrine, even though he made a number of very important contributions to the doctrine's development. Dr. Sandilands, of the University of Strathclyde, encouraged me in the task of writing about the main currents in cumulative causation as well as providing a number of his articles and the final paper of the late Lauchlin Currie (prior to its publication in HOPE). My doctoral thesis supervisor, Dr Gavan Butler of the University of Sydney, was very encouraging, and his supervision prevented much conceptual murkiness that would otherwise have appeared in this book. He also kept shepherding me back to the central task of the thesis by cautioning against chasing too many conceptual rabbits down too many black holes. Dr Evan Jones of the University of Sydney provided important editorial advice (convinced as he is that the English language is but a foreign tongue to me!). Dr George Argyrous of the University of New South Wales regularly urged upon me the central role of Thorstein Veblen in the development of CC theory.

This book is dedicated to the memory of my parents and to my wonderful wife Anna and children Huw and Kate.

List of Abbreviations

BIE   Bureau of Industry Economics
CC   Circular and Cumulative Causation
HOPE   History of Political Economy
R-R   (Paul N.) Rosenstein-Rodan

Chapter 1
Introduction

1.1 SCOPE OF THE STUDY

The purpose of this book is to critically examine the logical structure of the concept of circular and cumulative causation and the evolution of this structure over time. The study demonstrates that a coherent model of growth and development has evolved over the past seventy years founded on the concept of circular and cumulative causation. Further, it is argued that the proponents of this theory constitute a distinct and coherent school within the discipline of growth and development studies. This study identifies the central propositions of this theory, establishes the boundaries of this theory, and critically evaluates the principal contributions of the theory's chief proponents.

The analysis begins by placing the development of concept of circular and cumulative causation in the context of the cost controversy of the 1920s and 1930s, when the validity of Marshall's partial equilibrium methodology and his concept of internal and external economies and increasing returns were widely defended and contested. Allyn Young's (1913, 1928, 1929[a] [b] [c]) original formulation of circular and cumulative growth theory in his famous 1928 paper was a central contribution to this controversy. In this paper he sought to present 'a clear view of the more general or elementary aspects of the phenomena of increasing returns' (Young 1928, p.527). Young's growth model remained largely ignored for fifteen years, until its re-emergence in the 1940s and 1950s in the balanced and unbalanced models of development economics. The representatives of the balanced growth model examined here are Paul N. Rosenstein-Rodan (1943, 1955, 1957, 1984), and Ragnar Nurkse (1952, 1956, 1958, 1963), and for the unbalanced growth model, Albert O. Hirschman (1958, 1984, 1987). Following publication of the works on balanced growth there was an upsurge of interest amongst the leading economists of the 1940s and 1950s in the idea of external economies and increasing returns. The level of interest, the outstanding calibre of the participants in the debates and the great intellectual clarity they brought to the subject are very similar to that which occurred throughout the 1920s. The contributors to this debate include Tibor Scitovsky (1954), J. Marcus Fleming (1955), J. Meade (1952), E.J. Mishan (1965, 1971), Hollis Chenery (1959, 1961, 1965, 1979, 1986, 1988), Heinz Arndt (1955), John Sheahan (1958, 1959), and Paul Streeten (1959, 1984, 1987). Aside from attempting to clarify inherently slippery concepts, these theorists provided an important foundation for Hirschman's (1958) critique of balanced growth and stimulus for his alternative model of unbalanced growth.

In the literature, the concept of circular and cumulative causation is most commonly associated with Gunnar Myrdal (1944, 1958, 1968, 1972, 1984). Aside from actually inventing the term 'circular causation of a cumulative process' (Myrdal 1944, 1958), Myrdal's major contribution was to argue that those market forces producing circular and cumulative growth or decline are equally applicable to both developing and advanced economies. Further, Myrdal focused on the circular and cumulative interaction between cultural, social, and economic factors in generating either vicious or virtuous circles. Most of the other writers considered here operated with purely economic categories. For Myrdal, race, class, religion, and culture directly enter into and cannot be separated from 'economic factors'.

It is arguable the theory of circular and cumulative causation (CC) reached its apotheosis in Lord Nicholas Kaldor (1934, 1935, 1957, 1962, 1966[a] [b], 1967, 1970, 1971, 1972[a] [b] [c], 1975, 1981, 1982, 1985, 1989, 1990). Kaldor, who was a student of Young's, spent the last twenty years of his life in an investigation and elaboration of Young's growth model. Among his many contributions was the attempt to statistically test this theory of endogenous productivity growth through the 'Verdoorn Law'.

The essay concludes with some critical observations on the current revival of interest in the notion of external economies and increasing returns, especially as represented by 'endogenous growth theory', and in certain studies of economic development in northeast Asia. The study also concludes with a brief critical overview of important contemporary writers in this tradition, including Lauchlin Currie (1981, 1997), Roger Sandilands (1990), John Eatwell (1982, 1987), A.P. Thirlwall (1979, 1983, 1987, 1991, 1994), John Cornwall (1977, 1991), and John McCombie (1983, 1985, 1994). Following this critical overview, which identifies several deficiencies in the methodology and research interests of contemporary theorists, a number of suggestions are made to advance the current research programme in this important field of political economy. One of the key conclusions of this study is that a number of important ideas on the growth process and methods for its analysis from early contributors to the CC doctrine have been lost in the doctrine's subsequent development. Accordingly, it is argued the contemporary CC research programme could greatly benefit from a rehabilitation of these earlier ideas and methods.

Given the constraints of this book, it was not possible, nor was it the intention, to write an exhaustive history of the concept detailing all of the participants in the development of this growth theory and firmly grounding each in the major intellectual debates of their times. The purpose of this book is to chart the evolution of the principal ideas or main currents flowing through CC thought, and not to navigate every tributary entering the current or explore the sources of these tributaries. As emphasized above, the objective is to critically examine the evolving logical structure of the theory. Whilst some of the writers in this tradition made significant contributions in several fields of economics, the focus here is solely on identifying and critically analysing their specific contributions to the development of this growth theory. These contributions involve, for example, providing a new application for an existing concept (e.g. Rosenstein-Rodan's use of Young's theory in the study of underdevelopment), or introduction of new analytical tools (e.g. Rosenstein-Rodan's notion of co-ordination failure, Hirschman's linkage concept, or Kaldor's 'Verdoorn Law'). Moreover, given these constraints the survey has been necessarily selective in its coverage of economists who contributed to the theory. It is arguable that the work of Ingmar Svennilson (1954), W. A. Lewis (1955), Raul Prebisch (1961), Luigi Pasinetti (1981), Thomas Balogh (1982), and Jane Jacobs (1984) warrant substantial coverage in any account of the CC tradition. (Reference to these writers is restricted largely to footnotes where their work illuminates the other theorists who are the main subject of this study.)

In addition, this account has been necessarily selective regarding the works of those actually included in the survey. Lord Kaldor's oeuvre, for example, extends to over twenty substantial volumes. Many of these are directly concerned with theoretical and applied studies of growth and critiques of neoclassical economies that are either germane to, or directly engage with, CC concepts. The criteria used for selection were to identify those works where the major contributions of the chosen writers were originally formulated. In most cases such as Young, Rosenstein-Rodan, Scitovsky, Hirschman, Streeten, Myrdal and Kaldor, this is reasonably self-evident. For other less well-known writers, such as Sheahan, it was based on the genuine novelty of their contribution, as well as the level of bibliographic citings by either proponents or opponents of their work.

At various points in the essay, this group of theorists is referred to as a 'school'. This denotes that in their analyses of growth in industrial societies they employed similar analytical tools and cited one another's work in their articles and books. I do not mean that any formal relation or organization existed between the writers. For instance, I am unaware of any joint writing or joint-editorship of any works. Nor did they seek to establish an institutional structure such as a foundation or journal to propagate their ideas. Nevertheless, their relations extended beyond mutual citation, as evidenced by extensive personal contacts among at least some of the authors dealt with here. Space does not permit the detailing of these, nor is it the purpose of the study to dwell on these matters, so only a few of the more important or better-known points at which their lives crossed are noted below.

Lord Kaldor was a student of Young at the LSE in the late 1920s, and in Kaldor's own assessment his growth theories from the mid-1960s are largely elaborations and extensions of Young's original ideas (Kaldor 1972[c]; Thirlwall 1991, p.35). Lauchlin Currie was a student of Young's at Harvard, and both Kaldor and Currie engaged in vigorous debate over the correct interpretation of their intellectual mentor (Sandilands 1990, pp.294–303). In the 1930s Kaldor and Rosenstein-Rodan, among others, attended seminars by Robbins and Hayek at the London School of Economics. In 1933 Kaldor read Myrdal's *Monetary Equilibrium*, 'which partially prepared [him] for the Keynesian revolution to come' (Thirlwall 1991, p.18). In 1947 Myrdal invited Kaldor to become the first Director of the Research and Planning Division in the newly created Economic Commission for Europe. In this position Kaldor employed several outstanding economists, one of whom was P.J. Verdoorn (Thirlwall 1991, p.27). Verdoorn's empirical work on increasing returns in manufacturing industry (published in 1949) was later adapted by Kaldor as key evidence in support of his famous Growth Laws. An interesting sidelight on the leading members of this school is that whilst they worked outside the theoretical mainstream of economics, they nevertheless attained senior academic positions in prestigious universities. At the time of his death in 1929, Allyn Young was Professor of Economics at the London School of Economics. Rosenstein-Rodan was Professor of Economics at MIT and Director of the Centre for International Studies. Gunnar Myrdal held a number of chairs at Stockholm University for nearly forty years (and won the Nobel Prize for Economics in 1974). Ragnar Nurkse was a Professor at Columbia University. Albert O. Hirschman was a Professor at Yale, Columbia, and Princeton. Lord Kaldor was of course, a Professor of Economics at Cambridge (though elevated to this position only in his late fifties). It is surely also relevant to an understanding of the school's distaste for equilibrium modes of thinking that each of the leading figures in the CC school had an active engagement in government economic policy formation. Rosenstein-Rodan and Hirschman were initially involved in post-World War II Reconstruction and acted as advisers over many decades to Latin American and southern European states. Myrdal and Kaldor were also advisers in developing nations as well as playing prominent roles in Social Democratic governments in their own countries.

1.2 WHY THE STUDY IS WARRANTED

1.2.1 Failure to Recognize the Principle of Circular and Cumulative Causation

There is virtually a complete absence in standard references on the history of economic thought, growth theory, or development economics, to circular and cumulative causation or any group or school with whom the concept could be associated.[1] The exception to this would be the recognition of Nicholas

Kaldor's or Gunnar Myrdal's use of the theory. It was the latter who first used the term 'circular causation of a cumulative process' and 'vicious' and 'virtuous circles' in his 1944 work on the economic and social position of black people in America. However, even here, both Kaldor and Myrdal's work is generally discussed in isolation, with no recognition of a connection between them or of their relation to a wider group of economists who employed similar analytical tools. Moreover, it is common for accounts of Kaldor in texts on growth theory and elsewhere (Jones 1981, pp.194–205; Solow 1994; Rostow 1990, pp.337–339) to selectively focus on his earlier work on the 'technical progress function' (Kaldor 1957, 1962), largely ignoring his later work. In these later 'mature' works (post-1966), Kaldor fully developed his ideas on circular causation based on the mechanism of increasing returns identified by Young, and formalized in the Verdoorn Law. It should also be noted that in these later works he became more openly dismissive of equilibrium economics.

Where linkages between CC authors are recognized, an undue emphasis is given to the work on underdevelopment. Hollis Chenery (1975) for example, classified most of these authors as 'structuralists':

> Structuralist analysis attempted to identify specific rigidities, lags, shortages, and surpluses, low elasticities of supply and demand, and other characteristics of the structure of developing countries that affect economic adjustments and the choice of development policy... Lewis, Myrdal, Prebisch, Singer, and Rosenstein-Rodan departed from the flexibility and substitutability of neoclassical economics and introduced elements of structural analysis'.
> (Meier 1984, p.20)

An important deficiency with this classification is its failure to recognize that key figures in structuralist analysis, especially Myrdal and Kaldor, regarded their analytical apparatus as equally applicable to the study of advanced capitalist development.

One of the very few secondary accounts of circular causation, Ricoy (1987) provides an excellent synthesis of the principal elements of the theory ('increasing returns', 'effective demand', 'manufacturing as the engine of growth'). It also provides a useful summary of the major policy implications of the theory, especially the rejection of comparative advantage as an explanation of trade patterns, and the tendency to growing international and regional per capita income disparities arising from virtuous and vicious circles. However, because it is a synthesis, there is no sense of the incremental development of key concepts, nor of the frequent and significant differences between theorists over fundamental matters of principle. In addition, any criticism of the concept or of particular contributors is absent in Ricoy's account. Similarly, Eatwell (1982, especially Chapter 3, 'The Principle of

Circular and Cumulative Causation') provides an excellent non-technical exposition of the doctrine, but it too presents the doctrine in its fully developed 'received' state. Eatwell presents Kaldor's model of CC as the progeny of a 'marriage' between Young's views on increasing returns and Keynes's principle of effective demand. The very significant contributions of Rosenstein-Rodan, Hirschman, and Myrdal to the paternity of the concept are discreetly ignored. Eatwell also fails to acknowledge the manifold difficulties confronting Kaldor in reconciling Young's classically inspired growth model (based for example on a barter economy) and Keynesian economics.

Modern proponents of the concept appear to have shown very little interest in the evolution or origins of the doctrine over the twentieth century. (See for example, the substantial posthumous works on Kaldor, by Thirlwall 1987, 1991; Lawson, Palma, and Sender 1989; and Nell and Semmler 1991). By focusing almost exclusively on Kaldor's work, contemporary CC theorists either have not given important ideas from earlier contributors the emphasis they deserve or have neglected some of these ideas altogether. Important ideas from earlier theorists which have received insufficient attention include, for example, Hirschman's emphasis on the study of dis-aggregated industry structure for an understanding of the development process. Hirschman's methodology for analysing these industry structures, especially the use of input–output techniques, have not been taken up by contemporary CC theorists. By contrast, Kaldor and contemporary CC theorists have concentrated on manufacturing in the aggregate. (This is despite the fact that Hirschman's concerns and methods have spawned a vast literature in the fields of development, regional, and input–output economics.)

This study seeks to address these deficiencies in the literature, firstly, by demonstrating the continuity and evolution of fundamental principles amongst the major proponents of the growth theory originally enunciated by Allyn Young. Secondly, the study identifies and evaluates the significant original contributions to the theory by Rosenstein-Rodan, Hirschman, Myrdal, and Kaldor. This study also argues strongly that contemporary CC research would greatly benefit from drawing on many of the ideas and methods of the doctrine's pioneers.

1.2.2   Recent Interest in the Notion of External Economies and 'Disequilibrium Growth'

From the mid-1980s, there has been a powerful revival of interest in the role of externalities and disequilibrium growth in economic development. Firstly, a number of detailed empirical studies of post-war East Asian economic development seek to provide an alternative to neoclassical explanations of this rapid and sustained growth.[2] Secondly, external economies are also the analytical core of 'endogenous growth theory', and the related doctrine, 'strategic trade theory'.[3] The present study has significant implications for these recent developments. These implications are explored in the conclusion to this study, though a brief account is provided below to indicate the direction the argument will follow.

Concepts such as external economies, increasing returns, learning by doing, and the interdependence of investment decisions, are central to the explanation of rapid and sustained East Asian growth in several influential studies of development, such as those of Taiwan by Wade (1990), and Japan by Johnson (1982), Johnson, Tyson and Zysman (1991) and Stein (1993). These studies identify mechanisms of growth in an industrial economy that are identical to those used by earlier CC theorists. These economic histories provide an enormously detailed accretion of empirical material about the East Asian development process and industry policy. It is argued in the Conclusion that these histories furnish no coherent theory to explain these empirical findings and that the explanatory power of these histories would be greatly enhanced if they embraced CC theory. On the other hand, these histories provide considerable empirical support for the CC account of growth and development. CC theory also has major implications for endogenous growth theory, as represented for example by the work of Paul Romer (1986, 1991, 1994). From the perspective of CC growth theory, there are a number of major deficiencies in endogenous growth theory, which arise mainly from its singular concentration on 'technological' externalities. This in turn, is the outcome of a dismissive attitude by some proponents of endogenous growth to CC growth theory and especially the latter's focus on 'pecuniary' externalities. The concentration on technological externalities and rejection of CC growth theory are due to the preoccupation of endogenous theorists with the construction of mathematically tractable equilibrium models.

1.3 CLARIFICATION OF KEY TERMS

One of the principal difficulties presented to the student of the CC growth model is that many of the key terms used by its proponents, such as 'increasing returns', 'external economies', 'technological change', and 'complementarity', are identical to those used in orthodox analysis, though their meanings and/or applications may differ substantially from orthodox usage. This is exacerbated by the fact that these proponents (with the exception of Kaldor) frequently do not explicitly differentiate their terms from orthodox analysis, so these differences must be inferred from their usage or application. Secondly, there are also very significant differences *within* the CC school in the

use of these terms. These differences arise largely from competing conceptions of the sources of increasing returns and external economies, and of the
applicability of these concepts to different stages of industrial development.
Given that the primary purpose of this study is to critically examine the logical
structure of CC thought and changes in this structure over time, it is therefore
essential that these competing conceptions be understood. Lastly, no member
of the CC school, either past or present, nor any secondary source, has
produced a comprehensive account of CC production theory which integrates
the views on increasing returns, externalities, technological change, consumption theory and the distribution of income.[4] Kaldor (1972[c]; 1985) came
closest to such a synthesis, though this synthesis reflected only his particular
contributions.

The purpose of this section is to briefly compare and contrast neoclassical
and CC usage of these key terms and briefly identify differences in the use of
these terms within the CC School.

1.3.1   Increasing Returns

1.3.1.1   *Orthodox Conception of Increasing Returns*

The concept of increasing returns has presented many difficulties for
equilibrium and neoclassical analysis.[5] Foremost amongst these is that identification of the marginal contribution of factors of production to output
becomes problematic; increasing returns may lead to oligopoly or monopoly, and with marginal costs below average costs 'prices computed from
marginal costs would not even cover the expenses of firms' (Dorfman 1964,
p.138).

Alfred Marshall's (1920) analysis of increasing returns is both subtle and
complex. In its simplest terms, increasing returns are mainly due to increased
mechanization, increased specialization of production across firms and the
division of labour within firms, as the output of an industry increases. Increasing returns are the result of internal economies flowing from growth in the
size of an individual firm, and external economies resulting from the growth
of an industry to which a firm belongs.[6] Marshall's analysis of increasing
returns was very influential in the formulation of Young's growth model and
the subsequent development of CC theory. Given that this section is
restricted to a discussion of neoclassical and CC views on key economic
terms, a more detailed analysis of Marshall's notion of increasing returns
and its relation to CC theory is provided in Section 2.1.

Within the neoclassical system, increasing returns are generally examined
via the concept of scale economies, which in turn is derived from the theory
of costs. Scale economies are present 'where unit costs of production decline
as the size of a plant is increased' (Pratten 1971, p.7). Specifically,

scale economies are present where an equi-proportional increase in factor inputs results in a more than proportional increase in output (Devine, Jones, Lee, and Tyson 1976, p.95).[7] Strictly defined within the neoclassical system, or 'the received theory of costs', scale economies apply solely to plants (Devine *et al*. 1976, p.95). A plant is defined as the 'buildings or area in which productive activity is carried on, and it includes as well as most items of capital equipment, some of the labour inputs involved in managerial, supervisory, and maintenance tasks' (Asimakopulos 1978, p.159). A firm is an independent legal entity, which may comprise a single or several plants, producing one commodity or many different commodities (Asimakopulos 1978, p.237). Devine *et al*. are critical of the failure to distinguish between scale economies applying to plants and economies to scale of the *firm*:

> [T]he distinction between classical economies of scale and economies of the firm is not always drawn, even though many of the assumptions of the latter negate the assumptions upon which the traditional concept is based, eg. that large firms may exert downward pressure on factor prices'.
>
> (Devine *et al*. 1976, p.95)

Examples of economies of the firm include economies of bulk purchasing or selling, advantages of vertical and horizontal integration, risk reduction through diversification of investment and markets, or cost benefits of multi-product operation (Devine *et al*. 1976, pp.95–96). The latter has been the subject of much interest in recent years, and is commonly referred to as economies of scope (BIE, 1988).[8]

The shape of the plant envelope average cost curve is governed by the effects of scale economies (or diseconomies).[9] Neoclassical analysis assumes the plant envelope average cost curve is U-shaped. Scale economies result in declining marginal costs as output increases, but at some point diseconomies of scale set in, increasing marginal cost. It is assumed diseconomies set in at a sufficiently low level of a plant's output to prevent the growth of oligopoly or monopoly. Neoclassical analysis of scale economies is also 'static', as it is assumed 'that the state of technical knowledge is given, and that factor prices are given' (Devine *et al*. 1976, p.95). Technology and prices are given, to permit the identification of scale effects proper, as opposed to productivity gains arising from technological change, or increases in a firm's output arising from reduced input costs (Asimakopulos 1976, p.210). Static analysis also entails the notion of 'reversibility'; a reduction in output results in a movement back along the LRAC curve to another equilibrium position. (This contrasts with dynamic scale economies, whereby some of the productivity gains achieved at higher levels of output are permanently retained even if output falls.)

In the literature the sources of plant scale economies, strictly defined, include:

(i) *indivisibilities* – 'factors of production, in the world as we know it, consist of indivisible units.... If all the factors of production were finely divisible, like sand, it would be possible to produce the smallest output of any commodity with all the advantages of large scale industry. But... [factors and 'instruments of production'] for technical reasons, cannot be divided without limit. It is therefore impossible for an industry to equip itself to produce one unit of a commodity without immediately providing capacity to produce more than one unit' (Robinson 1933, p.334).[10] In other words, there are technical and economic limits to the minimum scale and/or output of plants. Pratten's (1971) examples of indivisibilities include capital goods, management personnel, calls by salesmen on customers, identifying sources of supply, perusal and drafting of contracts, and research and development;

(ii) *specialization* – the division of labour as emphasized by Adam Smith – provides productivity gains from employment of more specialized skills and equipment. Increasing a plant's output allows for the exploitation of these benefits;[11]

(iii) *economies of increased dimensions* – physical laws determine that the volume of solids increases proportionately greater than the surface area. In continuous process technologies such as oil refining employing tanks and pipelines, a doubling of volumetric capacity can be achieved at a 60 per cent increase in cost;[12]

(iv) *economies of massed resources* – the law of large numbers results in scale economies, when, for example, a plant operating several identical machines need stock proportionately fewer spare parts than a firm operating fewer machines;

(v) *superior techniques* – increased output may permit the introduction of more efficient techniques, such as the replacement of batch production with automated flow techniques. In other words, increasing the scale of a plant may facilitate the adoption of the most efficient production technique (Pratten 1971, pp.7–14).

It is clear that some of these sources of increasing returns may violate the assumption of fixed factor proportions.[13] Neoclassical scale economies are generally ascribed to increased specialization; the existence of indivisibilities; economies of increased dimensions and economies of massed resources (Devine *et al.*, p.96).

The strength of the neoclassical conception of increasing returns lies in its rigorous statement of the conditions necessary to identify such returns, although in the opinion of some industry economists this is also its primary weakness.[14]

1.3.1.2 *Increasing Returns in Circular and Cumulative Causation*

Having outlined the neoclassical view of increasing returns, a brief account of increasing returns in CC theory is provided which highlights the differences with neoclassical analysis.

Following the classical distinction between industry and agriculture, most CC theorists regard increasing returns as restricted largely to manufacturing industry. This is based on the claims that the scope for the division of labour increases in capital – labour ratio, and technological change is virtually unlimited in manufacturing. In addition, key factors of production in manufacturing are not fixed, but are themselves produced means of production. CC theory violates a number of key assumptions in the neoclassical conception of scale economies. Firstly, factor and input costs are not constant. For example, scale economies within the CC framework can result from firms' reducing factor costs through volume buying. More generally, increasing returns within the economy are assumed to result in lower input costs, especially intermediate and capital goods, since these are produced means of production subject to increasing returns. Reductions in costs and prices act to reinforce the further exploitation of increasing returns. Producers are assumed to respond to a reduction in costs by increasing output, and manufactures have a high price elasticity of demand, so that a reduction in price results in a more than proportionate increase in demand. Increases in supply, reductions in costs, and increases in demand mutually reinforce one another in a circular process of increasing output, increasing productivity and rising consumption.

Secondly, the key role of reduced factor costs in the CC account of increasing returns also highlights the fact that writers in this tradition generally make no clear distinction between plant and firm scale economies. Plant-level scale economies are certainly important in CC growth theory, with particular emphasis given to overcoming indivisibilities in the employment of capital and economies of specialization within a given industrial operation. Equally, some CC theorists emphasize economies to scale of the firm. Rosenstein-Rodan, for example, placed considerable emphasis on economies to scale of the firm, especially horizontal integration. He likened the benefits flowing from the co-ordination of investments by the state to those which arise from integrated investment planning within some 'giant firm or Trust' (Rosenstein-Rodan 1943, p.250).

Thirdly, in contrast to neoclassical theory, technological change is an integral and inseparable part of changes in factor proportions. CC theory recognizes that productivity growth arising from an increase in the capital–labour ratio is in many instances linked to technological change, in that the former is a primary transmission mechanism for the latter. Further, there is assumed to be a strong positive correlation between the rate of economic growth and the rate of technological change. Technological change is thus largely endogenous to the economic system. (This is examined in more detail in Chapter 2.)

In addition to static scale economies, a number of 'dynamic' economies are also central. Dynamic economies occur when 'unit costs decrease with the cumulative total volume of production' (Jacquemin and de Jong 1977, p.31). In contrast to static scale economies, the benefits of dynamic economies are not 'reversible', in that a reduction in output does not result in a loss of productivity gains achieved at a higher level of output. Within CC growth theory, dynamic economies are associated primarily with 'learning by doing'.[15] There is considerable ambiguity in the economics literature over the term 'learning by doing'. In the first usage, it refers to the fact that experience with a production process is often necessary to produce an optimal output, that is, on-the-job experience is required to reach the production possibility frontier. (This is one of the traditional arguments used to defend 'infant industry' protection.) The classic example of this type of learning by doing is the empirical observation that 'the labour-hours expended in the production of an airframe... is a decreasing function of the total number of airframes of the same type previously produced' (Arrow 1962, p.156). In the second usage, cumulative experience with a production process leads to technological change, that is, experience pushes the production possibility frontier outward (Vassilakis 1987[a], p.151). The second meaning is the one most commonly employed by CC theorists.[16] Kaldor (1972[c]) in particular ascribed to learning by doing a key role in the explanation of technological change and growth of per capita income.[17]

1.3.1.3   *Differences in the Treatment of Increasing Returns Within CC Theory*

There are, however, important differences within the CC school regarding several key aspects of increasing returns. Firstly, what are the *sources* of increasing returns – are they derived primarily at the firm, industry or inter-industry level? To what industries do they *extend*? Are industries other than manufacturing subject to increasing returns? And what are the *conditions* for the initiation and/or continuation of a virtuous circle of growth? This last point encompasses a number of questions, such as: is the CC understanding of growth in a developed mature industrial economy applic-able to an underdeveloped region, and to what extent is the growth process unbounded or does it generate contradictions or impediments to continued growth?

As regards the sources of increasing returns, Young held there are definite limits on the capacity of individual firms to exploit the benefits of increasing returns, broadly defined. The scope for increasing returns within the firm is constrained, though the reasons for this are largely unspecified. Following Marshall, this assumption is required to make the notion of internal economies of the firm compatible with competitive conditions. Increasing returns occur through growth in output of individual firms, though Young argues the more important effect is the entry of new firms commonly engaged in the manufacture of new specialized inputs utilizing new and more specialized equipment and skills. For this reason, Young's focus is on external economies (the generation of productivity gains at an inter-industry and economy-wide level), rather than internal economies. In contrast to Young, later theorists, including Rosenstein-Rodan, Nurkse, and Hirschman, focused largely on internal (plant and firm) economies. Within 'small' underdeveloped markets these scale economies result in an oligopolistic industry structure. However, like Young, they also argued that the scope for these plant and firm scale economies is constrained, so that within a 'large' industrial economy competitive conditions are maintained. The scope for scale economies within a given plant is largely the same in developed or underdeveloped economies. This follows from the premise that the

> plant capacity most economical to build and operate is not very different in different countries; but, as a percentage of an industry's total capacity, it is very much greater in underdeveloped than in fully industrialised economies. In under-developed countries, therefore, investment is likely to have a greater impact on prices, give rise to greater pecuniary external economies and thus cause a greater divergence between private profit and social benefit. (Scitovsky 1954, p.306)

The assumption that the optimal 'size' of a given investment project is 'independent of the level of development' is, of course, highly contentious (Bohm 1967, p.69). The work of Pratten, for example, would indicate that plant scale economies are highly elastic, so that the 'optimal size' plant for many commodities increases with the growth in total output of that commodity. Both Myrdal and Kaldor advocated a very broad view of the sources of increasing returns, including plant, firm, dynamic and external sources in their analysis. In addition, Kaldor regarded the scope for scale economies within the firm to be very large indeed. Consequently, for Kaldor, the typical industrial structure in an advanced economy is oligopolistic.

Finally, within the CC school there is a major divide or bifurcation over the conditions for growth, and in particular whether the interdependent process of expansion in demand and increasing returns is largely self-generating and self-governing or whether it is highly unstable and even capable of generating counter-forces to continued growth. Allyn Young and, to a lesser extent,

Lauchlin Currie focused on the self-perpetuating properties of the CC growth model. Others, such as Rosenstein-Rodan and Hirschman, emphasized the very great impediments to the initiation of the growth process in under-developed regions. Nicholas Kaldor highlighted the instability in the growth path and the potentially contradictory forces arising from growth (such as spiralling regional and international income inequality and the existence of long-term balance of payments disequilibria).

1.3.2   External Economies

The notion of external economies is also central to the CC account of increasing returns and growth. The notion of external and internal economies were, of course, introduced into economic literature by Alfred Marshall. Marshall described the benefits accruing to a particular firm from the growth of its industry as an external economy. These economies arise, for example, from reduced input costs resulting from increased specialization among suppliers of inputs within the industry. Marshall regarded external economies as entirely compatible with competitive conditions and the attainment of equilibrium (Arndt 1955, p.211). For Young as well, external economies are compatible with the efficient operation of a competitive market economy, and certainly do not constitute as they do for later CC theorists a fundamental reason for state intervention in market processes. (A detailed account of Marshall and Young's use of external economies is provided in Chapter 2.) As explained below, for later CC theorists, studying either underdeveloped regions or mature industrial economies, external economies are an important aspect of the divergence of private and social costs and benefits arising under imperfect market conditions.

Since Marshall and Young the term externality has come to have a variety of meanings in different economic theories such as general equilibrium and later CC growth theory.[18] The concept has, to use Heinz Arndt's (1955) metaphor, played several different parts in several different dramatic productions over its working life. Consequently, the 'concept of external economies is one of the most elusive in economic literature' (Scitovsky 1954, p.295). Probably, the most lucid account of external economies has been provided by Tibor Scitovsky (1954) and we rely substantially on this in the following. There is another compelling reason for relying heavily on Scitovsky's account: it was written directly in response to the work of Rosen-stein-Rodan and Nurkse, who Scitovsky believed employed the notion of external economies in a genuinely novel and – from a neoclassical point of view – paradoxical way.

Scitovsky begins his famous article by noting the general agreement that the notion of an external economy 'means services (and disservices) rendered free (without compensation) by one producer to another'. In other words, 'external economies are a cause for divergence between private profit and social benefit'. However, there is 'no agreement on the nature and form of these services or on the reasons for their being free' (Scitovsky 1954, p.295). The absence of agreement on the cause and effect of external economies is attributed to the fact that there are two entirely different usages of the term: one in 'equilibrium theory', the other in 'the theory of industrialization in under-developed countries' (Scitovsky 1954, p.295).

1.3.2.1 Technological Externalities

Within equilibrium theory, 'technological' externalities occur when there is 'direct interdependence among members of the economy'. This arises when the 'output of the individual producer may depend... on the activities of other firms.' These economies are not transmitted through the market mechanism via the exchange of goods and services, but 'are a peculiarity of the production function.' This definition of direct interdependence among producers, and the examples used by Scitovsky, are taken from Meade (1952). These include the free pollination service provided by bee keepers to apple orchardists, and economies of agglomeration arising from the concentration of firms in a locality, leading to the creation of skilled labour markets that may benefit other firms and industries (Scitovsky 1954, pp.298–99).[19] Using Meade's (1952) notation, technological externalities exist when the output (x_1) of a firm depends not just on the factors of production (l_1, c_1) used by the firm, but also on the output (x_2) and/or factor utilization (l_2, c_2) of another firm or industry. This is given in the production function, $x_1 = F(l_1, c_1; x_2, l_2, c_2)$ (Scitovsky 1954, p.298).

1.3.2.2 Pecuniary Externalities

The second type of externality, pecuniary externality, arises from 'interdependence through the market mechanism', although it also entails direct interdependence. According to Scitovsky such market interdependence is 'all-pervading' (Scitovsky 1954, p.300). Pecuniary externalities are given by the function, $P_1 = G(x_1, l_1, c_1; x_2, l_2, c_2)$, where the profits of a firm P_1 depend on its own output and factor utilization, and on the output and factor utilization of other firms or industries (Scitovsky 1954, p.300).[20] Where these benefits accrue to firms as profits, Scitovsky notes that Marshall would have regarded them (together with benefits accruing to persons), as producer and consumer surpluses respectively (Scitovsky 1954, p.301).

By contrast, in the 'theory of industrialization in underdeveloped countries' these pecuniary external economies 'should be explicitly taken into account when investment decisions are made; and it is usually suggested that this should be done by taking as the maximand not profits alone but the sum of profits yielded and the pecuniary external economies created by the investment' (Scitovsky 1954, p.301). Scitovsky notes the paradox whereby market interdependence may create a discrepancy between private and public benefits whereas, in equilibrium theory, the market is meant to optimize and equalize private profitability and the socially desirable allocation of resources. For Scitovsky the origins of this discrepancy are to be found in 'limitations of general equilibrium theory [which] render it inapplicable to the problems of investment' (Scitovsky 1954, p.301). In particular, this limitation is especially evident 'in the theory of industrialization of underdeveloped countries... in connection with the special problem of allocating savings among alternative investment opportunities' (Scitovsky 1954, p.299).[21] Hollis Chenery explained that in a competitive equilibrium, firstly, the effects of an entrepreneur's action on others' are known to all economic agents, given the assumption of perfect knowledge and foresight; and secondly, these effects are adequately signalled in relative prices.

> The maintenance of competitive equilibrium over time requires that pres-
> ent prices must accurately reflect future as well as present demand and
> supply conditions and that investors should react in such a way that their
> price expectations are continuously realized. These are very strong condi-
> tions. Under these assumptions, the pecuniary or market effects of one
> investment on the profitability calculations of other investors are part of the
> mechanism by which the market co-ordinates action among investors and
> eliminates the differences between private and social profitability of the
> initial investment. When the continuous adjustments needed to maintain
> competitive equilibrium are not assumed to take place, these market effects
> have a quite different significance.   (Chenery 1959, p.175)

1.3.2.3   *The Sources of Pecuniary Externalities*

The special features of investment which undermine general equilibrium conditions and create pecuniary external economies are twofold. Firstly, indivisibilities in the employment of capital goods: indivisibilities introduce a discontinuity into a production function so that either more or less output will be produced than that which will equate marginal costs and price. One of the possible range of capital – labour ratios will yield for the producer 'a higher profit than all others; but this need no longer be the one that is also the best from society's point of view. Hence the need... to take society's point of view explicitly into account' (Scitovsky 1954, p.302). Whilst Scitovsky is correct in noting that Rosenstein-Rodan and Nurkse emphasized indivisibilities in production as a difficulty for general equilibrium, later CC theorists such as Myrdal and Kaldor gave equal prominence to other sources of increasing returns, such as learning by doing and economies of the firm in their critique

of equilibrium reasoning. Secondly, 'general equilibrium theory... is static... whereas the allocation of investment funds is not static at all' (Scitovsky 1954, p.303). In particular, investment projects occur in real historical time, with such projects changing future demand and supply conditions. However, market prices only 'reflect the economic situation as it is and not as it will be' (Scitovsky, 1954, p.305). It is necessary, therefore, to have an additional signalling system for the transmission of information and the co-ordination of 'information about present plans and future conditions as they are determined by present plans' (Scitovsky, 1954, p.306). As noted earlier, Rosenstein-Rodan, Nurkse and Hirschman regarded the problem of market imperfections as applicable mainly to underdeveloped economies. The small size of these economies not only gives rise to market failure (due to their inability to overcome indivisibilities) but these economies also suffer from inadequately developed product and factor markets. For example, 'institutional and cultural' practices create 'obstacles' to factor mobility (Chenery 1959, p.178). Consequently, these authors stressed the need in underdeveloped economies for a signalling system in addition to the price mechanism to co-ordinate investment and consumption activity. These writers assumed that such market imperfections were either absent or comparatively minor in fully developed economies. These conditions significantly reduce the need for an 'additional signalling system' in advanced economies.

The combination of imperfect information about future market conditions, indivisibilities and the existence of adjustment lags in the volume and industry composition of investment gives rise to disequilibria and pecuniary externalities. These economies arise, for example, when industry (or firm) A invests in new plant which cheapens its supplies to industry (or firm) B, which in turn increases its demand for A's output. In this situation, equilibrium 'is reached only when successive doses of investment and expansion in the two industries have led to the simultaneous elimination of profits in both'. At this stage, investment in A is 'clearly greater than that which is profitable at the first stage, before industry B has made adjustment... We conclude, therefore, that only if expansion in the two industries were integrated and planned together would the profitability of investment in each one of them be a reliable index of its social desirability' (Scitovsky 1954, p.304). Other circumstances in which pecuniary economies may arise are when the output of industry (or firm) A expands, and

(i) the output of industry B is complementary to A;
(ii) the output of industry C is a substitute for inputs into the production of A;
(iii) the output of B is used in the production of A;
(iv) the demand for industry D is increased due to a rise in income following increased output of A (Scitovsky 1954, p.305).

1.3.2.4   Vertical and Horizontal Externalities

As well as Scitovsky, Hollis Chenery made important contributions to clarifying CC theorists' use of the term 'pecuniary externality'. Chenery notes that CC theorists used the term to describe two different types of market interdependence (though usually they did not make the distinction explicit). The first is 'market interdependence in production' or economies arising from productivity improvements in the supply of capital or intermediate goods used in production (Chenery 1959, p.178n). For example, an investment in electricity generation which results in lower price or improved quality to users represents a pecuniary externality. This type of externality is also known as a vertical externality.[22] The second is 'interdependence through increased consumer incomes', which describes a benefit accorded one industry or firm through increased sales to consumers, resulting from an expansion in activity of another firm or industry (Chenery 1959, p.178n). This is also known as an horizontal externality.

This distinction between interdependence through production and/or consumption is central within CC thought. Allyn Young combined both vertical and horizontal externalities in his growth model (though he did not use these terms explicitly). Increasing returns in capital or intermediate goods sectors lead to reduced input costs for purchasers – which, given certain assumptions, leads to an expansion in output and investment in both producer inputs and consumption sectors. Rosenstein-Rodan and Nurkse concentrated exclusively on horizontal pecuniary externalities, especially the benefits arising from a simultaneous expansion of plants within the consumer goods sector. Investment and increased output across several plants will increase real incomes and provide mutual support for this expansion. Hirschman, Myrdal and Kaldor emphasized both vertical and horizontal pecuniary externalities.

1.3.3   Complementarities in Production and Consumption

Complementarity is included in Scitovsky's list above as only one of several potential sources of externality. However, it has a central place in CC thought, and the various roles it plays in CC production and consumption theory highlight once again the radically different conception of economic processes compared to the neoclassical view.

Complementarities, like increasing returns and externalities, fit uncomfortably within the neoclassical system. Producer and consumer optimization with given resources requires ready substitution between factors and consumption goods respectively. The assumption of ready substitution is essential for convexity conditions and determinate mathematically tractable solutions to 'the economic problem'. It is for this reason that neoclassical economists have been attracted to 'the fair face of substitutability' and repulsed by 'the ugly mug of complementarity' (Newman 1987, p.545).[23] In neoclassical production theory '[m]any of the variable inputs are complements within the given plant in any particular short period; that is, an increase in the rate of output generally requires an increase in the rates of input of other variable inputs' (Asimakopulos 1978, p.163). In the longrun, however, all factor proportions are assumed to be variable and substitutable.

Within CC theory complementarity in production and consumption is far more pervasive and significant than the neoclassical principle of substitution. Three aspects of complementarity are examined here. Firstly, CC assumes fixed-factor coefficients in production. CC production theory emphasizes the indivisibility of factors, which leads CC theory to generally assume complementarity between factors. 'If a production element is indivisible, it combines with the other elements through a relationship of complementarity rather than of substitutability; that is to say, a fixed-coefficient type of production prevails. On the other hand, flexible coefficients need total divisibility' (Morroni 1992, p.28).

Secondly, CC theory rejects the notion of diminishing returns to a factor, especially capital, and generally regards increments to a capital stock as complementary to this stock. For Young and his followers, diminishing returns to a factor do not apply, since additional capital investments are complementary (and not, as assumed by the neoclassicals, competitive) and lead to an increase in productivity. In his excellent study of the development of external economies in growth theory, Heinz Arndt (1955) gave particular attention to this aspect of complementarity. Arndt highlighted the view of Young that capital investments may be complementary because new technology embodied in new capital and intermediate goods improves the productivity of these new goods and may also improve the productivity of existing capital goods and other factors.[24] This contrasts with the neoclassical view that 'each additional unit of capital, by definition, competes with the existing stock, and the marginal productivity of capital necessarily declines as the stock of capital grows' (Arndt 1955, p.201). In addition, aside from technological change, Young argued that growth in the size of the market gives rise to the production of new commodities and increasingly specialized inputs of capital and intermediate goods. These new commodities and more specialized inputs are a crucial aspect of the division of labour or increasing returns. These more heterogeneous or specialized inputs were presumed to improve the efficiency of the production system into which they enter. This effect captures the better utilization of existing technologies. Rosenstein-Rodan also emphasized those classes of investment goods, especially infrastructure, which must be supplied jointly. For example, electricity generation, transport, communications, etc., must be supplied collectively or in an indivisible bloc for their individual economic benefits to be realized.[25] Hirschman refers to these diverse processes as the 'complementarity effect of investment... i.e. that the investments of one period are often the principal motivating forces behind some additional investments of subsequent periods' (Hirschman 1958, p.44).

Finally, in neoclassical consumption theory, goods are complements if 'the satisfaction derived from the consumption of one depends entirely on the concurrent availability of the other in some proper proportion' (Asimakopulos 1978, p.111). Pairs of complementary goods have a negative cross-price elasticity of demand. Complementarity in consumption in CC theory is entirely different from this conception. The focus is on the causes and consequences of the growth of real per capita output and not on the optimal allocation of a given income. Neither consumer preferences nor the variety of goods are assumed to be fixed, but constantly adjust to changes in total output, real prices and per capita income. A key element in the CC account of complementarity in consumption is the effect of growth in per capita income leading to demand for a greater variety of commodities.[26] Young's notion of complementarity in production and consumption is central to CC growth theory.[27] Young's growth model is firmly grounded in the tradition of classical economics, and he accepted (though with some modifications) Say's Law of Markets.

> [M]aking abstraction of the use of money as a medium of exchange, the supply of any one commodity is an expression of the demand of its producers for other commodities and services... There is a sense in which supply and demand, seen in the aggregate, are merely aspects of a single situation.
> (Young 1929[a], p.580)

Young employed the notion of 'reciprocal demand' to capture these effects. Reciprocal demand is an expression of strong complementarity in the demand for the products of diverse industries. '[E]nlarging of the market for any one commodity, produced under conditions of increasing returns, generally has the net effect... of enlarging the market for other commodities' (Young 1928, p.537).

1.4   THE ROLE OF INCREASING RETURNS AND EXTERNALITIES IN CC THEORY

From the above it is clear that increasing returns, externalities and complementarities in production and consumption are central to CC growth theory. The theorists examined in this essay have differing conceptions of the *sources* of increasing returns, the industries to which increasing returns *extend* and the *types* of externality. There are also differences in the significance attributed to increasing returns and externalities in the growth process at different stages of industrial development. This last point encompasses differences in the *conditions* identified for the commencement and/or continuation of a virtuous circle of growth. The following represents a very brief summation of the manner in which increasing returns, externalities and complementarities interact in the growth process.

Increasing returns in manufacturing are pervasive and result from a number of sources. Growth of total output allows, for example, increased specialization of production across firms and industries, increase in the capital–labour ratio and introduction of more specialized capital equipment. Growth in total output is associated with improved productivity through learning by doing (and learning by using), and the more ready adoption of technological change (especially where this change is embodied in new capital goods). A number of economies of agglomeration are also important, such as ready supply of skilled labour, ready communication of trade and technical know-how, and advantages of nearness to markets, be they intermediate suppliers or final demand. Productivity gains through increasing returns are cumulative. Manufactures are assumed to have a high price and income elasticity of demand, so that a reduction in real price resulting from increasing returns is assumed to result in a more than proportionate increase in demand. This expansion in output and consumption ('widening of the market') in turn gives rise to additional increasing returns. 'Any increase in real income represents a widening of the market for goods and services in general, which yields increasing returns in the form of further increases in productivity and real income, which further widens the market, and so on' (Arndt 1955, p.204). These successive rounds of increasing returns, real price reductions, demand and output expansion, investment, and increasing returns, act not to equilibrate supply and demand but to perpetuate disequilibria. Growth, says Albert O. Hirschman, should be viewed 'as a chain of disequilibria... that nightmare of equilibrium economics, the endlessly spinning cobweb, is the kind of mechanism we must assiduously look for as an invaluable aid in the development process' (Hirschman 1958, pp.65–66).

1.5   OVERVIEW OF THE STUDY

Chapter 2 introduces Allyn Young's growth theory as a response to Marshall's conception of increasing returns and external economies in the context of the 'cost controversy'. The cost controversy engaged the leading economists in the 1920s and 1930s in a debate over fundamental principles of economic theory and method, and the results of this debate were to have a profound effect on the course of economic theory over the twentieth century. For Allyn Young, economic progress or increase in real per capita income in a market economy is the result of productivity growth which, in turn, is primarily a consequence of increasing returns. Increasing returns are due to growth in the market (increase in total output), which allows for increases in the division of labour. For Young, division of labour takes its most important forms in the expansion of 'roundabout methods of production' and specialization of production within firms and across industries. Roundabout production methods have a number of characteristics, but chief among them are an increase in the capital–labour ratio and increased use of more specialized or dedicated capital equipment. Growth in total output allows for the overcoming of indivisibilities in the employment of capital equipment, utilization of more specialized or dedicated equipment, and increased specialization of production across firms and industries.

Growth in the size of the market (total output) is due primarily to increases in productivity, which reduces the real price of goods and services. Growth in the market is a function of increasing returns (elastic supply) and elastic demand for manufactures or goods produced under conditions of diminishing cost. This interdependence is expressed in Young's famous aphorism: 'the division of labour depends on the size of the market, but the size of the market depends on the division of labour' (Young 1928, p.539). Young argues that the division of labour (increasing returns) is a process that occurs primarily at an industry and inter-industry level. Consequently, Young regards these benefits as external economies. As with Marshall, external economies serve the purpose of explaining endogenous productivity growth whilst allowing for a competitive industry structure. In Young's system a competitive industry structure is essential to ensure that real price reductions flowing from increasing returns are passed onto producers and consumers. The passing on of these price reductions is essential to growth in demand for manufactures, as Young assumes manufactures are subject to high price and income elasticities of demand.

The principal criticism of Young's analysis is that it presents an unnecessarily restricted view of the sources of increasing returns. For example, Young ignores the scope for economies arising from vertical integration, and regards the scope for scale economies within an individual firm as limited. In other words, Young stresses the realization of increasing returns through what he terms 'industrial differentiation' as opposed to 'industrial concentration'. Young's restricted view of the sources of increasing returns and the limited scope for economies within a given firm arises from the requirement (as with Marshall before him) to make increasing returns compatible with competitive conditions. The other major criticism is of Young's failure to consider the issue of effective demand in his growth model.

Chapter 3 examines the use of Young's theory in the balanced growth model of development economics. Allyn Young derived his growth model from analysis of a mature industrial economy in which resources were fully employed, markets were competitive, and the supply of capital and factors were elastic. By contrast, Paul N. Rosenstein-Rodan and Ragnar Nurkse are principally concerned to construct a model of development in an underdeveloped economy with a small total output and poorly functioning factor and product markets. A consequence of these market failures is that the coordination function of the market, upon which Marshall and Young relied, must be performed by the state. Balanced Growth envisages significant state intervention to exploit increasing returns and external economies as the means to accelerate growth in aggregate output and per capita income. To sharply distinguish the CC theory from growth models of the Swan-Solow type, Rosenstein-Rodan aptly described the former approach as a 'disequilibrium growth model' (R-R 1984, p.207).

Balanced growth accepts Young's contention that the overcoming of indivisibilities in the employment of capital is a function of the size of the market, and increases in the size of the market are largely determined by productivity gains (increasing per capita output). Rosenstein-Rodan and Nurkse thus set themselves the task of devising a solution to the joint problems of inadequate demand and investment in an underdeveloped region. In both the balanced and unbalanced models of development, external economies are used as the fundamental criteria for the volume, industry composition and timing of investment. For underdeveloped economies with limited capital, factor and product markets and poor information flows, it is argued that external economies are particularly important in their development. In the balanced growth model, if an economy is caught in a vicious circle of low investment and demand a growth path may be created by simultaneously establishing several large-scale efficient wage goods plants, where the demand for output of these plants is linked or complementary. This notion of complementary demand is analogous to Young's model of 'reciprocal demand' whereby an increase in the output of one commodity is effectively an increase in the demand for another commodity. The complementarity exploited by the balanced growth model is that arising from the structure of demand for basic wage goods such as processed food, clothes, transport, housing, etc. In a developing economy these wage goods would absorb almost all of the income of workers in the newly established wage goods industries. The structure of demand, relatively low real incomes and state import restrictions prevent a leakage of workers' income into other industries or imports.

The balanced growth model of development is dependent upon the significant externalities it generates. The principal pecuniary externality is the increase in effective demand for wage goods created by the incomes of workers in the new wage goods industries. A single-large scale investment by an individual capitalist in an underdeveloped region would fail owing to insufficient demand for its output; but the planned creation of several complementary industries generates the income and demand that will validate these investments. Rosenstein-Rodan also introduced a number of important applied economic tools to assist the planning and implementation of his development model. One of the key differences between Young's model and that of balanced growth is that the former emphasized productivity growth through external economies at an inter-industry level, whereas balanced growth focused on productivity growth through scale economies at a plant or firm level. Further, Young focused on the vertical and horizontal transmission of externalities, whereas Rosenstein-Rodan concentrated exclusively on the horizontal transmission. In other words, Rosenstein-Rodan emphasized only the benefits to producers and consumers arising from an expansion of consumer demand or lowering of real consumer prices, respectively. Young emphasized this benefit, as well as the vertical transmission of externalities arising mainly from a reduction in input costs to users of intermediate and capital goods as a result of productivity gains in these sectors.

In the period following publication of Rosenstein-Rodan's work there was renewed interest in the concept of external economies. Chapter 3 also briefly considers the critiques of balanced growth by Fleming (1955), Streeten (1959), and Sheahan (1958, 1959), which are an important background to the unbalanced growth model. Although Streeten, Sheahan and Hirschman supported many of the general principles advanced by Young and Rosenstein-Rodan to explain industrial growth, they objected to the specific programme for economic development propounded by Balanced Growth.

Chapter 4 considers the principal work of A.O. Hirschman, *The Strategy of Economic Development*, published in 1958. Hirschman is sharply critical of the balanced growth doctrine and focused on three shortcomings. The principal criticisms are that underdeveloped economies lack the managerial expertise to implement the type of large-scale simultaneous expansion envisaged by Rosenstein-Rodan. Secondly, the balanced growth model exhausts the quantum of externalities rather than generating a sequence of inducements to invest. Hirschman claimed, incorrectly as we shall argue, that the balanced growth model proposed a form of equilibrium, a simultaneous increase in inter-industry production which, once achieved, would fail to provide incentive for further expansion. Thirdly, Balanced Growth utilized limited externalities drawn only from the production and consumption of wage goods and largely ignored those greater benefits derived from the vertical transmission of externalities which arise from expansion of the capital and intermediate goods sectors.

In contrast to Rosenstein-Rodan's approach to development, Hirschman's theory of unbalanced growth is based on the planning of sequential investments in which the output of external economies from each investment 'induces' or 'compels' subsequent investments. Moreover, the output of external economies from each sequence of investments is designed to be greater than the input of external economies that went into the investment.

One of Hirschman's major contributions was the attempt to employ input–output techniques to describe the relation between growth in the size of the market and the progressive division of labour. Input–output was also used to quantify the magnitude and inter-industry flow of externalities. Using input–output technical coefficients of production (and derived multipliers), industries having the largest backward and forward 'linkages' can be identified, permitting the selection and sequencing of an optimum pattern of investment. Hirschman uses these input–output concepts as empirical analogues for the broader idea of externalities. Various forms of state assistance may be provided to promote such investments in a broad strategy of import-substitution.

Hirschman defines underdevelopment as the general absence of economic 'interdependence'. He simply means there are limited input-output relations, that is, comparatively few of the domestic production cells in the national transactions table have entries. Supply is mostly met by imports of manufactures and production consists principally of agricultural and/or mineral commodities. The focus of Unbalanced Growth is the promotion of manufacturing, especially intermediate and capital goods industries, in contrast to balanced growth which only emphasized wage goods. It is concluded that Hirschman's intention of sharply distinguishing balanced and unbalanced growth models is not well founded, and that the core analytical tools of both models are substantially the same. The models are substantially elaborations on the concept of circular and cumulative causation as developed by Allyn Young.

Chapter 5 considers Gunnar Myrdal who developed the concept of CC as the general methodology of the social sciences. It was Myrdal who first used the term 'circular causation of a cumulative process', and in the history of economic thought he is the one (other than Kaldor) most identified with the concept. Interestingly, Myrdal did not advance any new mechanism of increasing returns or externality to account for cumulative growth or decline, nor did he develop or apply new analytical tools (such as input–output) to examine the growth process. Nevertheless, he made a number of vital contributions. Firstly, in his methodological work especially, he made the vital contribution of clearly stating the logic or abstract principles of the CC model. The exposition of this methodology is the primary focus of this chapter. Myrdal also clearly stated the strong opposition of CC theory to neoclassical equilibrium. Secondly, Myrdal regarded the principle of CC as applicable to both underdeveloped and developed regions. In contrast, R-R and Hirschman maintained that external economies are much less important in the growth process of developed regions. Thirdly, Myrdal emphasized the effect of trade, capital flows and migration between rich and poor regions as an active cause of underdevelopment. Again in contrast, both R-R and Hirschman regarded the cause of underdevelopment as largely endogenous to poor regions. Myrdal highlights the 'development of underdevelopment', through free trade for example, which may constrain the size of the market in poor regions by inhibiting the expansion of domestic manufacturing. The final innovation was to give equal prominence to economic and non-economic factors (that is, to social, cultural and political influences) in the explanation of growth and decline.

The first three of Myrdal's innovations were to have a profound effect on Nicholas Kaldor's treatment of the CC doctrine (although the magnitude of the debt to Myrdal is not acknowledged in the secondary literature, nor unfortunately, by Kaldor himself). Chapter 6 considers Lord Kaldor, through whom the CC doctrine is generally regarded as having reached its apotheosis. Kaldor made several major contributions to the development of CC theory. These included the adoption of a very broad conception of the sources of increasing returns encompassing internal and external economies, plant scale economies, economies of the firm, and dynamic scale economies. Kaldor did not place *a priori* limits (unlike Young, R-R and Hirschman) on the growth of internal economies and consequently regarded oligopoly as the typical industrial structure of advanced economies. Kaldor also developed novel theories of the role of markets and price formation in concentrated markets. In addition, Kaldor enunciated a number of important methodological objections to general equilibrium theory. The role and significance of foreign trade in development was also extensively investigated and formalized in the 'balance of payments constraint to growth'. Kaldor was also the first to formulate the CC understanding of increasing returns so as to be subject to empirical examination. Kaldor's 'growth laws' are a simple yet robust empirical formulation of the causes and effects of increasing returns. Following their original formulation, these Laws have been subjected to comprehensive theoretical and empirical study. Although Kaldor accepted Young's view that demand creates its own supply, he rejected the classical presumption that supply creates its own demand. Kaldor combined the classical insights of Young, regarding the sources of endogenous productivity growth in an industrial economy with the Keynesian principle of effective demand. Finally, Kaldor is the only CC theorist to seriously ponder the question as to whether there are constraints to growth within the economic system. It is arguable the models of earlier CC theorists predicted growth without bounds. The ultimate constraint to growth in Kaldor's two sector-two stage model is the rate of productivity growth in the supply of raw materials from land-based activities (agriculture and mining) which are subject to diminishing returns.

A number of criticisms of Kaldor's contribution are advanced and explored. Firstly, he did not adequately develop 'the marriage of the Smith-Young doctrine on increasing returns with the Keynesian doctrine of effective demand' (Kaldor 1972[c], pp.1245–6). For example, Kaldor does not have a model of income distribution within concentrated markets, even though a specific distribution of productivity gains is central to ongoing growth in the system. Secondly, there are several difficulties with Kaldor's argument that increasing returns are restricted largely to manufacturing industry. A wider or 'global' view of the sources of increasing returns requires a significant revision of Kaldor's view of the growth process. Finally, it is argued that Kaldor's two sector-two stage model is not consistent with some important long-run 'stylized facts', and does not allow for the diversity of historical patterns of industrialization. Further, the two sector-two stage model may be inconsistent with certain fundamental principles of the CC model of development.

One of the important conclusions of this study that a number of important ideas from early contributors to the CC doctrine on the growth process and methods for its analysis have been lost in the doctrine's subsequent development. Accordingly, it is argued, the contemporary CC research programme could greatly benefit by a rehabilitation of these earlier ideas and methods. The essay also concludes with some critical observations on the current revival of interest in the notion of external economies and increasing returns, especially as represented by 'endogenous growth theory' and certain studies of economic development in Northeast Asia.

Chapter 2
Allyn Young (1876–1929): Increasing Returns and Economic Progress

> To say merely that the inducement to invest depends on the extent of the market... is not very revealing, indeed it is almost tautologous. Only by adding that the extent of the market also depends on the inducement to invest is the process of cumulative growth illuminated.
>
> (Streeten 1959, p.168)

2.1 INTRODUCTION

The doctrine of circular and cumulative causation received its initial exposition in Professor Allyn Young's famous 1928 article in the *Economic Journal*. Young died in March 1929, victim of an influenza pandemic, just three months after publication. The 1928 article was intended as prolegomena to a fuller investigation of his disequilibrium growth model (Newman 1987, p.937). Surprisingly, later writers in the CC tradition and the secondary literature generally have not provided a detailed account of Young's growth model nor an exhaustive critical appraisal.[1] Because Young's model is the foundation for subsequent CC theory, it is essential that this model be clearly articulated. Accordingly, this chapter provides an analytical account of Young's dis-equilibrium growth model and exposition of its principal shortcomings. Young's CC model was a product of the cost controversy of the 1920s. Young incurred considerable intellectual debt to Alfred Marshall and his commentators, especially John Clapham and Pierro Sraffa. Young's model broke new ground, focusing on the mechanisms of increasing returns and the way in which increasing returns and growth in total output are mutually reinforcing. The chapter also highlights the principal differences between Young's model of growth and development and that advanced by later writers in the CC tradition, as well as the differences with neoclassical growth theory.

2.2 CUMULATIVE CAUSATION IN CONTEXT

The origins of the theory of circular and cumulative causation are complex and diffuse, but are to be found mainly in the classical tradition of political economy, notably Adam Smith, Jean-Baptiste Say, Charles Babbage, John Stuart Mill and Karl Marx. CC theory for example, focuses on production, emphasizes the unique feature of manufacturing in being subject to increasing returns, regards technological change as largely endogenous, identifies capital accumulation as the key element in growth and the never-ending search for new markets as the driving force in capitalist economies. Other sources may include writers such as Friedrich List, whose dynamic analysis of trade and protection predates by nearly a century many of the ideas developed in the CC tradition (Haddad 1989). The impact of the methodology of the American Institutionalists on circular and cumulative causation, especially Thorstein Veblen (with whom Allyn Young worked at Stanford), has also been identified (Kapp 1976; Argyrous and Sethi 1996). A detailed investigation of these influences is outside the scope of this essay.

The immediate context for the development of CC theory was the so-called 'cost controversy' during the 1920s and early 1930s, which involved the leading economists of the period in a debate over fundamental principles of economic theory and methodology. The outcome of these debates proved to be critical to the subsequent course of economic theory and economic policy over the twentieth century. The debates centred largely on Professor Alfred Marshall's theories of increasing returns, the 'representative firm' and partial equilibrium methodology. Professor Allyn Young's 1928 article was only one of many contributions to the debate which sought to defend or contest Marshall's principles. In the literature on the controversy, Young's article and its relation to other contributors to the controversy is frequently ignored or given a minor role.[2] It is therefore instructive to briefly and selectively examine those aspects of Marshall's economics and the subsequent debates that were especially influential in the development of Young's theory.

2.2.1 Marshall's Theory of Increasing Returns

The central role Marshall gave to increasing returns in the growth of per capita income and his explanation of the sources of these returns had a profound effect on Young's model of growth in a mature industrial economy. Especially influential was Marshall's strong endorsement of Adam Smith's account of increasing returns, most notably, the role of mechanisation and the division of labour within the firm and its industry. The precise manner in which increasing returns operate within the firm as internal economies, and within the firm's wider industrial environment as external economies, is absolutely central to the CC model.

Marshall regarded increasing returns as one of the chief sources of economic progress. Increasing returns arise where 'an increase of labour and capital leads generally to improved organization, which increases the efficiency of the work of labour and capital' (Marshall 1920, p.265).[3] Increasing returns apply especially to manufacturing since there is far greater scope for the division of labour and mechanisation compared to agriculture and mining. The latter are generally subject to diminishing returns (p.127). Increasing returns or 'economies arising from an increase in the scale of production' fall 'into two classes, those dependent on the general development of the industry, and those dependent on the resources of the individual houses of business engaged in it and the efficiency of their management; that is, into *external* and *internal* economies' (p.262). The principal sources of internal economies or 'advantages of production on a large scale . . . . [within] a large establishment' are economies of 'materials', 'machinery', 'skill' and 'buying and selling' (pp.232–233).

Economies of 'materials' arise when a large establishment generates sufficient waste (such as offcuts), or by-products from its own production to make economic use of these materials in the manufacture of new commodities or other aspects of the production process. Marshall regarded such economies as relatively unimportant, due more to 'inventions' which make the use of waste and by-products economical, rather than economies arising strictly from an 'increase in labour and capital' (p.232).

Economies of machinery arise primarily from indivisibilities in the use of specialized equipment. 'For in a large establishment there are often many expensive machines each made specially for one small use' (p.234). The large output of such establishments in comparison with smaller establishments makes it economical to introduce more expensive and/or more specialized equipment. The large size of an establishment also makes it more economical to devote resources to keeping up to date with the latest innovations from capital goods producers and distributors. It also makes it possible to 'experiment' with production processes and equipment, and even to manufacture their own machinery (p.234). Marshall explains that economies of machinery are integral to the division of labour. There are two aspects to Marshall's argument. Firstly, with the 'ever-increasing minuteness of the subdivision of labour' production tasks have 'been reduced to routine'. When 'any manufacturing operation . . . can be reduced to uniformity' such tasks will 'be taken over by machinery' (pp.211–212). 'Thus machinery constantly supplants and renders unnecessary that purely manual skill, the attainment of which was, even up to Adam Smith's time, the chief advantage of the division of labour' (pp.212–213). Secondly, the division of labour and more intensive use of specialized equipment is positively related to growth in the size of the market.

Thus the two movements of the improvement of machinery and the growing subdivision of labour have gone together and are in some measure connected. But the connection is not so close as is generally supposed. It is the largeness of markets, the increased demand for great numbers of things of the same kind that, and in some cases of things made with great accuracy, that leads to subdivision of labour; the chief effect of the improvement of machinery is to cheapen and make more accurate the work which would anyhow have been subdivided.   (p.212)

Economies of skill are those most commonly identified with Smith's advantages of the division of labour. Marshall argues these advantages are more readily realized within larger firms. The larger a factory the more readily it may 'contrive to keep each of its employees constantly engaged in the most difficult work of which he is capable, and yet so to narrow the range of his work that he can attain the facility and excellence which come from long-continued practice' (p.236). Important economies of skill also apply to management (pp.236–237).

Larger firms also benefit from economies of buying and selling. 'A large business buys in great quantity and therefore cheaply; it pays low freights and on carriage in many ways... It often sells in large quantities and thus saves itself trouble... It can spend large sums on advertising by commercial travellers and in other ways' (p.235).

In a style of reasoning typical of Marshall, for every 'tendency' to concentration resulting from internal economies, there is a 'counter-tendency' identified with external economies promoting the continued growth of smaller firms. 'Many of those economies in the use of specialized skill and machinery which are commonly regarded as within the reach of very large establishments, do not depend on the size of individual factories' (p.220). Marshall identified many different sources of external economy.[4] Some of the principal sources include the growth of 'Trade-knowledge: newspapers, and trade and technical publications of all kinds are perpetually scouting for him [the small producer] and bringing him much of the knowledge he wants' (p.237). There is also the growth of 'correlated branches of industry which mutually support one another' (p.264). For example, crucial inputs to production such as transport and communications 'are accessible to any branch of production [and] do not depend exclusively upon its own growth'. In addition, 'economies of localization' or concentration of production within a region make it possible to realise the benefits of the division of labour without the growth of large establishments.

[T]he economic use of machinery can sometimes be attained in a very high degree in a district in which there is a large aggregate production of the same kind, even though no individual capital employed in the trade be very large. For subsidiary industries devoting themselves each to one small branch of the process of production... are able to keep in constant use machinery of the most highly specialised character, and to make it pay its expenses, though its original cost may have been high, and its rate of depreciation very rapid.   (p.225)

Advantages of increased specialization of labour within large firms can also be realized by economies of localization through increased specialization of labour across firms. The ultimate effect of these external economies, Marshall asserts, is that 'in short there remains no very great difference between the economies available by a large and by a very large firm; and the tendency of large firms to drive out small ones has already gone so far as to exhaust most of the strength of those forces by which it was originally promoted' (p.239).

In addition to a variety of external economies promoting the continued growth of smaller firms, Marshall identified a number of impediments to the continued growth of large firms. The chief impediment is that 'the continued very rapid growth of [a large] firm requires the presence of two conditions which are seldom combined in the same industry' (p.238). Even where a firm might have scope for considerable internal economies, Marshall asserts it is most unlikely the firm could find a market for its output, since 'many commodities with regard to which the tendency to increasing return acts strongly are, more or less, specialities... In all such cases the sales of each business is limited' (p.239). Another factor preventing continued exploitation of internal economies is the mortality of the entrepreneur (p.238). Like trees in a forest, he argued by metaphor, even the largest forest giants lose their vigour and are replaced by smaller saplings. This principle applies even to 'vast joint-stock companies, which often stagnate, but do not readily die' (pp.262–263). Marshall concludes that the scope for internal and external economies respectively is that 'an increase in the aggregate volume of production of anything will *generally* increase the size, and therefore the internal economies possessed by... a representative firm;... [but] it will *always* increase the external economies to which the firm has access' (p.265, my italics).[5]

Although Marshall gave considerable emphasis to increasing returns in explaining the growth of per capita output and made important advances in their study, the analysis was necessarily restricted by the partial and static equilibrium framework he proposed for the general study of economic phenomena. The primary purpose of the *Principles* was the 'investigation of the equilibrium of normal demand and normal supply in their most general form' (p.284). Necessary for the study of equilibrium is the assumption of '*Caeteris Paribus*'. This method entails

> the breaking up of a complex question, studying one bit at a time, and at last combining [the] partial solutions into a more or less complete solution of the whole riddle... breaking [up the problem]... segregates those disturbing causes, whose wanderings happen to be inconvenient, for the time in a pound of *caeteris paribus*. The study of some group of tendencies is isolated by the assumption *other things being equal*: the existence of other tendencies is not denied, but their disturbing effect is neglected for a time.
> (p.304)

This method is both partial and static. It is partial in the sense that the object of study is the individual firm or industry to which it belongs. It is static in the sense that in studying equilibrium conditions, it is 'assumed that the general circumstances of the market remain unchanged... that there is, for instance, no change in fashion or taste, no new substitute which might affect the demand, no new invention to disturb supply' (p.285). In other words, it is necessary to assume a given demand curve and given supply curves, and that the forces governing one do not affect the other. Marshall was emphatic that these assumptions, though essential to the scientific study of economics, were unrealistic. The world is neither partial nor static but dynamic: change occurs in real historical time, not logical time, and the forces governing demand and supply could not be confined to the 'pound of *caeteris paribus*'. Of the assumptions necessary for the study of equilibrium, Marshall claimed

> nothing of this is true in the world in which we live. Here every economic force is constantly changing its action, under the influence of other forces which are acting around it. Here changes in the volume of production, in its methods, and in its cost are ever mutually modifying one another; they are always affecting and being affected by the character and extent of demand. Further all these mutual influences take time to work themselves out, and, as a rule, no two influences move at equal pace. (p.306)

In particular, 'the uses of the Statical method in problems relating to very long periods are dangerous... [and these] difficulties and risks reach their highest point in connection with industries which conform to the law of Increasing Return' (p.315n). In the famous Appendix H to the *Principles*, Marshall detailed some of these difficulties. Chief among them are multiple and unstable equilibria, and irreversibilities in production functions.[6]

There are thus a series of tensions in Marshall's work: in particular, the conflicts between the conditions essential for competitive equilibrium, including the partial and static method necessary for its analysis, and the existence of increasing returns and the methods appropriate for its analysis. Allyn Young's 1928 paper can be seen as an attempt to resolve these tensions, essentially by abandoning Marshall's partial and static methodology and his focus on equilibrium. Instead, Young emphasized the study of growth and dynamic transformation of the economy caused by increasing returns and external economies, though also maintaining a key role for competition in his model.

2.2.2 The Cost Controversy and Allyn Young

The wide-ranging debate on the methodology and subject matter of economics in the cost controversy of the 1920s and 1930s traversed the compatibility of increasing returns and competition, the relevance of static and ceteris paribus methods to the study of growth and dynamics, and the extent and sources of increasing returns. The scope of this section is limited to a brief and selective examination of those aspects of the cost controversy that (it may be argued) were especially influential in the development of Young's theory of circular and cumulative causation. From this perspective, the most important contributors were the economic historian J. H. Clapham and Pierro Sraffa.

In his classic article, Clapham (1922[a]) made use of wit and irony to make a number of insightful and devastating observations on 'the Great Analytics' – Marshall and Pigou's partial equilibrium methodology and treatment of increasing returns. Clapham is critical of Marshall's conceptual apparatus for being a collection of 'empty economic boxes' or *a priori* and deductive categories devoid of empirical content.[7] Given the problem of heterogeneous inputs and outputs, how, asks the economic historian, is one to construct units of inputs and outputs to determine whether a firm or industry is subject to increasing or diminishing returns?[8] How is one to conceive of an 'industry'? Is it local, regional, national, or international? (Clapham 1922[a] 305–306). The concept of an 'industry' is central to Marshall's analysis of scale economies, but he uses the term ambiguously. At 'many times Marshall conveys the impression of confining external economies in the straightjacket of a single-product, homogeneous industry' (Becattini 1987, p.890). At other times some sources of increasing returns, such as the growth of scientific and trade-knowledge, are described as being dependent 'on the aggregate volume of production in the whole civilized world' (Marshall 1920, p.220). A similar argument holds for the external economies derived from the growth of infrastructure such as transport and communications. Expansion of this infrastructure and its external economies depends on 'an increase in the aggregate scale of production' (Marshall 1920, p.264). Marshall also emphasizes advantages arising not only from the growth of a particular industry, but also the growth of 'subsidiary industries' which provide inputs to the industry under study (Marshall 1920, p.233). For example, it is implied that increasing returns realized in capital goods industries and passed on in the form of cheaper inputs to another industry are to be regarded as an example of scale economies applying to an 'industry'.

Clapham argues that difficulties in constructing unambiguous indexes of inputs and outputs, as well as ambiguities in the definition of an 'industry' make it difficult, and possibly impossible, to identify whether a particular industry or firm is subject to scale (dis)-economies or to determine the sources of such (dis)-economies. In addition, Clapham is critical of the statical requirement to exclude technological change as a source of increasing returns. It is practically difficult if not impossible, to separate these two elements in the analysis of economic progress. Its exclusion reflects the *a priori* imperatives of equilibrium analysis (Clapham 1922[a], p.310).[9]

Clapham concluded that his critique was not to be regarded as a 'denial of the reality of increasing returns, only a denial of their measurability' in the very precise manner Marshall and Pigou had required for their partial equilibrium analysis. He suggested that if 'we widen the conception... so as to cover all inventions' and consider only the very long run, it is possible to 'arrive at certain tolerable historical results' regarding the sources and extent of increasing returns (Clapham 1922[a], p.314).

Whereas Clapham's objections were largely to Marshall's *a priori* and deductive methodology and the empirical vacuum of key categories, Sraffa's focus is primarily on the very restrictive assumptions in Marshall's system and the logical difficulties for it if certain key assumptions are relaxed or altered. Sraffa rejected the premise, essential for Marshall's partial equilibrium analysis, that the demand and supply conditions of a particular industry could be examined in isolation from the effects of these conditions upon other industries (Sraffa 1926, p.538). If an industry consumes even only a small quantity of a factor of production, it is necessary to reject the *ceteris paribus* assumption essential for partial equilibrium analysis. Such analyses are appropriate only for those rare instances where an industry consumes all of a particular factor, so that variations in the industry's use of this factor do not affect the supply schedule of other industries. In other words,

> when a variation in the quantity produced by the industry under consideration sets up a force which acts directly, not merely on its own costs, but also upon the costs of other industries; in such a case the conditions of the 'particular equilibrium' which it was intended to isolate are upset, and it is no longer possible, without contradiction, to neglect collateral effects.
>
> (Sraffa 1926, p.539)

Secondly, Sraffa also highlighted Marshall's ambiguity regarding the sources of external economies. Were they derived solely from the expansion of an 'industry', or were they the product of general industrial expansion? Sraffa claimed they were largely of the latter type, and consequently there is the 'impossibility of confining within statical conditions the circumstances from which they originate' (Sraffa 1926, p.541).

Finally, Sraffa rejected Marshall's compromise on increasing returns. To maintain competitive conditions Marshall conceived of increasing returns as being internal to the industry but external to the firm. Whilst Marshall allowed for internal economies resulting from improved organization within the firm, etc., these economies which may otherwise have led to the dominance of a few firms in an industry were undercut by Marshall's claim that the life expectancy of an individual firm was limited. With the device of external economies, Marshall was able to account for significant endogenous productivity growth whilst maintaining a competitive industry structure.

The beauty of external increasing returns was that it preserved much of the apparatus of economic theory (e.g., supply and demand curves that summarize the actions of price taking agents) while at the same time departing from the convexity assumptions that seemed inimical to a complete understanding of growth.   (Romer 1991, p.87)[10]

Sraffa argued that these types of increasing returns, internal to an industry but external to a firm, were precisely those most seldom encountered (Sraffa 1926, p.540). A more realistic view of increasing returns is where such returns are largely generated internally within the firm and their advantages primarily realized within the firm. Such an outcome is incompatible with competitive conditions. The appropriate mode of analysis for the firm producing under such conditions is monopoly theory, which is focused on the individual firm with a downward sloping demand curve (Sraffa 1926, p.540). Given these several difficulties in realising *ceteris paribus* conditions, Sraffa concluded that competitive equilibrium was unattainable in the presence of increasing returns.

Having outlined selected aspects of Marshall's system and his critics, we now consider how these provided a crucial influence on Allyn Young's contribution to the cost-controversy. Young's intellectual debt to Marshall was enormous. Marshall reiterated Smith's view on the central role of the division of labour in the explanation of the growth of per capita output. Young accepted Marshall's view that the division of labour takes its most important forms in increased use of more capital-intensive production methods (increased mechanization), the use of more specialized equipment and the specialization of production within the firm and across industries, and that this process is governed primarily by growth in the size of the market. Young also accepted Marshall's down-playing of Smith's emphasis on the refinement of 'manual skill' produced by the repetition and narrowing of production tasks. These aspects of the division of labour are a central element in Young's growth model. The crucial additional element which Young contributed was that the division of labour, by reducing the cost and price of commodities, acts to continually expand the 'size of the market'.[11] Young also accepted Marshall's very broad conception of the sources of increasing returns. Young allowed for non-equiproportional increases of inputs and permitted flexible input prices. This contrasts with the neoclassical analysis of increasing returns, which requires equi-proportional factor changes and fixed input costs. However, in contrast to Marshall, Young did not exclude technological change from the analysis of increasing returns.

The introduction by Marshall to the economics literature of 'external economies' in the explanation of increasing returns was wholeheartedly embraced by Young, and indeed by all subsequent CC theorists. However, there is one critical difference in the CC use of the concept. Whereas

Marshall viewed external economies as primarily arising within a particular industry, Young, like Clapham and Sraffa, viewed external economies as operating at an inter-industry and economy-wide level. 'What is required is that industrial operations be viewed as an interrelated whole' (Young 1928, p.539). Young's innovation was 'to widen the concept to include all cost reductions accruing to firms (or industries) from the expansion of output of goods or services in general' (Arndt 1955, p.195). Moreover, once this wider perspective is adopted, Young contends, like Clapham before him, that the possibility of practically isolating the various sources of increasing returns becomes exceedingly difficult. 'With the extension of the division of labour among industries, the representative firm, like the industry of which it is a part, loses its identity. Its internal economies dissolve into the internal and external economies of the more highly specialized undertakings which are its successors' (Young 1928, 538).

However, Young also accepted Marshall's view (and explicitly rejected Sraffa's) that internal and external economies were not generally associated with increased concentration of economic activity in fewer firms.[12] The typical pattern of industrial development was 'industrial differentiation' or increased specialization, whereby a growing market makes increased division of labour across firms and industries profitable (Young 1928, p.537). Young is notably vague as to exactly what are the limits to continued growth of an individual firm, as he did not explicitly embrace Marshall's biological analogy or identify any internal diseconomies. Nevertheless, the basic assumption that increasing returns did not lead to the continuing concentration of production in fewer and fewer firms in advanced industrial economies was accepted by Rosenstein-Rodan, Nurkse and Hirschman. Only Myrdal and Kaldor argued that the scope for internal economies was very elastic, and that increasing returns led generally to an oligopolistic industry structure in mature economies.

Like Clapham and Sraffa, Young rejects statical assumptions and the notion of competitive equilibrium. The factors governing supply and demand are not independent of each other. Changes in one industry cannot be partitioned from changes elsewhere; consumer preferences and technological change 'mutually modify' each other and are themselves altered with increases in output and per capita income. Central to Young's world view is dynamic change. '[T]he counter-forces which are continuously defeating the forces which make for economic equilibrium are more pervasive and more deeply rooted in the constitution of the modern economic system than we commonly realize' (Young 1928, p.533). However, whilst rejecting notions of stable equilibrium, Young retained an essential role for competition. Competition is necessary to ensure the passing on of productivity gains via real price reductions arising from increasing returns, with such reductions being essential to continued growth in the system.

These debates over internal and external economies and increasing returns eventually produced three schools of thought: the theory of imperfect competition in Robinson (1933) and Chamberlin (1933), Sraffa's own classical model of reproduction and growth in *Production of Commodities by Means of Commodities* (1960), and Young's dis-equilibrium growth model which focused on the dynamic and cumulative effects of external economies and increasing returns. An analytical account of Young's dis-equilibrium model is provided in the following section.

2.3   INCREASING RETURNS AND ECONOMIC PROGRESS

The purpose of Allyn Young's famous 1928 paper is to present 'a clear view of the more general or elementary aspects of the phenomena of increasing returns'. He defines increasing returns as the process whereby 'industries... can increase their output without increasing their costs proportionately' (Young 1928, p.527). Young begins his analysis by considering

> Alfred Marshall's fruitful distinction between the internal productive economies which a particular firm is able to secure as the growth of the market permits it to enlarge the scale of its operations and the economies external to the individual firm which show themselves only in changes of the organization of the industry as a whole.   (Young, 1928, p.527)

Young is critical of Marshall's 'view of the nature of the process of industrial progress which is implied in the distinction between internal and external economies.' Such a distinction leads to a 'necessarily... partial view' of the process of productivity growth or economic progress (Young 1928, p.528). Specifically, 'not all of the economies which are properly to be called external can be accounted for by adding up the internal economies of all the separate firms' (Young 1928, p.528). Rather, the source of increasing returns is in the interdependence of economic relations between industries. A change in the technology or organization of production within a firm or industry is simultaneously a cause and effect of changes in the wider economy. Young's level of analysis is primarily at the inter-industry and even economy-wide.

Young claimed this broad or 'inclusive view' of economic processes was a feature of classical economic reasoning.[13] The inclusive view of the classical economists led them to contrast increasing returns in manufacturing against diminishing returns in agriculture (Young 1928, p.528).[14] Increasing returns in manufacturing, according to Adam Smith, are primarily due to the division of labour, which in turn depends upon the extent of the market. (Indeed, Chapter 3 of the *Wealth of Nations* is actually entitled 'That the Division of Labour is Limited by the Extent of the Market'.) Young states that this 'theorem, I have always thought, is one of the most illuminating and fruitful generalizations which can be found anywhere in the whole literature of economics' (Young 1928, p.529). However, to Smith's theorem Young adds an important caveat: 'we mean by the division of labour something much broader in scope than that splitting-up of occupations and development of specialized crafts which Adam Smith mostly had in mind' (Young 1928, p.529). Young regarded this as a particularly limited vision of the mechanism of increasing returns, and in fact argued that Smith 'missed the main point' (Young 1928, p.530). Young does not expand on his differences with Smith, but he seems to consider that Smith did not adequately emphazise the growth of mechanisation (increase in the capital–labour ratio) associated with the division of labour.

Young's critical assessment of Smith is not justified, since he has failed to acknowledge the breadth of Smith's sources of increasing returns. For example, Smith regarded increases in the capital–labour ratio and increased specialization of capital equipment essential elements in the division of labour (Vassilakis 1987[b], pp.761–765).[15]

2.4 THE MECHANISMS OF INCREASING RETURNS

For Young, the division of labour, broadly conceived, generates increasing returns through the growth of roundabout or 'capitalistic' methods of production and the specialization of production within and across industries. These two mechanisms are interdependent (Young 1928, p.529).

2.4.1 Roundabout Production Methods

Young considered 'the principal economies which manifest themselves in increasing returns are the economies of capitalistic or roundabout methods of production' (Young 1928, p.531). Roundabout production methods involve the division of complex production processes and tasks into more specialized and simpler processes. A central feature of this division of labour is the more intensive utilization of capital equipment. Moreover, these increasingly specialized tasks are undertaken with increasingly specialized capital equipment, which is designed to perform only a limited range of functions (Young 1928, p.530). Interestingly, Young does not provide any reason why an increase in the capital–labour ratio generally, and the increased use of specialised equipment in particular, should improve productivity.[16] He simply accepts it as self-evident. This may be due to the fact that the concept of roundabout production methods was used extensively in classical political economy, and at the turn of the century by leading economists such as Wicksell and Bohm-Bawerk. They advanced the proposition that more roundabout methods of production, yield more output per unit input, but require more time because the capital goods they use have to be produced, too. This proposition in turn has been associated with the idea that the roundabout methods of production depend on the division of labour as well as on the fact that production takes time... The gist of their argument is that more roundabout methods of production are both more capital intensive and more productive.

(Hennings 1987, p.224)

The 'economies of roundabout methods even more than the economies of other forms of the division of labour, depend upon the extent of the market' (Young 1928, p.531). By the term size or extent of the market, Young means 'buying power, the capacity to absorb a large annual output of goods' (Young 1928, p.533). Because roundabout methods are related positively to the size of the market, Young explains this 'is why we discuss them under the head of increasing returns' (Young 1928, p.531). The relation between roundabout production methods and the extent of the market is explained by the example of mass production methods in the automobile industry.

It would be wasteful to furnish a factory with elaborate equipment of specially constructed jigs, gauges, lathes, drills, presses, and conveyors to build a hundred automobiles; it would be better to rely mostly upon tools and machines of standard types... Mr Ford's methods would be absurdly uneconomical if his output were very small, and would be unprofitable even if his output were what many other manufacturers of automobiles would call large.   (Young 1928, p.530)

In other words, factor utilization and factor proportions in production are not a function of relative factor prices; the size of the market determines the most efficient factor proportions in production. One assessment of Young's model is that 'the chief analytical innovation in (1928)... was to make the degree of roundaboutness depend primarily not on the rate of interest but on the scale of production, taken in a broad sense' (Newman 1987, p.939).[17]

2.4.2 Specialization of Production Across Industries

Young's 'particular thesis with respect to the way in which increasing returns are reflected in changes in the organization of industrial activities' is that increasing returns do not give rise to 'industrial integration' or concentration of production in fewer firms, but to 'industrial differentiation'. Industrial differentiation 'has been and remains the type of change characteristically associated with the growth of production' (Young 1928, p.537). Young rejects Sraffa's (1926) claim that increasing returns must necessarily lead to a concentration of production over time in fewer and larger firms. Whereas Sraffa's focus is on the firm and its capacity to generate and exploit increasing returns, Young's focus is on the generation of increasing returns at an industry and inter-industry level. These returns are associated principally with *'large'* production, not *'large scale'* production or the concentration of output in fewer firms or industries (Young 1928, p.531). '[W]e assume, as we must, in most industries there are effective, though elastic, limits to the economical size of the individual firm. The output of the individual firm is generally a relatively small proportion of the aggregate output of an industry.' (Young 1928, p.539). The reason for this industrial differentiation and increased capital intensity of production is primarily the existence of indivisibilities. The employment of a more efficient specialized technique of production and specialized capital equipment requires a level of demand or output greater than that which can be had by an individual firm engaged in a broad range of industrial activities. For many firms the

> degree in which it can secure economies by making its own operations more roundabout is limited. But certain roundabout methods are fairly sure to become feasible and economical when their advantages can be spread over the output of the whole industry. These potential economies, then, are segregated and achieved by the operations of specialized undertakings which, taken together, constitute a new industry. (Young 1928, p.539)

The processes that lead to an increased capital – labour ratio within the firm also lead to the creation of more specialized firms. Increases in the size of the market

> increase vertical disintegration and production roundaboutness for the same reason: it pays to exploit economies of scale more fully now, both by sharing fixed costs with other buyers instead of bearing them unilaterally, and by reducing variable cost through increases in fixed cost. In this sense, market size determines the degree of division of labour.
>
> (Vassilakis 1987[b], p.762)

Industrial differentiation takes a particular form, such that 'over a large part of the field of industry an increasingly intricate nexus of specialized undertakings has inserted itself between the producer of raw materials and the consumer of the final product' (Young 1928, p.537). In other words, the division of labour across industries occurs especially in the intermediate and capital goods sectors. Compared with the increased 'complexity... of goods offered in consumers' markets, the increase in the diversification of intermediate products and of industries manufacturing special products or groups of products has gone even further' (Young 1928, p.537). Young provides a detailed account of this process of industrial differentiation in the printing industry. He describes the growth of specialized firms supplying inks, type metal, paper, printing machines, as well as suppliers of machine tools for the manufacture of printing machines, inks and paper (Young 1928, pp.537–38). Young's familiarity with the printing industry and production processes generally arises from his work as a printer before embarking on an academic career (Newman 1987, p.937; Blitch 1995). Young's insistence that increasing returns are associated only or primarily with industrial differentiation is critically assessed in section 2.9. There are several other ancillary economies flowing from industrial differentiation. These include a higher degree of specialization in management and advantages from improved geographical location such as nearness to transport, source of supply, or final markets. The benefits of improved geographical location appear to result from the fact that a more specialized firm need make fewer compromises about its location compared to a firm engaged in diverse activities with diverse inputs and final markets (Young 1928, p.538).

In addition to the growth of industrial differentiation, Young describes how a large market permits the exploitation of increasing returns in the supply of 'standardized semi-finished… or intermediate goods'. The large size of the market permits the existence of large-scale capital-intensive intermediate and capital goods industries supplying standardized inputs, which in turn promotes the growth of specialized suppliers of finished products. The type of capital-intensive industry subject to significant scale economies that Young presumably had in mind includes intermediate inputs such as steel, glass, gas, chemicals, electricity, water, transport and concrete. A multitude of specialized 'industries… take over the standardized semi-finished products and convert them into a diversity of finished products'. Young notes this process gives the 'appearance of a paradox [as]… never before in the world's history has so large and varied an assortment of goods been within reach of the average man as in these days of 'standardization'!' (Young 1929 [c] p.165).

Finally, central to the notion of roundabout methods is that production occurs in historical time. The existence of indivisibilities and the fact that growth in the size of the market to overcome these indivisibilities takes time means that growth does not proceed in a smooth linear way. '[P]rogress is not and cannot be continuous. The next important step forward is often initially costly, and cannot be undertaken until a certain quantum of prospective advantages has accumulated' (Young 1928, p.535).

By arguing that increasing returns are realized primarily through industrial differentiation Young was able to reconcile increasing returns and competition.[18] The crucial aspect of competition in Young's model of growth is the passing-on of price reductions to producers and consumers of productivity improvements arising from increasing returns. This is examined in the next section.

2.5 THE CIRCULAR AND CUMULATIVE NATURE OF INCREASING RETURNS

It has been demonstrated how Young organized his analysis around a model of productivity growth based on increasing returns arising from the interdependent processes of increases in the capital–labour ratio, increased use of specialized capital equipment and increased industry specialization. These processes apply particularly to the intermediate and capital goods industries. The scope for increasing returns is governed principally by the extent of the market which is 'defined by the volume of production' (Young 1928, p.533). Building on these premises, Young introduces certain additional features which give the system a dynamic and growth-oriented impetus. A model of productivity growth alone is not enough to ensure continuing growth in the system. Young's key innovation was to argue that the processes of increasing returns which depend upon the extent of the market have the effect of increasing the size of the total market. This circular and cumulative growth model is expressed in Young's famous aphorism, 'the division of labour depends upon the extent of the market, but the extent of the market also depends upon the division of labour' (Young 1928, p.539).[19]

Young adapted Say's Law of Markets to explain how the market grows, absorbing the continually growing per capita output arising from the division of labour. Unlike Say, who devoted many years to formulating his model and identifying the equilibrating mechanisms that would ensure an 'equality' of production and consumption, Young did not provide detailed reasoning for his adoption of Say's Law.[20] Young regarded Say's approach and the assumption of goods exchanging for goods as applicable to 'some special types of economic analysis [where] it remains convenient to assume that trade is conducted by barter, without the use of money' (Young 1929[b] p.932). This approach is particularly apposite to the study of the interdependence of economic relations within an aggregate economy and to the conditions for long-run growth. (Young's use of Say's Law and its relation to the Keynesian principle of effective demand is examined in more detail in Section 10.1.) The process of long-run growth and exchange within the aggregate economy is best conceived of in terms of barter; or goods exchanging for goods. In other words 'making abstraction of the use of money as a medium of exchange, the supply of any one commodity is an expression of the demand of its producers for other commodities and services... There is a sense in which supply and demand, seen in the aggregate, are merely aspects of a single situation' (Young 1929[a], p.580).

Young was of course aware of gaps between supply and demand and the complications caused by the introduction of money. Say's Law is 'misleading' in the sense that 'there may be and often are maladjustments of supply and demand. Furthermore, production in general may at one time outrun and another time fail to keep pace with the expansion of money incomes' (Young 1929[a], p.580). Nevertheless, it is evident from Young's adaptation of Say's Law that he regarded this Law as the appropriate apparatus for the study of long-run growth in which technology, the organization of industries, and consumer tastes are all subject to interdependent change.

Young used the term 'reciprocal demand' to describe the process whereby an increase in the supply of one commodity results in increased demand for other commodities. One reason why Young focused on a barter economy or goods exchanging for goods is that he conceived of increasing returns in terms of an increase in the physical quantity of goods produced within the economy. On several occasions Young defined increasing and decreasing returns in terms of 'displacement costs' – or the extent to which an increase in one commodity displaces or reduces the output of another commodity. 'It is best to think of increasing and decreasing returns as displacement costs. Decreasing returns exist where the increase of one product is to be had only at the sacrifice of proportionally greater quantities of other products' (Kaldor 1990, p.33); alternatively, when an increase in one 'commodity can be had only by sacrificing progressively larger amounts of the other' (Young 1928, p.541). Graphically Young depicted decreasing (eè) and increasing returns (ìì) as production possibility frontiers, with the former being concave to the origin and the latter convex to the origin (Young 1928, p.540). The type of returns obtaining in the production of commodities *y* or *x* will determine the quantity of the other commodity 'displaced' as the output of one of the commodities increases (Figure 1).

To Say's broad conception of a barter economy, Young introduced the notion of demand elasticity for particular products and the output of whole

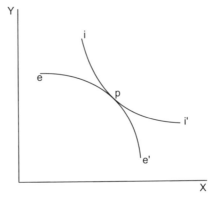

Figure 1:   Increasing and Decreasing Returns as Displacement Costs
(*Source*: Adapted from Kaldor 1990, p.33).

industries (such as manufactures), to explain the growth or decline in demand for particular commodities or output of whole industries.[21] A virtuous circle of growth is created when the production of commodities is subject to increasing returns and these commodities have a high income and price elasticity of demand. The high price and income elasticity of demand ensures that the market for these commodities expands as the price of these commodities declines. This increase in the volume of production, in turn, creates increasing returns which permits further price reductions for the commodities. Young argued that the conditions for continuing growth in per capita output are established when

> commodities exchanged are produced competitively under conditions of increasing returns and when the demand for each commodity is elastic, in the special sense that a small increase in supply will be attended by an increase in the amounts of other commodities which can be had in exchange for it. Under such conditions an increase in the supply of one commodity *is* an increase in the demand for other commodities, and it must be supposed that every increase in demand will evoke an increase in supply.
> (Young 1928, pp.533–534)

The requirement that production occur under competitive conditions is to ensure that any reduction in the costs of production brought about by increasing returns will be passed on in lower prices. This is essential to exploit the high elasticity of demand with respect to price and income for manufacturing commodities, which Young assumes generally applies (Blitch 1983, pp.368–69). In the orthodox system prices serve to equilibrate supply and demand, ensuring a uniform rate of profit and optimal allocation of resources. For Young prices, or more correctly reductions in the real price of commodities, play an important but entirely passive role. Reductions in real prices are essential to the realisation of elastic demand for manufactured goods, whereby a reduction in the cost of a manufactured commodity will stimulate a more than proportionate increase in demand. Young does not provide a detailed analysis of competition or income distribution within this dis-equilibrium growth model.[22]

Young argues that 'enlarging of the market for any one commodity produced under conditions of increasing returns, generally has the net effect ... of enlarging the market for other commodities'; nevertheless growth across industries and commodities is not uniform. (Young 1928, p.537). 'The rate at which one industry grows is conditioned by the rate at which other industries grow, but since the elasticities of demand and of supply will differ for different products, some industries will grow faster than others' (Young 1928, pp.534).[23] Growth of the total market when viewed from the point of view of the individual firm or industry is an external economy that acts simultaneously to lower the costs of production (via increasing returns on inputs for the firm or industry) and expand the market for its product. Of course, the scope for increasing returns (elastic supply) and elasticity of demand for particular commodities differs across commodities and industries. Generally, however, it is a feature of manufacturing that it is subject to increasing returns, and the demand for its product is elastic. Young applied this model to explain the concern of entrepreneurs to expand sales and market share. 'The businessman's mercantilistic emphasis upon markets may have a sounder basis than the economist who thinks mostly in terms of economic statics is prone to admit'. The entrepreneur's 'persistent search for markets' is to be partly explained by the quest to exploit increasing returns or 'augmenting profits by reducing costs' (Young 1928, pp. 536–537).

2.6   COMPLEMENTARITIES IN CONSUMPTION AND PRODUCTION

Young's notion of complementarity in consumption and production is central to CC growth theory. This approach to complementarity differs substantially from that employed in neoclassical theory.

Within consumption, 'reciprocal demand' is an expression of strong complementarity in the demand for the products of diverse industries. On the demand side, 'enlarging of the market for any one commodity, produced under conditions of increasing returns, generally has the net effect... of enlarging the market for other commodities' (Young 1928, p.537). Furthermore, 'enlarging the market for other commodities' entails not just deepening the market for an existing array of products, but also widening production by the introduction of new commodities. It is one of Young's fundamental assumptions that an increase in real per capita income gives rise to 'an increase in the complexity of the apparatus of living, as shown by the increase in the variety of goods offered in consumers' markets' (Young 1928, p.537). Underlying this growing diversity of consumer wants is the 'infinite variety of human needs and... the human passion for novelty and change' (Young 1929 [c] p.165). Young does not adequately emphasize the point that the growing diversity in consumer wants as per capita income increases is essential to continued growth in the size of the market. If the array of consumer wants and consequently consumer products were fixed as to their type and quality, presumably a point of saturation of demand would be reached for many of these commodities. For example, it is conceivable that the demand for television sets may become saturated, but a change in the 'quality' of this product (such as the introduction of colour TVs), or the introduction of a new product such as CD players results in a significant lift in the demand for consumer electronic products. In the absence of these new products, the main determinant of the growth of demand would be population growth and depreciation of the existing stock of consumer goods.

On the supply side, a dynamic and growing economy provides both the means and the incentive to introduce new commodities. The ever-growing diversity of consumer wants has been satisfied by 'a multitude of specialized industries [which] fashion the bewildering varieties of goods, which are sold in the world's markets' (Young 1929 [c] p.165). However, these specialized industries can only supply these markets because of high-quality and low-cost inputs from intermediate and capital goods producers.

Young's view of the consequence of the division of labour in stimulating growth in the variety of consumer and producer goods is important and novel. Firstly, the effect of increased productivity and increased per capita income flowing from the division of labour is to increase the variety of consumer wants and the production of consumer goods. Secondly, increasing returns take one of their most important forms in the increased diversity of intermediate and capital goods inputs to production. In other words, the division of labour is associated with increased specialization of tasks and output across firms and industries, and directly linked to an increase in the diversity of goods produced. This contrasts with traditional arguments regarding the effect of the division of labour, which emphasize the tendency towards and benefits obtained from (national) specialization in the production of a limited number of commodities (Groenewegen 1987, p.904).

In the subsequent evolution of CC thought there arose a significant difference of opinion over the optimal industrial structure for a newly developing country. Rosenstein-Rodan advocated a broad-based pattern of import substitution to create a 'large' market and thereby overcome indivisibilities in the use of efficient capital-intensive production methods and infrastructure. Hirschman argued for import substitution to create a 'large' market to realize the benefits of specialization in producer inputs industries. (The broad approach of Rosenstein-Rodan and Hirschman was supported by the work of Leontief and Chenery in the 1950s and 1960s.) Kaldor, in contrast, argued that the benefits of the division of labour and increasing returns would be more readily exploited by concentrating investment in only a limited number of industries. By concentrating production on exports, these industries would have access to much larger markets than those available within a single national economy. This bifurcation in CC thought is examined in some detail in later chapters, and a resolution of these differences is provided in the Conclusion to this study.

Another aspect of complementarity was highlighted in Heinz Arndt's (1955) explanation of external economies in growth theory. Arndt argues that Young and Rosenstein-Rodan regarded investments in capital goods as complementary. This is due to the supply of increasingly specialized capital goods and technological change resulting in 'improvement in the *quality*' of capital (Arndt 1955, p.200). Implicit in Young's analysis is a rejection of the neoclassical notion of diminishing returns to a factor, which holds that *ceteris paribus* increasing the quantity of one factor relative to others will reduce the marginal productivity of that factor. In Young's model increasing the capital–labour ratio is one of the principal sources of productivity growth. One of the reasons diminishing returns to capital do not set in is that, for Young, capital investment is a primary transmission mechanism for technological change. Indeed, Young goes even further and argues that rates of technological innovation and capital investment are linked in a circular and cumulative way. Aside from technological innovation embodied in new capital goods, it will be recalled, Young claims that increases in the size of the market lead to the supply of increasingly specialized or heterogenous inputs to production. These new specialized capital goods and intermediate inputs 'have a presumptive claim to be regarded as embodying more economical uses of productive resources than those which they replace' (Young 1928, p.535).[24] In this instance improvements in the quality of inputs results from the better utilisation of existing technologies.

The presence of heterogeneous capital goods is another reason why equilibrium conditions cannot exist within Youngian production theory. In the context of criticizing the marginal productivity theory of income distribution, Young notes that 'capital once fixed or invested in permanent forms is generally irretrievably committed to the fortunes of a particular type of enterprise, whatever those fortunes may prove to be' (Young 1929[b], p.931).

To conclude this section, Young largely ignores both the neoclassical 'economic problem' arising from the scarcity of factors and the neoclassical principles of substitution and diminishing returns. Given his concern with the forces governing long-run growth of output per worker and per capita consumption, for Young the quantity of factors is not fixed, nor is their supply especially constrained. The focus is not on factor substitution but on factor creation and the complementary effect of output and investment stimulating additional production and investment in the same or other sectors. One of the principal inferences Nicholas Kaldor (1972[c]) and Lauchlin Currie (1981) made from Young's system was that key resources such as capital, labour and, to a lesser extent, raw materials are created and not given as natural endowments. Many inputs are produced means of production and as such their supply is subject to increasing returns (Kaldor 1972[c], p.1251). In contrast to neoclassical growth models, expansion of output is not determined by an exogenously given increase in factor supplies and technological change, rather the rate of output growth is determined by the rate of growth of demand.

2.7 INCREASING RETURNS AND TECHNOLOGICAL CHANGE

In conventional neoclassical growth theory, technological change or an increase in output per unit of input is conceived as an upward shift in the production function. The neoclassical model draws a sharp distinction between productivity gains arising from utilization of an existing stock of knowledge and that resulting from technological innovation. Technological change is also assumed to be exogenous, that is, the time-rate of change is independent of the economic system. Figure 2 illustrates technological change as a shift in the original curve $f(k, t_0)$ to the new position $f(k, t_i)$, so that at any level of the capital-labour ratio (except 0), more output per worker can be produced.

It also demonstrates the general assumptions that the production function is continuously differentiable (e.g., absence of indivisibilities), and that diminishing returns to a factor apply – as the ratio of capital to labour increases, the marginal product diminishes (Jones 1982, Chapter 6).

Young's model is entirely different from this orthodox approach. Young's discussion of technological change is inchoate and fragmentary, but since it appears to play a role in his account of productivity growth it is important to try to consider his arguments. Young identified 'various factors which reinforce the influences which make for increasing returns. The discovery of new natural resources and of new uses for them and the growth of scientific knowledge are probably the most potent of such factors' (Young 1928,

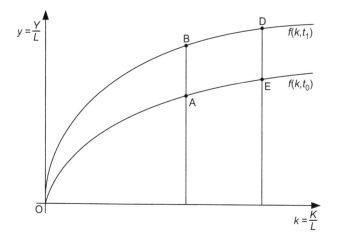

Figure 2: Neoclassical Representation of Technological Change
Source: (Jones 1982, p.159)

p.535). Technological change is largely endogenous to the system. Young assumes a circular and cumulative relation between the growth of new scientific knowledge and the growth of total output. 'The causal connections between the growth of industry and the progress of science run in both directions, but on which side the preponderant influence lies no one can say' (Young 1928, p.535). Young implies there are a number of reasons why this relation should hold but identifies only one explicitly. This is the growth of what is now called industrial research and development, 'a scientific interest conditioned by economic interest – is beginning to infiltrate industry' (Young 1928, p.536). Moreover, the primary mechanism for the transmission of technological change is capital investment. Investment in new capital and intermediate goods involves the replacement of less efficient productive techniques by a more efficient vintage. Growth in scientific knowledge applied in new products and processes directly raises the productivity of capital.

Technological innovation plays a role in Young's growth model but he does make the claim that the division of labour by itself is both a necessary and sufficient condition for continual growth. 'Even with a stationary population and in the absence of new discoveries in pure and applied science there are no limits to the process of expansion except the limits beyond which demand is not elastic and returns do not increase' (Young 1928, p.534). These 'new discoveries' are contrasted with 'such new ways of organizing production and such new 'inventions' as are merely adaptations of known ways of doing things, made practicable and economical by an enlarged scale of production' (Young 1928, p.534n). However, the claim that there are virtually 'no limits' to the growth process in the absence of technical innovation is surely an overstatement of the capacity to wring continuing productivity gains from roundabout production methods. Notwithstanding Young's claims regarding growth 'under these hypothetical conditions' of 'stationary population' and 'absence of new discoveries', on balance it is arguable that Young regarded technical innovation as central to growth (Young 1928, p.534).[25]

Kaldor's long-standing opposition to the neoclassical conception of technological change, expressed in his 'technological progress function', embodied the principal elements of Young's fragmentary thoughts (Kaldor 1957; 1962). This is evident in Kaldor's summary of his critique of orthodox economic theory.

The use of more capital per worker ... inevitably entails the introduction of superior techniques ... On the other hand, most, though not all, technical innovations require the use of more capital per man – more elaborate equipment and/or more mechanical power ... It follows that any sharp or clear-cut distinction between the movement *along* a 'production function' with a given state of technology and a *shift* in the 'production function' caused by a change in the state of knowledge is arbitrary and artificial.

(Kaldor 1957, pp.595–96)

2.8   THE APPROPRIATE LEVEL OF ANALYSIS

Reference has already been made to Young's advocacy of an

inclusive view, considering the market not as an outlet for the products of a particular industry, and therefore external to that industry, but as the outlet for goods in general ... it is a conception of a market in this inclusive sense [as] ... an aggregate of productive activities tied together by trade [that] ... carries with it the notion that there must be some sort of balance, that different productive activities must be proportioned one to another.

(Young 1928, p.533)

Young seems to be proposing an elementary input–output conception of the economy, whereby goods and services embodying the benefits of increasing returns are traded and positively affect directly and indirectly virtually all productive activity.[26] This intimation of input-output methods is significant as thirty years later A. O. Hirschman and Hollis Chenery were to employ the Leontief model in their 'disequilibrium' analysis of growth in underdeveloped economies. Their emphasis on the development of intermediate and capital goods sectors reflects the priority Young gave to these industries in the explanation of productivity growth. Inter-industry trade is the means whereby decreasing costs and increasing demand in one sector are transmitted to another sector. 'Every important advance in the organisation of production ... alters the conditions of industrial activity and initiates responses elsewhere in the industrial structure which in turn have a further unsettling effect. Thus change becomes progressive and propagates itself in a cumulative way' (Young 1928, p.533).

This line of reasoning led Young to the view that the appropriate level of analysis for understanding the process of economic progress was an inter-industry or economy-wide level. This represents a clear rejection of Marshall's apparatus of partial equilibrium with its focus on the 'representative firm' or a particular industry which could be studied under *ceteris paribus* conditions.

With the extension of the division of labour among industries the representative firm, like the industry of which it is a part, loses its identity. Its internal economies dissolve into the internal and external economies of the more highly specialized undertakings which are its successors and are

supplemented by new economies ... the mechanism of increasing returns is
not to be discerned adequately by observing the effects of variations in the
size of an individual firm or of a particular industry, for the progressive
division and specialization of industries is an essential part of the process by
which increasing returns are realized. *What is required is that industrial
operations be seen as an interrelated whole*.

(Young 1928, pp.538–39 my italics)[27]

Young's emphasis on external economies arising from the division of labour
across firms and industries is a continuing theme in the subsequent development of CC thought. Kaldor expressed this view succinctly: 'as Allyn Young
emphasized, increasing returns is a "macro-phenomenon" ' (Kaldor 1966 [a],
p.9). After Young there is a major divide within CC theory as to whether
increasing returns apply only to 'industrial operations' or also to other economic activities, especially agriculture, mining and services. Kaldor, in particular, argued forcefully that increasing returns only apply to industrial
activities, with primary and tertiary industries subject to diminishing and
constant returns respectively. On the other side, Lauchlin Currie argued
strongly that increasing returns were a 'global' phenomenon and that the
benefits of the division of labour are accessible to all industries. This dispute
within the CC tradition is in part due to Young's conflicting statements as to
whether increasing returns extend to industries other than manufacturing.
(For example, Young's 1928 article emphasized that increasing returns do not
extend to agriculture. In his LSE Lectures 1927–1929, Young argued that
'[s]ome industries never seem to show increasing returns, e.g. agriculture'
(Kaldor 1990, p.54). Contrary statements by Young are cited in Sandilands
(1990, pp.308–310). This fundamental dispute is analysed in more detail in
Chapter 6.)

2.9   EXTERNAL ECONOMIES AND ECONOMIC PLANNING

Having outlined his growth model, Young reflects on the possibility that
external economies may be employed by the state to accelerate growth
rates. An 'industrial dictator', Young speculates, 'could hasten the pace' of
economic development 'somewhat, but he could not achieve an Aladdin-like
transformation of a country's industry, so as to reap the fruits of half a
century's ordinary progress in a few years' (Young 1928, p.534). This is due
to the long gestation periods required for the training of skilled labour, and
the necessary growth of large industrial centres that generate and exploit
economies of agglomeration. The accumulation of the necessary capital is
also a lengthy process (Young 1928, p.534).

In subsequent formulations of CC theory in balanced and unbalanced growth, significant market imperfections are assumed in underdeveloped economies. These imperfections arise from a number of factors, such as the presence of uncertainty in the formation of investors' decision-making, and the assumption that indivisibilities may prevent the introduction of modern capital-intensive production techniques and/or give rise to an oligopolistic industry structure. Consequently, an 'industrial dictator' in the form of the state is essential to co-ordinate those progressive rounds of investment and secure the necessary demand that Young regarded as inherent to a mature competitive economy. In the work of Myrdal and Kaldor, the state also plays a central role in the maintenance of growth, counter-acting the tendency to unequal growth in the analysis of advanced industrial economies.

2.10   CRITICISMS OF YOUNG'S GROWTH MODEL

At least two aspects of Young's model deserve critical attention. These are the failure to consider effective demand, viewed broadly, and Young's partial view of the sources of increasing returns. The notion of effective demand has received intensive analysis by subsequent CC theorists. In general, they have been much less accepting of the capacity of the market alone to generate self-sustaining growth.

2.10.1   Effective Demand

It has been demonstrated how Young constructed a barter economy in which goods exchange for goods along their respective 'offer curves', and accepted Say's Law in which supply creates its own demand. He does not employ notions of savings and investment but seems to use a classical notion of accumulation, whereby a surplus is converted into means of production to ensure continued growth of production. Thus 'the accumulation of the necessary capital takes time, even though the process of accumulation is largely one of turning part of an increasing product into forms which will serve in securing a further increase of product' (Young 1928, p.534). Young regards the forces of economic progress as inherent to an industrial market economy and provides a simple, albeit insightful model of the circular and cumulative relation between growth in productivity and aggregate output whilst discounting those factors that may lead to economic regress. These latter factors include, for example, instability in the volume of investment induced by entrepreneurial uncertainty about future demand, natural resource constraints, changes in income distribution that prevent the passing-on of real price reductions to consumers and balance of payments constraints to growth.

Young was obviously aware of the potential gap between supply and demand; indeed, it is his inherent in his 'disequilibrium' model of dynamic growth in which constantly changing consumer tastes, new technology and new production methods not only make existing occupations and capital equipment redundant but also require alterations to the spatial distribution of economic activity. Thus the 'enlarging of the market' results in a 'displacement [that] may be considerable and the repercussions upon particular industries unfavourable' (Young 1928, p.537). Moreover, Young was acutely aware of the complications caused by the introduction of money. '[M]odern processes of price-making and distribution depend upon the use of money and credit, not only in the sense that processes so complex would be unthinkable otherwise, but also in the further sense that the use of money and credit has certain special and discernible effects upon the outcome' (Young 1929[b], p.932). These sources of disequilibrium led Young to criticise 'some of the older [classical] economists who held that general overproduction is impossible – a theorem which, though not really erroneous, has proved to be misleading.... There may be and often are maladjustments of supply and demand. Furthermore, production in general may at one time outrun and another time fail to keep pace with the expansion of money incomes' (Young 1929[a], p.580). Nevertheless, it would seem that Young regarded 'maladjustments' and the influence of 'money and credit' as short-term effects; complications within his long-run growth model. In the long run, and looking at the economy in the aggregate, Young held that 'making abstraction of the use of money as a medium of exchange, the supply of one commodity is an expression of the demand of its producers for other commodities and services. There is a sense in which supply and demand, seen in the aggregate, are merely different aspects of a single situation' (Young 1929[a], p.580).

Later CC theorists were much less sanguine about the capacity of the market, unaided and undirected, to generate virtuous circles of growth. Most CC theorists after Young quite correctly stressed factors which either inhibit the initiation of the 'self-perpetuating' growth process or, once initiated, may limit or even reverse the rate of growth. Rosenstein-Rodan, Hirschman and Myrdal envisaged an extensive role for the state in the planning of industrial development and the management of demand through policies such as government spending and import substitution. The subsequent development of CC thought does not reflect a simple opposition between Young's classical and later Keynesian inspired analyses of demand and investment. For example, although Rosenstein-Rodan and Hirschman identified a central role for the state in development and the management of demand, they did not adopt an orthodox Keynesian approach to the issue of effective demand. For Rosenstein-Rodan (as well as Lauchlin Currie), Say's Law is an important element in their explanation of the self-reinforcing growth of supply and demand in underdeveloped economies. Hirschman largely ignores monetary considerations in his account of investment and has a very mechanistic model of the determination of investment. Only Kaldor, amongst the CC theorists examined here, criticized Young in explicitly Keynesian terms by highlighting the key role of investment (and exports) as the essential element of autonomous (or exogenous) demand, and emphasizing the potential for divergence between consumption and production due to the existence of money and expectations. There are however, unsatisfactory aspects to Kaldor's criticism of Young's classical model and his attempt to integrate Young's growth model and Keynes theory of income determination. Kaldor's analysis of 'effective demand' is detailed in Chapter 6. This chapter also provides a resolution of the conflict within the CC tradition between the 'Sayian' analyses of demand of Currie and Rosenstein-Rodan and Kaldor's emphasis on Keynesian or 'monetary' mechanisms.

2.10.2   Problems in Young's Treatment of Increasing Returns

Three aspects of Young's treatment of increasing returns demand critical scrutiny. First, Young does not justify the assertion that a firm's internal economies are exhausted at a level of output which is small compared to the total output of its industry. Second, Young does not identify the significant problem indivisibilities present for the maintenance of competitive conditions. Third, Young's conception of the sources of increasing returns is selective and ignores those sources which are strongly related to the growth of oligopoly.

It is important to delve more deeply into the argument of both Young (and Marshall) that increasing returns are compatible with competitive conditions (Young 1928, p.527). Competition plays a central role in Young's growth model, since he relies on competition to ensure the passing-on of real price reductions to producers and consumers. Real price reductions, combined with the assumption of high price and income elasticity of demand for manufactures, generates growth in total output. Yet Young does not provide a detailed definition of what he means by 'competition'. The key elements implicit in Young's model are an industry structure with a sufficient number of producers (of consumer and producer goods) to ensure the passing-on of cost reductions via lower prices. Further, competition seems to be the essential driving force in the adoption of new techniques of production, new investment, establishment of new industries and product innovation. Young's focus on external economies and on minimizing the scope for the continued realisation of internal economies within a firm follows from his fundamental premise.

> [W]e assume, as we must, in most industries there are effective, though elastic, limits to the economical size of the individual firm. The output of the individual firm is generally a relatively small proportion of the aggregate

output of an industry. The degree in which it can secure economies by making its own operations more roundabout is limited.

(Young 1928, p.539)[28]

Marshall identified a number of internal diseconomies, in addition to biological life-cycle arguments regarding the limited period of growth and 'vigour' a firm could experience. In contrast, Young provides no argument for a firm's inability to continually exploit internal economies. In Young's defence, it is possible to infer from his analysis, or impute to it, a number of countervailing forces to the increased concentration of an industry's production within a few firms. Young's proposition that vertical disintegration is the form most characteristic of the growth in the market would seem, at least partly, to be derived from Marshall's view that a restraint on continued growth of the firm are internal diseconomies arising from production of an increased variety of commodities. Increasing the variety of commodities produced by a single firm offsets the benefits of specialization. Increasing the variety of commodities thus tends to stimulate the introduction of new specialized firms (Vassilakis 1987[b], p.764). Young argues that the growth of real income produces a demand for an increased variety of commodities amongst consumers, and an increased supply of specialized producer inputs. Consequently, it may be imputed that growth in the market tends to produce *pari passu* countervailing barriers to increased concentration of production.

Against this, recent research indicates there may be considerable benefits arising from economies of 'scope' or the joint production of different commodities (BIE 1988[a]). Chandler's monumental study of the growth of large (oligopolistic) American corporations in the nineteenth century, for example, identified the cause of their rise precisely in their capacity to exploit '*the unprecedented cost advantages of the economies of scale and scope*' (Chandler 1990, p.21. italics in original). Another countervailing factor, which, it may be argued, promotes a competitive industry structure, is the ongoing reduction in the real price of capital goods. Within Young's system the supply of capital goods as produced means of production is subject to increasing returns. A reduction in the real price of capital goods reduces the fixed costs of a firm and thus makes it easier to overcome indivisibilities in production. Reducing the real cost of capital goods lowers the potential barriers to entry of new firms which the high cost of capital goods may represent. However, against this line of reasoning, real price reductions may be a factor facilitating the entry of new firms, but it does not of itself imply any limit to the growth of existing firms; it is not, in other words, an internal diseconomy. It is concluded that Young does not provide a solid foundation for one of the key assumptions in his model, that there are significant internal diseconomies preventing the growth of oligopoly across a wide range of industries. The implication of this is examined in the following sections.

Ironically, there are a number of passages in the 1928 article where Young contradicts the assumption that growth in output occurs only, or primarily, via industrial differentiation. It would seem that the same processes of increasing returns which operate at an industry and inter-industry level could be generated almost without limit within a single firm. The following passage describes the operation of roundabout methods as applied to Henry Ford's auto plants.

> It would be wasteful to furnish with an elaborate equipment of specially constructed jigs, gauges, lathes, drills, presses, and conveyors to build only a hundred automobiles; it would be better to rely mostly upon tools and machines of standard types... Mr Ford's methods would be absurdly uneconomical if his output were very small, *and would be unprofitable even if his output were what other manufacturers of automobiles would call large.* (Young 1928, p.530, my italics)

In this case, the operation of roundabout methods is described as internal economies available to an individual firm. It is the very large size of Ford's particular firm in relation to the output of the industry and other manufacturers which accounts for its capacity to employ comparatively more productive techniques.

The second flaw in Young's analysis of increasing returns is the failure to adequately identify the problem indivisibilities present for the maintenance of competitive conditions. In one of his earliest published articles, Kaldor noted that

> the mathematical economists in making 'perfect competition' as their starting point, weren't such fools after all. For they assumed perfect divisibility of everything; and where everything is perfectly divisible, and consequently economies of scale completely absent, 'perfect competition' must necessarily establish itself. (Kaldor 1935, p.394)

Like the classical economists, Young does not argue for perfect competition, but he does assume that indivisibilities do not require a very high share of a commodity's output to be overcome. He ignores the possibility that indivisibilities may produce high barriers to entry due to very high fixed costs and lead to concentration of production within fewer firms. The level of capital investment required to enter production in industries such as the steel, cement, motor vehicles, aircraft, pharmaceuticals, building materials and aluminium production, etc. generally results in an oligopolistic structure for these industries (Blair 1972). In addition to capital costs there are a variety of 'sunk' or irrecoverable costs, such as marketing and R&D, which may preclude the entry of many firms to an industry.[29] This of course, is not to argue that indivisibilities must lead to oligopoly, or that 'industrial differentiation' is not a very important mechanism of increasing returns. Rather, the case against Young is simply that he has provided a one-sided model. In the economics literature, indivisibilities along with other scale economies are identified as one of the causes of oligopoly (Asimakopulos 1978, p.312). Empirical data also supports this contention. '[T]he achievement of the maximum economies of scale is not, on our evidence, compatible with the existence of competition of many firms for a large number of products within the U.K.' (Pratten 1971, p.313).

Finally, Young has a limited view of the sources of increasing returns, which he identifies primarily as the overcoming of indivisibilities and the advantages of specialization (within the firm and across industries). Young ignores economies to scale of a firm which arise, for example, from advantages of vertical and horizontal integration, risk reduction through diversification of investment and markets, or cost benefits from multi-product operation, etc. These economies of the firm are more directly related to growth in the size of the firm in relation to its industry, and consequently, they are much more awkward to incorporate into a competitive industry structure. This would seem to be a plausible explanation for their omission from Young's work. The effect of Young's restricted view of the potential sources of internal economies, and his unwillingness to admit the possibility that the scope for internal economies within a very broad range of industries may be very large indeed, is to reduce the realism of his analysis.

Later writers in the CC tradition redressed these deficiencies in Young's account of increasing returns by having a much broader conception of the origin of increasing returns. For example, they accepted the central role of external economies and industrial differentiation but also combined plant scale economies and economies of the firm. They also incorporate Young's view that technological change should be viewed (at least primarily) as endogenous. Rosenstein-Rodan, for example, placed considerable emphasis on economies to scale of the firm, such as advantages of horizontal integration. The benefits flowing from state co-ordination of private investments he likened to those which arise from integrated investment planning within some giant 'Trust'. Kaldor regarded the large scope for internal economies as the prime cause for the pervasiveness of oligopolistic industry structures across advanced industrial nations. Indeed, Kaldor was the only CC theorist to analyse the nature of competition and price formation within such concentrated markets.

2.11 SUMMARY OF YOUNG'S GROWTH MODEL

This chapter has provided a detailed analytical account of Allyn Young's disequilibrium growth model, identified some of the sources of this growth model in Marshall's economics and the cost controversy, determined the key differences in the assumptions of disequilibrium and neoclassical economics and contrasted some of the important assumptions of Young and latter writers in the CC tradition. Given the large 'territory' traversed in this chapter, we may assist the reader by briefly reiterating the key elements of Young's growth model.

Economic progress, productivity growth or increase in per capita real income are due to increasing returns. Increasing returns are caused primarily by the division of labour, which take their most important forms in increases in the capital–labour ratio, increased use of more specialized capital equipment and increases in the specialization of production within the firm and across industries. Increases in the capital–labour ratio, use of more specialized equipment and industry specialization are in turn caused by expansion in the size of the market (total output). Growth in the market allows for the overcoming of indivisibilities in the employment of capital equipment and permits increases in the specialization of production across industries. Growth in the market also reduces the real price of capital goods and intermediate inputs, since production of these goods is also subject to increasing returns. The division of labour has occurred especially in the intermediate and capital goods sectors. Productivity gains in the manufacture of these inputs to production are important in reducing costs of production for user industries. Reinforcing these effects is technological change, which is positively related to the rate of growth of output and transmitted primarily through capital investment.

Growth in the market is in turn primarily due to productivity gains. Continuing expansion in total output occurs when there is elastic demand for goods produced under increasing returns (elastic supply). The interaction of increasing returns and growth in total output generates a virtuous circle of cumulative growth. Young adapts Say's Law in the notion of 'reciprocal demand', to describe how an increase in the production (supply) of one commodity is effectively an increase in the demand for other commodities. The rate of growth of any one industry is determined by the rate of growth of all other industries. The rate of growth of a particular industry is governed by the price and income elasticity of demand for its product and its elasticity of supply. The latter is determined largely by the extent to which the commodity is subject to increasing returns in production. Growth in total output is associated with an increase in the diversity of output, and this diversity is an essential element in the growth of total output. This diversity occurs in capital/intermediate and consumer goods industries. Increased specialization and heterogeneity of inputs to production is an essential aspect of the division of labour, as explained above. In addition, within a dynamic economy an increase in real per capita income gives rise to 'an increase in the variety of goods offered in consumers' markets' (Young 1928, p.537). An essential mechanism of growth is a growing diversity of consumer preferences with rising per capita income whereby the introduction of new commodities has the effect of 'enlarging the market for other commodities' (Young 1928, p.537). Manufacturing is the engine of growth as it is generally subject to increasing returns (elastic supply), and the demand for its output is elastic with respect to price and income, though there is some ambiguity in Young's writings as to whether increasing returns extend to other industries. (This is examined in ch.6).

2.12 CONCLUSION

Out of the abstract and arcane methodological debates surrounding internal and external economies and the appropriate techniques for economic analysis, Allyn Young constructed a growth model and suggested tools of analysis that seriously question the orthodox understanding of economic processes. This growth model and these tools of analysis are the principal foundation for the theory of circular and cumulative causation.

The subsequent development of this theory has been dominated by three questions flowing from Young's original work. First, what are the principal *sources* of increasing returns? In particular, are these sources primarily internal and/or external to the firm? This is important not just for identifying the principal cause of per capita income growth in the circular and cumulative model; it is also critical in determining the type of industrial structure, either competitive or concentrated, to which this growth model gives rise. Second, to what industries do increasing returns *extend*? Does the division of labour, broadly defined, extend only to manufacturing, or can these benefits also be had by primary and tertiary industries? Finally, what are the *conditions* for the initiation and/or continuation of the circular and cumulative growth process? To what extent is the growth process either self-perpetuating and self-governing; or unstable, generating counter-tendencies which undermine the conditions for growth? A related and subsidiary question is, do the conditions for growth differ between underdeveloped and developed economies? These three questions are examined in the following chapters.

Kaldor argued that one of the truly remarkable events in the history of economic thought is that the economics profession largely ignored Young's paper. 'Economists ceased to take any notice of it long before they were able to grasp its full revolutionary potential' (Kaldor 1972[c], p.1243). The reasons for the neglect are not difficult to fathom. Increasing returns, fixed factor coefficients in production, heterogeneous capital and intermediate goods, endogenous technological change and complementarities in production and consumption and 'income effects' on consumption patterns are the principal elements in Youngian production theory. These elements contradict the assumptions integral to equilibrium analysis.[30] Nevertheless, Young's ideas eventually found a receptive audience, initially and somewhat improbably, amongst the pioneers of development economics in the 1940s and 1950s. It is to this application of the concept we now turn.

Chapter 3
Paul N. Rosenstein-Rodan (1902–1985): From Circular Causation to Balanced Growth

The market mechanism does not realise the 'optimum' either in one nation or between nations, because it relies on such unrealistic assumptions as linear homogeneous production functions, no increasing returns or economies of scale or of agglomeration, and no phenomenon of minimum quantum or threshold. This obscures the nature of the development process and the risks involved. Nothing in theology or technology ordains that God created the world convex downwards.

(Rosenstein-Rodan 1984, p.209)

3.1 INTRODUCTION

Paul N. Rosenstein-Rodan's early work in economics was firmly based in the Austrian School; he took his PhD. from Vienna University in 1927. Although he had mastered equilibrium economics and made substantial contributions to it, even in this early phase he was critical of equilibrium theory's 'tendency to put too much emphasis on the explanation of the end positions as such, and to neglect the importance of the intermediate positions which constitute the ultimate problem' (Rosenstein-Rodan 1934, p.89). In particular, Rosenstein-Rodan (R-R) made use of concepts such as indivisibilities, complementarities in demand, expectations and hierarchies of wants as these affect the path of adjustment to equilibrium. As an early contributor to the 'cobweb' theorem, R-R argued that these concepts could generate 'cumulative effects' resulting in perpetual movements away from equilibrium (R-R 1934, pp.95–96). By the time of his seminal (1943) article he had made a complete break with equilibrium reasoning and belief in the efficacy of the market mechanism. 'Not traditional equilibrium theory, but an analysis of the *disequilibrium growth process* is what is essential for understanding economic development problems' (R-R 1984, p.207, my italics).

This chapter begins with an account of the theoretical structure of R-R's development model, concentrating on the use and adaptation of Young's growth theory. At numerous points in the chapter reference is made to the work of Professor Ragnar Nurkse, the great proselytizer of R-R's model. Aside from actually inventing the term 'Balanced Growth', Nurkse was frequently able to express these ideas in a more lucid and compelling manner than R-R. In the principal articles where R-R and Nurkse set forth their analysis, explicit reference was made to Allyn Young. R-R accepted the central role of increasing returns through overcoming indivisibilities in the employment of capital in the explanation of the growth of per capita income. He also argued Say's Law could be especially applicable to underdeveloped regions. In particular, if production were focused on goods which had strong complementary demand, and if these goods had an elastic supply and high elasticity of demand at income levels pertaining in the underdeveloped region, then Say's Law would obtain and a growth path of increasing supply and demand could be established. Also prominent in R-R's work is Young's argument for the stimulus external economies give to additional investment (R-R 1943, p.251; 1957 p.60).[1]

Whilst these received ideas are the core of his theory of growth, R-R made a number of significant contributions to CC theory. The major contribution was the claim that for a number of reasons the market mechanism may be inherently inefficient in determining the optimum volume and industrial composition of investment. It will be recalled that Marshall and Young identified externalities as one of the primary causes and effects of growth in an advanced industrial economy. Again, for Marshall and Young, the market is 'efficient' in the special sense that there is no or minimal divergence between 'private and social marginal net product'. For R-R the overcoming of indivisibilities in the employment of capital may require a firm to have a very large share of the output of a particular commodity. This is the case for many industrial products, according to R-R, and certainly applies in the provision of infrastructure which is frequently characterized as a natural monopoly. In a 'small' underdeveloped market such indivisibilities may preclude the introduction of modern capital-intensive production techniques and inhibit industrialization. The small size of the market in relation to the level of capital investment required to introduce modern production techniques also introduces 'risk' or uncertainty into private investment decision making. In addition, R-R argues entrepreneurs are incapable of incorporating externalities into their investment decision making. Accordingly, the state is required to co-ordinate the volume and industry composition of investments, using externalities both as a key criteria for the selection of investments and as an instrument in the development process.[2] Thus indivisibilities, risk and the investment criteria of entrepreneurs may result in the volume and industry composition of investment being less than, and different from, that which is optimal from society's point of view. To clarify this analysis of R-R's theory, a composite development plan is constructed from his writings to briefly illustrate how this theory was intended to operate in practice.

The chapter concludes with a number of criticisms of R-R's work. The principal criticism is the concentration of balanced growth on the exploitation of scale economies and complementarities in demand at the same stage of production – that is, balanced growth focuses on consumer goods industries and neglects producer goods industries. The concentration on 'horizontal integration' largely ignores the scope for productivity gains and increases in the elasticity of supply arising from the vertical integration of capital, intermediate and consumer goods industries. This section also evaluates criticisms of R-R's diversified import-substitution development strategy. Critics such as Sheahan (1958, 1959) proposed that increasing returns will be maximized and development best promoted by the concentration of investment in a small number of industries geared to export promotion. The debate over competing development models stimulated by R-R's work is a crucial stage in the development of CC thought. The conflict between strategies of import-substitution and export promotion as the best means of exploiting external economies and increasing returns is evident even in Kaldor's work some three to four decades later.

3.2   THE CRITIQUE OF EQUILIBRIUM ECONOMICS

The purpose of this section is twofold: firstly, to identify R-R's principal objections to equilibrium reasoning; secondly, to identify the similarities and differences in Young's and R-R's understanding of the forces in economic growth, and how these differences underlie the Balanced Growth model of development.

3.2.1   Indivisibilities

For R-R, like Young, a major source of increasing returns arises from overcoming indivisibilities in the employment of capital. R-R also accepts Young's view that the extent of the market is determined largely by the division of labour, one of the chief characteristics of which is increases in the capital–labour ratio.[3] R-R, like Young, assumes that more capital-intensive production methods are also more efficient.[4] R-R distinguishes two forms of capital investment which give rise to increasing returns. The supply of most manufactured commodities is subject 'to increasing returns, that is economies of scale', because the most efficient techniques of production 'require a high optimum size of firm' (R-R 1957, p.60). Indivisibilities also apply in the provision of infrastructure or 'social overhead capital', such as power, transport and communications, which have very high capital costs. These services must generally precede or be supplied concurrently with 'more quickly yielding directly productive investments' (R-R 1957, p.61). Allyn Young emphasized that one of the key sources of productivity growth was industrial differentiation, or specialization of production within and across industries. This specialization, combined with his general assumption of finite limits to the size of a firm in relation to its industry's output, led Young to downplay the scope for internal scale economies. Growth in the market allows for an economy-wide increase in the capital–labour ratio. For R-R, by contrast, the primary effect of growth in the market is to allow a firm to exploit internal economies. Productivity growth is largely a function of overcoming indivisibilities in the employment of capital, largely through increasing the scale of plants and firms. R-R argues that indivisibilities are not compatible with competitive conditions in underdeveloped regions, where the small size of the market permits only one or a few optimal size plants in any industry. Given these conditions there arises 'the obvious danger of monopolistic markets' (R-R 1957, p.60). However, like Young, R-R maintains that within a 'large' mature industrial economy indivisibilities are consistent with competitive conditions. This is because the optimal 'size of the investment project... can be assumed to be independent of the level of development' (Bohm 1967, p.69). In other words, the scope for scale economies within a given plant is largely the same in developed or underdeveloped economies.

> [The] plant capacity most economical to build and operate is not very different in different countries; but, as a percentage of an industry's total capacity, it is very much greater in underdeveloped than in fully industrialised economies. In under-developed countries, therefore, investment is likely to have a greater impact on prices, give rise to greater pecuniary external economies and thus cause a greater divergence between private profit and social benefit. (Scitovsky 1954, p.306)[5]

The assumption that the scope for economies of the plant and/or firm are largely the same in developed or underdeveloped regions is, of course, highly contentious. One of the leading contemporary theorists on external economies regards it as 'impossible to restrict the relevance of the allocation problems connected with price effects to underdeveloped countries' (Bohm 1967, p.74). The empirical work of Pratten (1971) indicates that the scope for plant scale economies is highly elastic, in that the 'optimal size' plant for many commodities increases with the growth in total output of that commodity. Kaldor rejected the arguments of Young and R-R, maintaining that the typical industrial structure of advanced economies was oligopolistic and that indivisibilities played a major part in causing these concentrated markets.

3.2.2   Complementarities in the Use of Capital

There is another notion of indivisibility which R-R introduces: the necessity for joint provision of infrastructure projects. It is no good, for instance, having a modern electricity supply without a good transport or communication system. There is an indivisible quantum of each type of infrastructure project necessary to create the conditions for development: 'an irreducible minimum social overhead capital industry mix is a condition for getting off the dead end' (R-R 1957, p.61). R-R describes the necessity for joint supply of infrastructure as an example of the complementarity of capital investment. The complementarity of capital investment explains the failure of the neoclassical prediction that capital will flow from regions where it is abundant to regions where it is scarce. This argument is reinforced by R-R's acceptance of Young's argument that increases in the capital–labour ratio do not produce a reduction in the productivity of capital owing to the presence of increasing returns. Neoclassical analysis predicts that given identical production functions and the same 'quality' of factors across nations, the income of factors will be determined by their relative scarcity. Given the ready mobility of factors, capital will flow from regions where it is abundant to regions where it is scarce, thereby equalizing the rate of return on capital. For R-R, these assumptions and predictions of neoclassical economics are invalid (R-R 1957, p.64). 'Because of complementarity between different forms of specific capital equipment, the marginal productivity of capital is very likely to be higher in rich countries endowed with a large and varied stock of capital equipment than in poor underdeveloped countries' (Arndt 1955, p.202).

3.2.3   Indivisibilities and Risk

Indivisibilities in underdeveloped regions with relatively small markets are a potentially insuperable barrier to industrialization. For R-R, indivisibilities exacerbate the risk or uncertainty an investor has about finding a market for their product. This is because indivisibilities 'make the minimum investment much larger' than in the case where all factors are perfectly divisible (R-R 1957, p.62).

The notion of risk or uncertainty is not subjected to detailed analysis by R-R. The risk attached to a particular investment seems to vary directly with the proportion of total output the investment is intended to supply. In underdeveloped regions where a single new investment may satisfy the whole demand for a commodity, R-R assumes this is more 'risky' than a similar – 'sized' investment in developed regions which may only represent an increment to existing supply.

3.2.4 Complementarities in Consumption

A method of reducing investor risk is to exploit complementarity in demand. R-R's notion of complementarity in demand is derived from two sources. Firstly, R-R argues like Young that an increase in the production (supply) of one commodity is effectively an increase in the demand for other commodities (Young 1928, p.534). R-R also argues like Young that the primary determinant of the demand for a particular commodity is its income elasticity of demand. It is a fundamental tenet of balanced growth that production should be planned to conform with current income elasticity of demand. Further, with increases in per capita income the composition of production should change over time if such increases in per capita income are associated with changes in the income elasticity of demand for particular commodities and increases in the variety of goods demanded and produced.[6]

Secondly, R-R employs a notion of complementarity in demand derived from the Austrian School and his early work in the 1930s on utility theory (Chakravarty 1983, p.73). At low levels of per capita income, demand for most goods is highly inelastic, since demand is directed solely to a small variety of basic wage goods. The income elasticity of demand for basic wage goods such as processed food, shoes, shelter, clothing, transport, etc. is very high. At low income levels any increase in income will be directed to these goods. Moreover, these basic wage goods have a strong natural complementarity in terms of satisfying basic human needs.[7]

The simultaneous establishment of several wage goods plants can exploit this complementarity since the pattern of demand is stable and highly predictable. The use of complementarity in demand as an investment criterion and the co-ordination of investment decisions to satisfy these demands is not appropriate in 'rich countries', since with 'their more variegated needs it is difficult to assess the prospective demand of the population' (R-R 1943, p.250). Exploiting complementarities in demand reduces the risk attached to investment decisions. The reduction in risk manifests itself in a larger volume of borrowing or equity funds available to investors or lower risk premia on projects (R-R 1957, p.61). 'The planned creation of... a complementary system reduces the risk of not being able to sell, and, since risk can be considered as cost [*sic*], it reduces costs. It is in this sense a special case of external economies' (R-R 1943, pp.249–50).

3.2.5 Technological Externalities

R-R identified another externality derived not from indivisibilities or planned exploitation of complementarities in demand, but from technological externalities or 'non-appropriabilities in production functions' (R-R 1984, p.209). It will be recalled that such technological externalities are economic benefits arising from production, though these benefits are not transmitted through the price mechanism, nor are they subject to legal ownership as private property. The primary technological externality is that related to vocational training. An employer's investment in the training of workers cannot be appropriated solely by the employer, since the worker is free to sell his labour power elsewhere. 'There are no mortgages on workers – an entrepreneur who invests in training workers may lose capital if these workers contract with another firm. Although not a good investment for a private firm, it is the best investment for the state' (R-R 1943, p.248).

Rather than seeing such externalities as a logical curiosity of little practical importance – as suggested, for example, by Meade (1952) – R-R regards them in the specific form of vocational training as absolutely central to successful industrialization (R-R 1984, p.209). The state is required to realize technological externalities in the training of industrial workers through state provision of training facilities and facilitating co-operation between firms in vocational training (R-R 1943, p.248). A second technological externality is the positive relationship between the growth of output and the growth of 'effective knowledge'. Although it received only passing comment by R-R, he regarded it as central to the explanation of both the cumulative growth of industrial output and persistent differences in cross-country income. Effective knowledge, or what is now termed learning by doing,

> cannot be acquired by reading a book, or by editorial exhortation. It can be acquired however, on the job! This possibility is a major source of increasing returns to the industrial system as a whole. Perhaps the most important yield of development is a cumulative increase in effective knowledge!
>
> (R-R 1957, p.64)

R-R regarded the growth of effective knowledge as an external economy. It is a function not so much of the growth of an individual enterprise (with the benefits largely appropriated by that enterprise as an internal economy), but is related to the growth of aggregate output, with the benefits of improved know-how diffused across manufacturing industry (R-R 1957, p.64).[8]

3.2.6   Co-ordination of Investment Decisions

It is R-R's contention that markets in underdeveloped regions exhibit major imperfections. These imperfections give rise to a variety of market co-ordination failures.[9] The principal co-ordination failures are 'risk' and the 'divergence between private and social marginal net product'.[10] Risk or uncertainty is reflected in the unwillingness of individual entrepreneurs to commit to large-scale (indivisible) projects. To exploit complementarity in demand and realize increasing returns, as conceived by R-R, investment on a large scale integrated across several industries is required. As noted above, the risk attached to a particular investment varies directly with the proportion of total output the investment is intended to supply. Given that the introduction of a modern large-scale consumer good plant to an underdeveloped region could supply most if not all of the region's requirements for a particular commodity, R-R assumes such investments are far more 'risky' than a similar investment in developed regions, where it may represents simply a small increment to existing supply. An additional source of risk or uncertainty is that a large-scale investment programme integrated across several industries requires a volume of data and capacity for analysis and planning well beyond the scope of any one entrepreneur (R-R 1943, p.250).

Positive external economies generated by an individual entrepreneur are not included in the entrepreneur's calculation of rate of return. It is a feature of a decentralized market economy that maximization of private profit is the only criterion for investment decision-making (R-R 1984, p.215). The level of analysis adopted by finance capital and individual entrepreneurs is the single plant or project. The 'single project approach' adopted by private investors effectively makes 'integration impossible' (R-R 1957, p.67).

> There is no incentive within their framework for many investments that are profitable in terms of 'social marginal net product', but do not appear profitable in terms of 'private marginal net product'. The main driving force of investment is the profit expectation of an individual entrepreneur which is based on experience of the past. Experience of the past is partly irrelevant, however, where the whole economic structure of a region is to be changed.   (R-R 1943, p.250)

R-R does not provide a detailed justification for these claims. It would have been worthwhile for R-R to have considered more deeply the impediments to widespread use of consortia or co-operation between private investors to redress these co-ordination failures.[11] For Marshall and Young, external economies were both a cause and an effect of growth in the size of the market and were 'automatically' realized with the growth of the economy. Marshall and Young assumed a competitive economy with many producers where the output of each producer was (generally) small in comparison to its industry. The benefits which an individual producer provides when they invest (and reduce their costs) or expand their output are relatively small, and it is assumed that the force of competition requires each producer to pass on cost reductions. In other words, the divergence between private and social marginal costs for firms creating or receiving external economies is minimal. By contrast, the structural conditions in underdeveloped regions with a small market and very small number of producers in any industry led R-R and

Nurkse to a different conception of the role of external economies. '[E]xternal economies, instead of covering those cases of increasing returns which occur independently of the output of individual firms (or industries), now cover those cases where the favourable repercussions of investment do not (fully) accrue to the investor in a given field' (Arndt 1955, p.197).

Nurkse identified two additional reasons for the necessity for co-ordination of investment decisions. Foreign private investment in underdeveloped regions is concentrated in commodity production. Apart from not contributing to the type of production envisaged by balanced growth, commodities are subject to widespread synthetic substitutes, low price elasticity of demand and declining and fluctuating terms of trade. Direction by the state, either in the form of incentives or threats, may be required to encourage foreign private investment in manufacturing (Nurkse 1952, pp.261–62). Further, economic co-ordination is required to address the problem of an inadequate savings rate in underdeveloped countries. There is a secular tendency in underdeveloped areas for an insufficient share of national income to be devoted to savings. The warranted rate of savings and investment is above the actual rate. The 'intervening variable', as it were, between increased incomes flowing from an initial investment and a subsequent increased savings rate is the growing relative difference in income levels between rich and poor countries. This differential has the tendency to 'push up the general propensity to consume of the poorer nations.' The objective needs of capital formation run up against the 'demonstration effect' of rich nations living standards, or simply, 'the temptation to copy American consumption patterns' (Nurkse 1952, pp.265–266).[12] The introduction of this constraint on the action of circular and cumulative growth processes is important, as it introduces sociological and psychological elements into what would otherwise be a mechanistic growth model.[13]

The implication for economic development of balanced growth is not simply that it accelerates the rate of per capita output. Rather, the industrial structure will be significantly different and significantly more productive.[14]

> If the industrialization of international depressed areas were to rely entirely on the normal incentive of private entrepreneurs, the process would not only be much slower, the rate of investment smaller and consequently the national income lower, but the whole economic structure of the region would be different. Investment would be distributed in different proportions between different industries.   (R-R 1943, pp.250–251)

At the very end of his career, R-R provided this summary of his thinking on the development process: 'The indivisibilities and the external economies to which they give rise, plus the technological external economies of training labour, were the theoretical foundations for my advocacy of an integrating, synchronizing "big push" to "jump" over the obstacles to development' (R-R 1984, p.215). R-R's arguments for the necessity of co-ordinated investment decisions and the 'Big Push' reverses Marshall's famous dictum of socio-economic evolution, *natura facit saltum* – nature does move in jumps (R-R 1957, p.57).[15]

3.3 ROSENSTEIN-RODAN'S GROWTH MODEL IN PRACTICE

3.3.1 Impediments to Growth in Underdeveloped Regions

In his famous article, 'Problems of Industrialization of Eastern and South Eastern Europe' (1943), Rosenstein-Rodan addressed the issue of post-war reconstruction in south-eastern Europe. The objective was to identify the means to promote 'industrialization in international depressed areas... to produce a structural equilibrium in the world economy by creating productive employment for the agrarian excess population' (R-R 1943, p.254). The symptoms of this structural disequilibrium were underemployment in agrarian societies and large differences in per capita income between developed and underdeveloped nations.

R-R's solution to the problems of underemployment and low per capita income was to advocate the promotion of industrialization by exploiting external economies and complementarities in demand. Two reasons are advanced to explain why the strategy should focus on industrialization. Industrial economies have a higher per capita income than those based on agriculture or other commodities. Manufacturing also generates more externalities than other economic activities (R-R 1984, p.211). R-R identified two major impediments to industrialization in underdeveloped regions such as south-eastern Europe. They were the problem of the small size of the market, which inhibits introduction of an 'optimum size of the industrial enterprises', and creating an environment conducive to 'lowering the marginal risk of investment' (R-R 1943, p.246). To redress the two impediments to development, R-R proposed 'a scheme of... industrialization comprising a simultaneous planning of several complementary industries' (R-R 1943, p.247). The balanced growth doctrine of R-R and Nurkse posits that the introduction of 'large-scale plants in a variety of increasing return industries' producing consumer goods for the home market will reduce the real price of these goods (Fleming 1955, p.276). This will 'tend to increase real income and hence real demand' for the product of these plants (Fleming 1955, p.273). Thus, the co-ordinated introduction of a number of plants, the demand for whose product is complementary, may be jointly profitable, even though each plant, if introduced separately, may be unprofitable. The simultaneous development of complementary industries gives rise to a set of positive externalities, which, it is claimed, will substantially overcome the impediments to development. R-R argues that external economies, especially those arising from growth in the market, are an important source of profitability and inducement to investment. 'If we create a sufficiently large investment unit by including all the new industries of the region, external economies will become internal profits' (R-R, 1943 p.251).

3.3.2   Exploiting Complementarities

R-R argued that the industrial structure of south-eastern Europe had adequate public infrastructure, such as rail and roads, but that the region suffered from low per capita income. This specific structure determined that wage goods industries should be subject to co-ordinated development. These industries allow for the exploitation of complementarities applying to basic consumer or wage goods. In other regions, which had a much lower level of basic infrastructure, such as Asia and Latin America, it would be more appropriate to 'favour a different programme of industrialization' designed to redress these specific capital requirements (R-R 1943, p.252).

R-R argued his case for exploiting complementarity as a means of addressing the problems of indivisibility and risk, with the famous 'shoe factory' example. The establishment of a single modern large-scale shoe factory in a poor region employing 20,000 workers producing for the local market only would be unlikely to make a profit. This is because the minimum economic output of a capital-intensive, large-scale factory may be greater than the annual consumption of shoes within the region at current per-capita income levels. Whilst the income of former underemployed agricultural labourers who may find work in the new modern shoe factory is certainly above that of their previous level, these workers cannot spend all of their income on their own production, as quite obviously they require other basic wage goods for survival.

3.3.3   Redressing Co-ordination Failure

The solution to this problem of deficient demand confronting a single large scale investment was to simultaneously establish a number of wage goods plants, the demand for whose output was linked or complementary. R-R used the analogy of a large integrated firm to describe this process. A planned system of complementary investments would simultaneously redress the problem of insufficient capital and deficient effective demand. Thus 'what was not true in the case of one shoe factory would become true in the case of a whole system of industries: it would create its own additional market' (R-R 1943, p.249). Given an appropriate matrix of industries in which there was no 'leakage' of demand into imports or other industries, supply could create its own demand. 'The new producers will be each other's customers and will verify Say's Law by creating an additional market' (R-R 1957, p.62).[16]

The envisaged instrument of planning was to be the 'Eastern European Industrial Trust', a multinational public sector body charged with selecting industries for development and raising private and public sector capital for their realization (R-R 1943, p.248). In the original 1943 article, and the equally famous 1957 article on the 'Big Push', R-R did not consider how the Trust would identify and quantify the complementarities and externalities central to the realization of the programmed investment approach. (This task would fall to Albert Hirschman, whose principal innovation was to use input-output methods to attempt to quantify some of the externalities identified by Young and R-R.)[17] Nevertheless, R-R's 1943 article was one of the first to employ a number of concepts and techniques that would later become essential tools in applied development studies and applied economics more generally (Rostow 1990, pp.408–409). R-R's ten-year plan for southeastern Europe employed the notions of capital–labour ratio (with estimates of capital per worker required for light, medium and heavy industries), and labour requirements per unit of output. Secondly, the plan applied the Keynesian idea that the savings rate increases with real income. (This implied that dependence on foreign capital would decline over time.) To repay foreign capital it would also be necessary to institute planned international trade by allowing the new industries of south-eastern Europe access to the markets of developed 'creditor countries'. Moreover, structural adjustment policies for creditor countries' would be essential to assist these economies to cope with the displacement of domestic manufactures caused by these imports (R-R 1943, pp.253–255).

In later applied work on development programmes for Italy, India and Indonesia, R-R and others at the MIT Centre for International Studies used more advanced methods, such as shadow prices and linear programming (R-R 1957; 1984, p.216). Given the assumption that market prices are not a good indicator of the optimum social allocation of resources, shadow prices are attached to inputs and outputs of selected industries, the goal being to maximize some objective function, such as income growth or employment creation, against linear constraints. The key constraints were to balance supply and demand, minimize the cost of investment across a range of industries, or minimize adverse balance of payments effects. The effects of scale economies and complementary demand, for example, could be incorporated into these models by assuming, respectively, declining average cost with increasing output, and the increased feasibility of installing new plant if other user/supplier plants are simultaneously established. There are, of course, a number of well-known problems in employing these models, such as the arbitrary estimation of shadow prices, or the opportunity cost of labour, capital, foreign exchange, etc. (Thirlwall 1994, p.269). Reflecting on the development of linear programming techniques in the 1950s, Hollis Chenery commented that, '[h]istorically speaking, the programming approach is thus the operational counterpart of the theory of balanced growth, from which much of its conceptual framework is derived' (Chenery 1961, p.288).

3.4　CRITICISMS OF BALANCED GROWTH

During the two decades the Balanced Growth model was being formulated, it was subjected to sustained attack.[18] Much of this criticism was ill-founded, such as certain static-equilibrium interpretations of the growth model, or Streeten's (1959) mis-understanding of R-R's ideas. Nevertheless, two lines of criticism of the balanced growth doctrine proved to be very influential for the future development of CC thought. These criticisms are the focus of this section. Fleming's (1955) attack, in particular, cut very deeply into the balanced growth edifice. Fleming noted that balanced growth advocated the exploitation of increasing returns, complementarities and externalities in the consumer goods sector only, and largely ignored the scope for industrial development and productivity growth through co-ordinated expansion of both the consumer and producer goods sectors. The broad vision of industrial development that Young had, Fleming argues, has been significantly narrowed by R-R. Somewhat ironically, the major deficiency in Balanced Growth is that it is not sufficiently balanced. The second important line of attack was that offered by Sheahan (1958, 1959). He accepted all of the criticisms of orthodox economics put forward by R-R and Nurkse, but proposed a model of industrialization based on international specialization of production, contrary to the diversified import-substitution model of Balanced Growth.

3.4.1　Inelasticity of Factor Supplies

A critical assumption in the balanced growth model is that factor supplies are sufficiently elastic so that the external economies which a new industry A creates for industry B are not negated by external diseconomies of rising factor prices due to installation of the new A plant. The balanced growth doctrine 'assumes that the relationship between industries is for the most part complementary'. In underdeveloped regions however, 'the limitations of factor supply ensures that the relationship is for the most part competitive' (Fleming 1955, p.279). Inelasticity of factor supply in underdeveloped regions significantly constrains the scope for simultaneous balanced growth across several sectors.

Nurkse (1956) responded to Fleming by noting that the balanced growth model assumed labour supply was elastic due to agricultural underemployment and potential for relocation of labour from existing inefficient cottage industries. R-R also emphasized that planned industrialization must give prominence to vocational training to improve the supply of skilled labour. Capital was also assumed to be available from overseas. Moreover, Fleming ignored the effects of scale economies and co-ordination of economic activity in reducing unit inputs per unit output. In other words, Nurkse was critical of Fleming for casting balanced growth in a static equilibrium framework and then criticizing the inevitable shortcomings arising from this approach.

3.4.2 FAILURE OF BALANCED GROWTH TO EXPLOIT 'VERTICAL INTEGRATION'

Whilst Nurkse was right to admonish Fleming for formulating balanced growth in static efficiency terms, Fleming did nevertheless identify a major flaw in Balanced Growth theory. Fleming criticized the concentration of balanced growth on the exploitation of scale economies and complementarities at the same stage of production, that is, the consumer goods industries. The focus of balanced growth on what he termed 'horizontal integration' largely ignores the scope for economies arising in the 'vertical integration' of capital and intermediate goods production with final demand industries (Fleming 1955, p.283). Just as consumer goods industries commonly 'operate under conditions of imperfect competition, where efficient production is hampered by smallness of the market... factor-producing industries' also operate under increasing returns that may be exploited to reduce input costs (Fleming 1955, p.284). Accordingly, Fleming advocated the joint planning of producer and consumer good sectors. External economies from this joint planning will exceed those if expansion occurred in the consumer and producer goods industries separately.[19] Fleming contends that the '"vertical" transmission of external economies – whether forward from supplying to using industry, or backward from using industry to supplying industry – are much more favourable than for a "horizontal" transmission between industries at the same stage' (Fleming 1955, p.285).

The force of Fleming's representation of balanced growth is reinforced by Nurkse. 'The notion of balanced growth... is a limited one, confined to the horizontal pattern of supply and demand for consumables. It is not applicable in any simple way to the relationship between the overhead facilities sector and the consumer goods sector, which is essentially a vertical relationship' (Nurkse 1963, p.250). Nurkse goes even further to admit he cannot even understand why the two sectors need be linked. 'The notion [of balanced growth] is sometimes used in a far wider connotation, embracing capital goods and public overheads as well as final consumer goods. I confess that I am not able to make sense of it [the balanced growth doctrine] except in terms of income elasticities and complementarities of demand' (Nurkse 1963, p.250n).

It may be objected that following Fleming's 1955 critique, R-R responded to this criticism in the 1957 'Theory of the Big Push', which emphasized the role of infrastructure in development. Whilst R-R identified indivisibilities in infrastructure as a major impediment to development, he did not identify the co-ordinated development of infrastructure and downstream user industries as a method of redressing these impediments. Nor did he consider in any but a cursory manner how these downstream users might benefit. R-R simply stated 'the most important products [of infrastructure] are investment opportunities created in other industries' (R-R 1957 p.60). Further, in the 1943 and 1957 articles he did not emphasise, as did Young, the crucial role of the capital goods and specialised industrial supplies in growth.

Fleming is certainly correct in emphasizing the role of vertical integration of industry, though he pushes his argument too far by claiming that 'Marshall and his commentators' regarded 'horizontal economies' as being 'relatively unimportant' (Fleming 1955, p.285). Fleming views the balanced growth doctrine as a reaction against this earlier devaluing of horizontal economies. This is an unbalanced interpretation of Young's model. Young certainly located the primary source of productivity growth in the overcoming of indivisibilities and 'industrial differentiation' in the capital and intermediate goods sectors. Equally, however – and Fleming is remiss in not emphasizing this point – 'industrial differentiation' and overcoming indivisibilities are only possible in the presence of an expanding market for final demand goods. It is precisely those complementarities in the demand for final demand goods, identified by Young and emphasized by R-R, which underpin growth in the market.

3.4.3   What is the Optimal Industrial Structure?

The concept of Balanced Growth has several meanings in the work of R-R and Nurkse. Some of these include:

(i) Balance of supply and demand;
(ii) Balance of production with changing income elasticities of demand;
(iii) A balance, or quantity of demand, sufficient to overcome indivisibilities in the employment of capital;
(iv) A balance in the production of commodities to exploit complementarities in demand that may exist between them;
(v) A balance of output and the sectoral composition of that output (agriculture, manufacturing, services) with the labour force to create full employment.

What is altogether absent is the notion of inter-industry balance, especially as noted above, between consumer and producer goods industries. One explanation for R-R and Nurkse ignoring the potential benefits of vertical integration is that they never addressed the question of the optimal industrial structure for which underdeveloped regions should be aiming.[20] In other words, the central concern of balanced growth is to identify the means of *initiating* the process of industrialization in underdeveloped regions, not with the end or goals of this process. R-R and Nurkse did not consider what happens after industrialization is initiated, what structural changes are required to continue the development path, and what an optimal or even desirable national industrial structure would look like. Consequently, they ignored the insight of Young as to one of the primary sources of productivity growth in a mature industrial economy, i.e. efficiency gains in the producer goods sector. Subsequently, Albert Hirschman was to give a central role in his strategy for development to the capital goods and intermediate inputs sector.

3.4.4 Diversification versus Specialization

The novelty of Sheahan's (1958) critique of balanced growth is that he accepted many of the arguments advanced by R-R and Nurkse, but rejected their advocacy of an integrated industrial structure founded on import-substitution. Balanced growth advocated a co-ordinated expansion and diversification of domestic production in accordance with changing income elasticities of demand.

Sheahan endorses the balanced growth view that difficulties arise from a concentration of national production in commodities, and accepts 'the real problem of capital indivisibilities' in the industrialization of underdeveloped regions, and the central role of increased capital intensity and scale economies in productivity growth. He also accepts the need for central co-ordination (subject to some caveats) of large-scale investment projects (Sheahan 1958, pp.187–197). Sheahan also concedes the central claim of balanced growth regarding 'the logical connections between returns on individual investment projects and aggregate growth' (Sheahan 1959, p.347).[21] However, Sheahan claims the 'error [of balanced growth] lies in linking returns on individual projects with increases in domestic production of other goods' (Sheahan 1959, p.347). Drawing on Fleming's analysis, Sheahan argues that balanced growth is invalidated by inelastic factor supplies, since 'the basic difficulty of balanced growth is it implies a serious limitation on efficiency unless relative costs remain constant in the expansion process' (Sheahan 1959, p.347). In the face of limited factor supplies, rapid diversification of the economy will result in increasing returns being offset by rising costs. Accordingly, Sheahan proposes the following alternative strategy: 'any co-ordinated program should be concentrated on those focal industries in which returns are highest, taking into account conflicting claims for scarce resources. Concentration on the few best industries should be the guiding rule of any program to raise income' (Sheahan 1958, p.196). In other words, the 'incentive to invest is *not* a function of the degree of balance in domestic production, but of the growth of real income' (Sheahan 1958, p.196). The investment criteria that will optimize the 'growth of real income' are the postulates of specialization and international trade. The identification of a 'country's relatively efficient industries [can be made on the basis of] efficient resource allocation through trade' (Sheahan 1958, pp.192–193). Sheahan's criterion for investment selection is comparative absolute cost as opposed to comparative advantage. In summary,

> the concept of balance may be very misleading for policy in so far as it suggests deliberate guidance of investment in directions matching the pattern of increases in domestic demand. It shifts attention away from the possibility of raising income more rapidly by concentration on production of those goods which fall in relative costs, and trading them for goods which rise in relative cost as domestic production proceeds. *Balancing domestic production and demand would make sense only in the most exceptional case that relative costs remained constant as output increased.*
>
> (Sheahan 1958, p.197, my italics)

Whilst Sheahan is correct in characterizing balanced growth as focusing on import-substitution and growth of the home market, R-R did envisage an important role for foreign trade in the balanced growth model. On the demand side, the 'world market can be a substitute for the additional domestic market' required to validate a large-scale investment. On the supply side, balanced growth did not of course, envisage autarky; 'international trade undoubtedly reduces the size of the minimum push required, so that not *all* the wage-goods need be produced in the developing country, but it does not eliminate it' (R-R 1957, p.63). In addition, the export of some proportion of production from the newly installed consumer goods plants was envisaged to repay the foreign borrowings required to fund the import of these consumer good plants (R-R 1943, p.251). Nevertheless, the key difference remains: for R-R international trade complements balanced growth; for Sheahan international trade is a substitute for it.

Sheahan's critique may itself be criticized on several grounds. Firstly, Sheahan under-mines his own case by readily conceding the compatibility of rising output and constant or even diminishing costs for most or all goods. '[W]here countries are starting from disequilibrium conditions... the borderline of diminishing returns may well be moving away faster than the supply of capital increases'. Rather than being an 'exceptional case... the presumption should ordinarily be that capital formation will, by increasing the total supply of productive factors in the economy, raise real income and have a net positive effect on many, though surely not all, other industries' (Sheahan 1958, pp.195–196).[22] Sheahan's acceptance of the complementarity of investment and the necessity of state co-ordination severely blunts the force of his argument and reduces his objection to Balanced Growth from one based on high theory to an empirical question of how 'many' industries may benefit from co-ordinated expansion. Indeed, it would seem from his comments that the benefits from the pursuit of balanced growth are pervasive. Secondly, Sheahan's use of current cost as the investment criterion (which maximizes present output and consumption) may result in lower long-run growth rates compared to alternative investment criteria. One of the central arguments of balanced (and unbalanced) growth is that not only may there be a difference between private and social marginal product of investments, but these respective returns are likely to differ over time. This is obvious in the case of social overhead capital or infrastructure, where satisfactory direct returns may not arise until the very long term. There are also other investments which are important for a variety of externalities they create, such as backward and forward linkages, skilled labour supply, or technology diffusion. As R-R emphasized, these benefits are not included in the entrepreneur's rate of return, though they are influential in determining the profitability of future investments. Thirdly, Sheahan wants to retain the postulate of efficient national and international resource allocation through trade, but accepts the balanced growth critique of orthodox trade theory. The problem therefore arises as to what are the criteria for the selection of investment projects if the lowest relative cost is dependent on the capital intensity and scale of the project and related inputs. There is, in other words, a circularity in Sheahan's argument, since the identification of industries within a country which have lower relative costs of production than imports is not independent of the scale and scope of previous and proposed investment decisions. Fourthly, Sheahan accepts that supplies of skilled labour, capital intensity and scale are key principal determinants of relative efficiency. It follows that possibly an under-developed nation will never be able to compete against more developed regions which, by definition, are much better endowed in these respects. If, as Sheahan implies, international trade is based on absolute cost advantage (achieved through increasing returns) and not comparative advantage, industrialization in some regions may never occur. Finally, as suggested by Young, R-R and Arndt, capital investments are essentially complementary. An advanced nation has a very broad range of high-quality inputs essential to support any single project. The achievement of 'lowest relative cost' in any particular industry is very dependent on an efficient, broad-based network of industrial supplies and infrastructure. In other words, there may be a conflict between Sheahan's objective of producing at 'lowest relative cost' and his proposed means of industrial 'specialization'.

Sheahan's identification of two approaches to the realization of increasing returns, one based on the establishment of (horizontally) integrated industries satisfying complementary consumer demands largely for the home market, and the other based on a concentration of resources in selected industries producing for export markets, highlights an important bifurcation in the development of CC thought. This conflict between the establishment of a broad interdependent industrial structure founded on the home market, or specialization in the production of a limited range of commodities for export is examined in more detail in Chapter 6.[23] This bifurcation is especially evident in a comparison of the two leading CC theorists, Albert Hirschman and Lord Kaldor. Albert Hirschman (1958) claimed underdevelopment could be defined as an absence of input–output linkages. This is not a tautology: rather, Hirschman argued for a causal connection between the growth of the capital and intermediate goods sectors (i.e. increasing the diversification of and interdependence between industries), and the rate of growth of per capita income. Hirschman's model focussed largely on the growth of the home market. By contrast, Kaldor's post-1966 work stressed the disadvantages and inherent limitations of import-substitution or growth of the home market and strongly advocated the benefits of specialization in the production of a limited range of commodities and export orientation.

3.4.5   Streeten's Arguments for Unbalanced Growth

Paul Streeten's (1959) critique of balanced growth is important for a number of reasons. Firstly, Streeten greatly extends Sheahan's approach of turning the arguments used to derive the theory of balanced growth into a justification for unbalanced development. Secondly, and more importantly, this work exemplifies the sterility of much of the debate between the proponents of balanced and unbalanced growth. By the conclusion to his famous article, the propositions stoutly advanced and defended by Streeten are so qualified and loaded with conditions as to practically dissolve any distinction between the competing growth models.

   The doctrine of Balanced Growth, Streeten observes quite correctly, is derived from indivisibilities in production and complementarities between and within production and consumption (Streeten 1959, pp.170–171). Streeten turns these arguments on their head to derive a case for unbalance between and within production and consumption (for the sake of brevity, we focus only on arguments relating to production in the following):

'The tenor of the argument ... is that in certain conditions unbalance may
stimulate rather than impair progress, that it may be a condition of, rather

than an obstacle to, rapid growth, and that too great an emphasis on balance may cause, rather than prevent, stagnation'.

(Streeten 1959, p.171)

Indivisibilities in production provide a powerful argument for concentration of investment in a limited number of industries. Underdeveloped 'economies without large markets' will not be able to support simultaneous expansion in several complementary industries in which 'economies of scale are important and the optimum size of equipment large'. Streeten interprets balanced growth as being incapable of realising scale economies, since it proposes the establishment of many 'sub-optimal' plants – a series of 'small advances on many fronts simultaneously' (Streeten 1959, p.182). From these conditions, Streeten draws the inference that a 'plan directed at the full exploitation of scale economies will be a plan for unbalanced growth'. The creation of a market to support exploitation of scale economies will involve 'distortion of demand' to direct demand to those industries selected for expansion. This distortion will be achieved through taxes and tariffs, planned shortages in commodities and the probable carrying of surplus capacity for several years in the industry or plant producing under increasing returns (Streeten 1959, pp.176–177).[24]

Given the smallness of the market, the installation of large scale plants in underdeveloped regions will often entail the creation of excess capacity for extended periods. Streeten argues that 'building ahead of demand' has historically given rise to important complementary investments. He argues this effect by way of historical example: 'The construction of railways in the nineteenth century... did not merely meet existing demand, but created new demand by encouraging a whole cluster of activities' such as new population and industrial centres and new sources of raw materials (Streeten 1959, p.180). Shortages and over-supply also create a conducive environment for technological innovation. Referring to several examples of invention during the English Industrial Revolution, such as the use of coal to produce iron owing to a shortage of wood, and the subsequent invention of the steam engine to remove water from coal mines, Streeten argues: 'scarcities and bottlenecks provided the stimulus to the inventions that revolutionised the... world's economic system. Necessity was the mother of invention, but invention was also the mother of necessity' (Streeten 1959, p.181).

Streeten's interpretation of balanced growth is incorrect in several respects. The first is the view that balanced growth is not able to exploit scale economies because it is committed to simultaneous expansion of all or most consumer industries, resulting in sub-optimal size plants for most goods. Nurkse responded to this line of criticism: 'The dispersal of investment over a variety of consumer-goods industries can undoubtedly be carried to excess. The balanced growth principle can be and has been interpreted far too literally. Producing a little of everything is not the key to progress' (Nurkse 1958, p.643). The objective of balanced growth is to raise per capita income through joint planning, not to immediately satisfy all consumer wants. It will also be recalled that R-R specifically saw a role for imports to satisfy some of these wants. Secondly, Streeten ignores the fact that balanced growth does not exclude the possibility of excess capacity or 'building ahead of demand'. Adequate infrastructure is a precondition to development and must precede downstream investment. Social overhead capital, in particular, is subject to considerable and varied indivisibilities, and these combined with 'considerations of deliberate development policy may lead to the building of overhead facilities well in advance of the demand for them. In the process of capital expansion, a lack of balance in the vertical structure of production may be unavoidable or even desirable' (Nurkse 1963, p.250). Finally, unbalanced growth provides only vague advice for the formulation of a development plan or of a criterion to 'decide upon the order in which investments should be carried out' (Streeten 1959, p.182). Streeten's development principles have a decidedly metaphysical quality. 'Only if the forward flow of energy is impeded in all directions by a succession of bottlenecks (if this were logically admissible), and if the backward pull of the passive sectors is stronger than the forward push of the active sectors, is balanced advance indicated' (Streeten 1959, p.183).

If one distinguishes between the contrived disputes and the actual content of the respective theories, it is arguable that balanced growth and unbalanced growth employ nearly identical concepts. Central to both are indivisibilities, externalities, increasing returns and complementarity in demand and investment. The successful exploitation of these factors requires state intervention in the market. One can only but agree with Nath's assessment 'that Streeten... has no real quarrel with balanced growth' (Nath 1962, p.306).

3.5   Conclusion

This chapter has shown, firstly, the evolution of the central concepts of circular and cumulative causation through the theory of balanced growth. Secondly, the chief criticisms of balanced growth were outlined and evaluated. Balanced growth accepted Young's argument that per capita income growth is strongly linked to increasing returns, which in turn is dependent on growth in the size of the market. Balanced growth also accepted Say's Law of Markets, with the mechanisms ensuring an equality of supply and demand being the high income elasticity of demand (at very low income levels) for basic wage goods, and the strong complementarity in demand for these wage goods. The principal innovations balanced growth introduced into CC theory are:

(i) The claim that development entails a shift from a commodity-based to an industrial-based economy;

(ii) Uncertainty amongst entrepreneurs, through expectations about the success of new investments;

(iii) Recognition that indivisibility in the employment of capital may represent a (possibly insuperable) barrier to entry of more efficient production techniques;

(iv) The claim that productivity growth arises mostly from internal economies, that is, increasing the size and capital intensity of individual enterprises;

(v) The claim that the typical industry structure in underdeveloped regions is an oligopoly. This follows from indivisibilities in modern capital-intensive production techniques and the small size of the market – the optimum size plant in underdeveloped regions requires a significant share of a commodity's or industry's output;

(vi) Recognition that indivisibilities, uncertainty and the inability of investors to incorporate external economies into their decision-making may prevent the market mechanism from equating 'private and social marginal net product';

(vii) Consequently, the state may be required to redress these 'co-ordination failures' by controlling the industry composition, volume and timing of investments.

Although Young rejected equilibrium economics, he still regarded 'the market' as providing a satisfactory solution to the allocation of investment, balancing of supply and demand and growth in the system. Whilst his model is built on indivisibilities and externalities, the market is sufficiently large to overcome barriers to the introduction of efficient production techniques, and the force of competition is sufficiently strong to ensure productivity gains are passed on and the means of production are continually revolutionized. For balanced growth, market imperfections produce a number of co-ordination failures such as uncertainty and the 'single project' focus of investors. These failures overwhelm the system preventing the operation of what R-R terms the 'disequilibrium growth process' (R-R 1984, p.207). In an underdeveloped economy co-ordination failures prevent the exploitation of those external economies that are essential to initiate the process of industrialization. In R-R's analysis market imperfections are much less prevalent in developed industrial economies; therefore external economies as a source of growth are less significant and the need for state co-ordination of investment decisions is greatly diminished. For other writers in the CC tradition, notably Myrdal and Kaldor, pecuniary and technological external economies in advanced industrialized regions are pervasive. Moreover, state control of market forces within and across developed economies is essential to ensure that the same factors which account for virtuous growth do not also lead to a vicious circle of decline in demand, productivity, and investment.

Balanced growth advocated a co-ordinated expansion and diversification of consumer goods production based largely on production for the home market. Whilst R-R and Nurkse invoked the name of Allyn Young to justify this strategy, their view ignored crucial aspects of Young's growth model. Balanced growth ignored Young's overwhelming emphasis on productivity growth in the intermediate and capital goods sectors. Subsequently, Hirschman gave priority to the establishment of these sectors in his strategy for development. It is to this adaptation of Young's model that we now turn.

Chapter 4
Albert O. Hirschman (1915–): From Balanced to Unbalanced Growth

> Ordinarily economists have been content with general references to the advantages of external economies, complementarities, cumulative causation, etc. But no systematic effort has been made to describe how the development path ought to be modified so as to maximize these advantages. (Hirschman 1958, p.100)

4.1 INTRODUCTION

A.O. Hirschman's principal work, *The Strategy of Economic Development* (1958), is the most systematic presentation of the case for unbalanced growth.[1] Fleming's (1955) critique of balanced growth provided a solid foundation for Hirschman's model of unbalanced growth. The key element on which Hirschman focused was the claim that inelasticity of factor supply may constrain growth, and consequently must be explicitly addressed in national development plans. Hirschman focused on investment criteria which give priority to improving the elasticity of factor supply through 'backward linkage' to the capital and intermediate goods sectors. Hirschman also concentrated (somewhat idiosyncratically) on limits to the supply of indigenous managerial and entrepreneurial 'decision-making' capacity. The inelasticity of factor supply is the primary reason why Hirschman rejected the programme of large-scale simultaneous investments proposed by balanced growth. In contrast, he favoured a 'sequential' pattern involving the development over time of increased capacity in capital and intermediate goods sectors.

Allyn Young conceptualized the process of growing markets within a mature industrial economy as generating new specialized industries and increased division of labour amongst existing industries in a process of 'industrial differentiation'. This occurred primarily in the intermediate inputs and capital goods sectors. Hirschman similarly conceptualizes the effect of growth in the 'size of the market' in underdeveloped countries as leading to the *creation* of an intermediate inputs and capital goods sector, which over time becomes ever more differentiated. In underdeveloped economies 'industrial development will proceed largely through backward linkage, that is, it will work its way from the "last touches" [simple processing of imported goods such as packaging bulk goods for sale] to intermediate and basic industry' (Hirschman 1958, p.158). The central concern of Hirschman's model is how to get this process of industrial differentiation underway. The major difference between developed and underdeveloped economies is that the latter do not have a complex web of intra- and inter-industry transactions characteristic of an advanced industrial sector. In underdeveloped economies supply of manufactures is largely met through imports. For an underdeveloped economy the act of 'filling in' the intermediate and capital goods sectors in the national input–output transactions table generates circular and cumulative increases in supply capacity and demand. Like Young, Hirschman argues for the circular and cumulative relation between the division of labour and the growth of per capita income and growth in the size of the market.

Hirschman introduced a number of important conceptual innovations into CC growth theory. Firstly, he concentrated on the detailed industrial structure to explain the phenomena of development and underdevelopment. (By contrast, R-R, Nurkse and Streeten were content with broad generalizations regarding the importance of manufacturing in the aggregate in raising per capita income.) Secondly, input–output techniques were used as the primary method for analysing the critical features of industrial structures. Thirdly, input–output multipliers (income, employment and output) were seen as providing a means of quantifying pecuniary externalities arising from complementarities in production and consumption. Lastly, the manipulation of final demand by the state was viewed as providing a means to alter the industrial structure by creating strong inducements to domestic investment in selected industries. These achievements however, are also subject to a number of serious faults. Hirschman 'oversold' the capacity of input–output techniques to capture important aspects of externalities and complementarities in production and consumption. He also proposed a very mechanical model of the relation between demand and investment.

The following account of Hirschman's model focuses on his analysis of the structural differences between developed and underdeveloped nations and his use of the 'linkage' concept in the analysis of these differences. His comments on the role of surpluses/shortages, and the relation between 'social overhead capital' and 'directly productive investments' are given only minor attention. This is because some of these ideas have been previously encountered in Streeten's work and, more importantly, it was Hirschman's structural analysis that provided the major innovation in CC thought.

4.2 THE CRITIQUE OF BALANCED GROWTH

Hirschman prefaced his famous work with a warning to 'the reader that I heartily disagree with the "balanced growth" doctrine. In fact...it was the experience of finding myself instinctively so much at variance with this theory that made me aware of having acquired a distinct outlook on development problems' (Hirschman 1958, p.50). This distinct outlook was the theory of unbalanced growth. The theory of balanced growth, which Hirschman associated with R-R, Nurkse, Arthur Lewis and Scitovsky, does not provide a solution to 'the interlocking vicious circles of underdevelopment' (Hirschman 1958, p.52). Hirschman gave a number of reasons for rejecting balanced growth.

Firstly, Hirschman simply denies that underdeveloped regions have the resources to simultaneously create several consumer goods industries capable of realizing economies of large-scale production. If 'a country were ready to apply the doctrine of balanced growth, then it would not be underdeveloped in the first place' (Hirschman 1958, p.54).

Secondly, Hirschman introduces a new resource constraint: the 'principal scarce resource' in an underdeveloped economy is the capacity for 'genuine decision making' (Hirschman 1958, p.63). Hirschman offers no empirical proof or any other supporting argument for this decidedly idiosyncratic claim. There is, he argues, a shortage of managerial and decision-making capacity to design and implement what he refers to as an 'efficient sequence of investments'. These are investments which simultaneously maximize the use of existing positive external economies and themselves generate external economies. Hirschman contends that the balanced growth model, which he equates with large-scale simultaneous development of several investment projects, 'requires huge amounts of precisely those abilities which we have identified as likely to be in very limited supply' (Hirschman 1958, p.53). One way to make sense of this claim is to view the shortage of capacity for 'genuine decision making' as analogous to R-R's assertion that co-ordination failures are endemic to underdeveloped regions. For both Hirschman and R-R one of the key problems is the incapacity of entrepreneurs to plan or co-ordinate investment so as to exploit external economies. Whereas R-R sought to overcome co-ordination failure through comprehensive state planning, Hirschman is more sceptical of the efficacy of centralized economic direction. The Balanced Growth model is premised on extensive state intervention which entails the raising of private capital and directly controlling the volume, industrial composition and timing of investments. In contrast, Hirschman claims state planning agencies are unlikely to realize the benefits from external economies:

The case for centralized investment planning as growth promoting per se would of course be entirely convincing if it permitted production to be organized in such a way that only external economies were internalized while all the external diseconomies and social costs...remained strictly external to the central authority. (Hirschman 1958, p.56)

There are very considerable external diseconomies arising from the 'ruthlessness and destructiveness of capitalist development', such as structural unemployment, devalued skills and capital and so forth. Further, the state has traditionally assumed responsibility for ameliorating these diseconomies. Hirschman concludes that contradictions in the role of the state, arising from the simultaneous promotion of development and internalization of external diseconomies flowing from that development, results in the state restricting innovation and investment (Hirschman 1958, pp.56–7).[2] In the case of state-run enterprises 'the process of "creative destruction" is constitutionally alien to it because 'destruction' here means self-destruction rather than destruction of somebody else' (Hirschman 1958, p.59). This is a genuinely novel perspective on the role of the state in development, and possibly the most damning argument adduced by Hirschman to a high level of state intervention. However, in concluding his discussion of this topic, he successfully parries the thrust of this argument by noting that 'centrally planned economies have abundant recourse to the old capitalist trick of shutting out of the economic calculus a variety of social costs that are being incurred in the process of growth. As a result they may well achieve accelerated growth' (Hirschman 1958, p.61). In other words, there is apparently no compelling reason for state planning to have an adverse effect on growth processes. Nevertheless, there is no doubt Hirschman's intention was to provide a critique of any growth models (balanced or otherwise) which relied on very large scale state intervention.

> [T]he balanced growth doctrine is usually invoked to provide a justification for centralised governmental direction and coordination of the development process. But this justification is hardly convincing. A task that private enterprise or market forces are unable to handle does not *ipso facto* become ideally suited to performance by public authorities. We must recognize that there are tasks that simply exceed the capabilities of a society...Balanced growth in the sense of simultaneous multiple development would appear to be one of them. (Hirschman 1958, p.54)

Thirdly, Hirschman denies that balanced growth occurs in the real world. When balanced growth theorists examine an economy at two different points in time, they confuse description of an outcome with the cause of growth. Looked at over two discrete points of time, a growing economy has increased output distributed across an increased number of industries in such a way as to give the appearance of growth occurring through a moving equilibrium of balanced intersectoral supply and demand. Such analyses are rejected as simple-minded exercises 'in retrospective comparative statics' (Hirschman 1958, p.62). In reality, growth proceeds as 'a series of uneven advances of one sector followed by the catching-up of other sectors' (Hirschman 1958, p.63). The implication of this argument is that whilst it may be possible to engineer a period of balanced growth, this pattern of development cannot be sustained indefinitely or independently of significant state intervention. Market processes inherently generate unbalanced intersectoral growth. Moreover, this unbalanced pattern of development optimizes growth.

Hirschman's fourth argument against balanced growth is that 'development is a lengthy process during which interaction...takes place...up and down and across the whole of an economy's input-output matrix, and for many decades' (Hirschman 1958, p.66). Economic relationships are enormously complex – in which the growth or decline of one industry or some technological innovation, for example, may have ramifications far from its origins. Such ramifications are generally difficult to predict. This complexity with respect to both interaction and prediction means that balanced growth policies may well be 'futile' (Hirschman 1958, p.69). Presumably this critique applies equally to all planning models, including his own. Nevertheless, the burden of Hirschman's argument is to favour comparatively smaller development projects.

Lastly, both balanced and unbalanced growth models identify externalities as the foundation of growth and use externalities as the criteria for the selection of investment projects. However, Hirschman criticizes the former because this development strategy simply exhausts these externalities and does not provide further stimulus or inducement to additional investment. Balanced Growth can provide 'isolated progress in one area...but only for a limited period; if it is not to be choked off, it must be followed by progress elsewhere' (Hirschman 1958, pp.78–79). The basis of this criticism, which is the central charge against balanced growth, is somewhat obscure, but seems to be based on two separate arguments. 'Hirschman...ridicules balanced growth by pretending that it recommends "balance" – a static equilibrium' (Nath 1962, p.303). Hirschman ignores the fact that a permanent increase in real income will occur under a balanced growth strategy, and this may induce further industrial development in other sectors that were not part of the original group of industries subject to simultaneous development. That is to say, development would not be restricted to the initial set of planned industries, and consequently there is no basis for the claim that externalities will be 'exhausted'. Hirschman is also critical of the reliance of R-R and Nurkse on consumption and production complementarities in the wage good industries. This criticism is similar to that of Fleming (1955). For Hirschman, creation and expansion of the producer goods sector is a crucial mechanism for expanding the size of the domestic market in underdeveloped regions. Not only does growth of this sector improve the elasticity of input supply; just as importantly, for any given expansion in final demand a larger stimulus to the domestic economy is created if both consumer and producer goods industries contribute to production. By proposing expansion only of the consumer goods industry, the balanced growth model implies that a large proportion of capital and intermediate inputs into the consumer goods sector 'leaks' directly into imports (Hirschman 1958, pp.168–169).

4.3   DEFINITION OF EXTERNALITIES AND COMPLEMENTARITIES

For Hirschman, as with Young and R-R, external economies are central to the growth process in both mature competitive industrial economies and in underdeveloped regions.

> The reason ... the theory of growth for advanced economies has not made much of these sequences [of external economies stimulating additional investment] is that they are expected to take place automatically and almost instantaneously; also, with a complete universe of commodities already in production, the needs aroused or opportunities opened up by additional investment result only in marginal adjustment in outputs from *existing capacity*. In underdeveloped countries, on the contrary, these processes are absolutely basic in determining the expansive path of the economy.
> (Hirschman 1958, p.42)[3]

Hirschman, like R-R before him, argues that a key feature distinguishing a mature competitive economy from an underdeveloped economy is that the latter exhibits a profound divergence between private and social marginal net product. Consequently, the state is required to mediate the level, timing and industry composition of investment. 'Underdeveloped economies tend to exhibit certain systematic discrepancies between private costs and social costs [so that] ... reliance on the market would lead to a misallocation of resources' (Hirschman 1958, p.76). Again, like R-R, this divergence is due to the small size of the market which results in an oligopoly market structure for most commodities and inadequate transport and communications, and poorly functioning product and factor markets in underdeveloped regions (Hirschman 1958, p.160). In his analysis of development, Hirschman focuses on pecuniary economies arising from increasing returns and complementarities in production and consumption. Three types of complementarity are identified:

(a)   Production complementarities arising from scale economies where an increase in output of commodity A lowers the costs of producing commodity B – for example, where A is an input to B, and A is subject to increasing returns;

(b) Production or consumption complementarities, excluding scale economies, 'where an increase in the demand for commodity A and the consequent increase in its output call forth an increased demand for commodity B at its existing price' (Hirschman 1958, p.67). In the production process this occurs where B is an input to the production of A, and the output of A increases. In consumption it occurs where A and B are 'joint products'; petrol, for example, is a directly derived demand from motor vehicles (Hirschman 1958, p.67);

(c) Hirschman refers to types (a) and (b) as 'technical complementarities' and notes they are familiar to orthodox economists. Excluding scale economies and derived demands, there are conditions 'where increased availability of one commodity does not compel a simultaneous increase in supply of another commodity, but induces slowly through a loose kind of complementarity in use, an upward shift in the demand schedule.' This is similar to Veblen's concept of 'entrained wants' generated, for example, by fashion and marketing (Hirschman 1958, pp.67–8). An example of this

> looser type of complementarity (entrained want) can be found in the way in which the existence of new office buildings strengthens the demand for a great variety of goods and services [including] . . . restaurant facilities, stylish secretaries, and eventually perhaps to more office buildings as the demonstration effect goes to work on the tenants of older buildings.
>
> (Hirschman 1958, p.68)

From these three types Hirschman derives the following broad definition: 'The common feature of the various complementary situations is that, as a result of the output of A increasing, the profitability of the production of B is being increased, because B's marginal costs drop, or because its demand schedule shifts upward, or because both forces act jointly' (Hirschman 1958, p.69).

4.4   INDUCED INVESTMENT

Hirschman locates increasing returns and complementarities in production and consumption at the centre of his growth theory because externalities 'induce' or 'compel' investments (Hirschman 1958, pp.69–71). Hirschman has a very mechanistic model of the determination of investment. Given an expansion in demand or reduction in costs of production, increased investment will automatically follow. Hirschman refers to this determination as the 'complementary effect of investment' (Hirschman 1958, p.41). This model of induced investment is a return to the pre-Keynesian world of Young in which the effect of money and expectations is absent, and where investment is a direct function of growth in the size of the market and/or reduced cost of inputs. Externalities induce a continuing sequence of increases in demand and supply. The circular and cumulative character of this growth process is well expressed in the following quotation:

> [E]ach move in the sequence [of growth] is induced by a previous disequilibrium and in turn creates a new disequilibrium that requires a further move ... at each step, an industry takes advantage of external economies created by previous expansion, and at the same time creates new external economies to be exploited by other operators.   (Hirschman 1958, p.67)

The model of induced investment in Hirschman's development strategy is analysed in detail in Section 4.8.

4.5   EXTERNALITIES AND DEVELOPMENT POLICY

Hirschman accepts R-R's idea that entrepreneurs are incapable of 'factoring' externalities into their investment equations. This is because private investors allocate capital between competing investment projects on the basis of direct pecuniary costs and benefits. Like R-R, Hirschman regards such orthodox investment criteria as inappropriate in underdeveloped regions. The role of the state is to redress co-ordination failures in investment arising from the inability of private capital to exploit external economies. Externalities provide a criterion for selecting between competing projects. For unbalanced growth the objective of development policy is to select and sequence investment projects, each of which has an output of external economies greater than the input of such economies derived from past and current ventures.

> 'The question of priority [between investment projects] must be resolved on the basis of a comparative appraisal of the strength with which progress in one of these areas will induce progress in another.'
>
> 'In practice, growth sequences are likely to exhibit tendencies towards convergence [of public and private benefits from a given investment] or potentialities of divergence, and development policy is largely concerned with the prevention of too rapid convergence and with the promotion of possibilities of divergence.'
>
> (Hirschman 1958, p.79; p.72)

The fundamental criterion is: to what extent does investment A generate externalities which act to induce or compel investment in projects B or C? A chain of investment decisions which maximize production and consumption complementarities and induces additional investments is an 'efficient sequence' (Hirschman 1958, p.82–83). The particular instruments the state uses in the co-ordination of investment are examined in Section 4.8.

4.6 LINKAGES

Hirschman's development model is founded on the argument that scale economies and complementarities are critical to inducing investment in underdeveloped regions. He asserts it is the role of development policy to create an 'efficient sequence' of investments which maximize the outputs of externalities, thereby perpetuating inducements to invest in a circular and cumulative manner. Hirschman introduced his growth model at a high level of abstraction, but subsequently seeks to operationalize the theory by identifying the tools which economic planners might manipulate to affect his model. In this regard Hirschman makes the bold, and indeed, disparaging remark about other development writers in the CC tradition. 'Ordinarily economists have been content with general references to the advantages of external economies, complementarities, cumulative causation, etc. But no systematic effort has been made to describe how the development path ought to be modified so as to maximize these advantages' (Hirschman 1958, p.100). Hirschman's response to this challenge was to develop the concept of 'linkages'.

4.6.1 Backward Linkage

In relation to private sector investment, 'two inducement mechanisms' operate (Hirschman 1958, p.100). 'Backward linkage' effects apply to intermediate and capital goods industries which supply inputs to the production of other commodities. In input-output terms, backward linkage effects operate on each of the j_i cells in the Jth column vector. The backward linkage of any jth sector (L_{b_j}) can be measured as the ratio of the sum of purchased intermediate inputs to the total value of production – that is:

$$\underset{i}{L_{b_j} = \sum X_{ij}/X_j}$$

A major inducement to invest is created when the output of the Jth industry expands to the point where output of the supplying ji industries reaches a 'minimum economic size . . . the size at which domestic firms will be able both to secure normal profits and to compete with existing foreign suppliers' (Hirschman 1958, p.101). As an empirical generalization, or 'general rule of thumb', Hirschman asserts that backward linkage in underdeveloped regions will take effect 'as soon as existing demand is equal to one half of the economic size of the plant... The additional demand... will come from the growth of existing demand and from the development of new demand through forward linkage' (Hirschman 1958, p.103n). Hirschman provides no evidence for this generalization, nor does he cite any source for the claim. An example of backward linkage would be the incentive to invest in domestic tinplate production as an input to an expanding vegetable or fish canning industry. Once the level of demand for inputs reaches a 'minimum economic size', the volume of which varies according to the type of input and its associated indivisibilities in production, a major stimulus is created to establish domestic supply of these inputs. Hirschman asserts that the typical pattern of development, most notably in South America, has been where

> imported goods have been gradually replaced by domestic production which has been called forth by the existence of a large and stable market. Of considerable importance are the backward linkage effects... The minimum economic size of many intermediate and basic industries is such that in small markets a variety of user industries needs to be established before their combined demand justifies substitution of imports... by domestic production.   (Hirschman 1958, p.113)

4.6.2   Forward Linkage

'Forward linkage' effects operate where an economic agent 'will induce attempts to utilize its outputs as inputs in some new activities' (Hirschman 1958, p.101). In input–output terms, this may be viewed as a row vector A, in which the ai cells in the A row show the industries which use the output of the Ath industry. Each a_i cell represents a proportion of the total sales of the Ath industry. The forward linkage of any ith sector (Lf_i) can be measured as the ratio of inter-industry demand to total demand, that is:

$$Lf_i = \sum_j X_{ij} \Big/ \frac{(\sum_j X_{ij} + Y_i)}{}$$

Generally, the larger the share of total inputs provided by the A industry to the a_i industry, the greater the incentive for an a_i industry to be established. Hirschman provides an example of the strong stimulus provided to the establishment of cement block manufacturing by the existence of a cement industry (Hirschman 1958, p.102). One can think of other examples, such as aluminium processing following on from the establishment of electricity generation capacity, or clothes-making following the establishment of a textile industry.[4]

Backward linkage is the dominant form of linkage, as

> forward linkage could never occur in pure form. It must always be accompanied by backward linkage which is the result of the "pressure of demand". In other words, the existence or anticipation of demand is a condition for forward linkage effects to manifest themselves...forward linkage cannot...be regarded as an independent inducement mechanism.
>
> (Hirschman 1958, pp.116–117)

Whilst the cement industry may stimulate creation of cement block manufacturing, the latter would not exist without a construction industry to absorb its output. To use the Keynesian metaphor, forward linkage which operates through expanding supply capacity, is 'like pushing on a string'.

4.6.3   Combined Linkage Effects

Whilst backward linkage is the dominant form of linkage in promoting investment, the strongest inducement applies where they act together (Hirschman 1958, p.117). Industries having both inducement mechanisms operating on them are 'intermediate or "basic" industries whose products are distributed through many other industrial sectors besides also going directly to final demand...such industries should be given preference over the "last" industries [consumption goods], if they are at all economically feasible' (Hirschman 1958, p.118). Hirschman cites the empirical work of Hollis Chenery (1958), who undertook detailed studies of the input–output structure of underdeveloped nations and its effects on growth and development. Industries having the highest combined backward and forward linkages are intermediate inputs such as iron and steel production, non-ferrous metals, textiles, chemicals and petroleum' (Hirschman 1958, p.106).[5] Transport equipment and machinery industries have a high backward but low forward linkage effect. Hirschman attributes this to the fact that in conventional input–output models the output of these industries is allocatd to the final demand category *Gross Capital Formation* (Hirschman 1958, p.107).

Linkage effects 'account for the cumulative character of development' – that is, they 'go far toward explaining the acceleration of industrial growth which is so conspicuous during the early stages of a country's development' (Hirschman 1958, p.104). Linkages provide the mechanism for simultaneous and progressive expansion in domestic demand and supply. On the supply – side, linkages increase the supply capacity of an underdeveloped economy, especially by expanding the intermediate and capital goods sector. On the demand side, they effectively retain demand in an economy that would otherwise have 'leaked' into imports (Hirschman 1958, p.119). An initial expansion in economic activity induces successive (diminishing) rounds of income, employment and output expansion through input–output multipliers.

4.7 LINKAGES AND ECONOMIC INTERDEPENDENCE

Hirschman defines underdevelopment as the relative absence of linkages or inter-industry interdependence (Hirschman 1958, p.109). An underdeveloped economy is one that has a very large leakage of demand for both intermediate and final demand goods into imports. In comparison with advanced industrial nations, input–output relations are limited – that is, there are a limited number of domestic intermediate and final demand industries and the intra- and inter-industry transactions are very restricted.[6] The structure of underdeveloped economies is such that the circular and cumulative mechanism of simultaneous expansion in demand and supply capacity resulting from investments in the intermediate or capital goods sectors is insufficiently developed for growth to occur. The goal of development policy is to create an interdependent or integrated industrial structure. The means for identifying 'the degree of interdependence shown by any one industry' is given by:

1. the proportion of its total output that does not go to final demand but rather to other industries, and
2. the proportion of its output that represents purchases from other industries. (Hirschman 1958, pp.104–105)

The first and second criteria respectively measure the extent of an industry's forward and backward linkage with other domestic intermediate and capital goods industries.[7] Industries which overwhelmingly possess these linkages – that is, those which are most interdependent in their inter-industry transactions – are in manufacturing. The significance of manufacturing for development is that there is 'a close correlation with both income per capita and with the proportion of the population occupied in manufacturing' (Hirschman 1958, p.109). Like Young, R-R and Nurkse, Hirschman discounts the role of agriculture and mining in economic development. The limited linkages between agriculture/mining and the rest of the domestic economy is 'the most important reason militating against any complete specialization of underdeveloped countries in primary production'. Agriculture has forward linkages with many industries, but these generate low value-added. Mining in underdeveloped regions is typically conducted as an 'enclave' development where exports 'slip out of the country without leaving much of a trace in the rest of the economy' (Hirschman 1958, p.110).

4.8 LINKAGES, INTERDEPENDENCE, AND DEVELOPMENT POLICY

By showing the linkages of demand and supply that exist between industries, input–output provides an essential tool to 'describe how the development path ought to be modified' (Hirschman 1958, p.100). The means of developing a more integrated input–output structure is to promote industrialization, primarily through import-substitution and growth of the home market. Hirschman does not discuss at length an alternative export-led development strategy. An export-led strategy is rejected on the basis that a developing country would not have the technical competence to supply those manufactured goods which are demanded in advanced industrial countries (Hirschman 1958, pp.170–172). In addition, it is reasonable to infer from Hirschman's analysis that the objective of developing an integrated industrial structure is more readily achieved on the basis of planning domestic growth in supply and demand. Another possible reason for his failure to consider an export-led growth strategy for an underdeveloped nation was the absence in the immediate post-war period of a real-world model of such a form of development. Japan and Taiwan, for example, were several years away from exporting even a modest share of their national output.[8] Hirschman's emphasis on developing an integrated industrial structure as the optimum means of raising per capita income is the antithesis of Sheahan's (1958) counsel. (It will be recalled that Sheahan advocated a nation should specialize in the production of a limited number of products and exchange these on international markets.)

Given the key role of linkages in promoting manufacturing, the major issue in development policy is 'how are linkage effects to be maximized?' (Hirschman 1958, p.104). State interference or direction is required to alter the pattern of consumption and investment towards those industries which possess the strongest linkages and are capable of being undertaken, given current technical capacities and output. Hirschman, however, provides only cursory suggestions as to the instruments and planning methods the state is to employ. The first is to provide adequate 'social overhead capital' as infrastructure, health and education provide an essential complement to private 'directly productive activities' (Hirschman 1958, p.83). Secondly, the state can alter the pattern of consumption and investment.

> [S]ome interference through tariffs, excise taxes, and subsidies, with the developing consumption of a country may be justified if it can be demonstrated that a certain growth pattern of consumption would exert far more powerful backward linkage effects than the pattern that is likely to develop in the absence of interference ... [In other words,] capital formation can be called forth merely by rearranging and concentrating the pattern of imports. (Hirschman 1958, pp.115–116)

Once the level of demand for imports reaches a minimum economic size, investment in domestic production of the imported product and/or production of inputs into the product is assumed to be automatically 'induced'. Hirschman's theory of induced investment is central to the operation of linkages and development policy. As noted in Section 4.4, the theory is notable for the absence of explicit consideration of income and savings and their relation to investment. In this regard, Hirschman is similar to Young and R-R, who largely ignore the monetary aspects of the economy. For Young, R-R and Hirschman, the volume of investment is determined by the size of the market. Hirschman considers the question of capital formation in input–output terms, where, for example, the output and investment in intermediate goods industries is a simple step-function of the level of final demand. As soon as demand for a particular commodity reaches a level equal to 'the domestic production threshold, i.e. the minimum economic size at which domestic production is undertaken', the requisite domestic investment in the import replacing activity will be made (Hirschman 1958, p.114).[9] This process is illustrated in Figure 3.

Let there be n activities, the first k of which are not carried on within an underdeveloped region at the beginning of the development process. The outputs of k industries are imported and are used as inputs to the $n-k$ industries or enter directly into final demand. In Figure 3 all imports are non-competitive. The first k columns of the matrix are filled with zeros because they correspond to the inputs of the k activities, which by assumption are not produced domestically. The imports M_1, M_2....M_k are

		Intermediate Demands from: $1\cdots k$	$k+1\cdots\cdots n$	Final Demand	Total Demand
Outputs from	1 2 ⋮	O⋯O	$M_{1,k+1}\cdots M_{1n}$	M_{1F}	M_1
		O⋯O	$M_{2,k+1}\cdots M_{2n}$	M_{2F}	M_2
	k	O⋯O	$M_{k,K+1}\cdots M_{kn}$	M_{kF}	M_k
	$k+1$	O⋯O	$X_{k+1,k+1}\cdots X_{k+1,n}$	$X_{k+1,F}$	X_{k+1}
	n	O⋯O	$X_{n,K+1}\cdots X_{nn}$	X_{nF}	X_n
Value added		O⋯O	$X_{V,K+1}\cdots X_{Vn}$	—	—
Total input		O⋯O	$X_{K+1}\cdots X_n$	—	$X+M$

Figure 3:   Hirschman's Model of Induced Investment

(*Source*: Hirschman 1958, p.114)

determined by specified final demands: this gives us directly the final demand component of the M's (M_{1f}, M_{2f}...M_{kf}) and, indirectly, via the inverse matrix, the intermediate import demand components. It is assumed that information is available on the trend rate of growth for imports, and the domestic production threshold of these imports, i.e. the minimum economic size at which domestic production is undertaken. Let the outputs defining these thresholds be T_1, T_2 ...T_k, and the corresponding capital requirements K_1, K_2...K_k. At the beginning of the growth process all the M's are smaller than the corresponding T's. But with the growth of final demands, a point will be reached where some M_j will be equal to or larger than T_j, and therefore the economy will make the investment K_j. 'In this way, one can derive an induced investment pattern' (Hirschman 1958, p.114).

Hirschman's model does not adequately emphasize the positive effects on the growth of final demand with each increment in the growth of domestic intermediate supply. For example, the model could be 'closed' by considering the growth in primary inputs (wages, gross operating surplus and taxes) and the positive effect of the income-multiplier on the growth of final demand, following each instance of import-replacement investment. Highlighting this mechanism would round-out the model and more clearly demonstrate the CC pattern of growth.

4.9 CRITICISMS OF HIRSCHMAN'S MODEL

4.9.1 Induced Investment

Three decades after his famous work, Hirschman (1987) was to regard the assumption of a strict deterministic relation between demand and investment as unwarranted. In the absence of either state ownership or very strong command over private investment decision making, it is not possible to accurately predict the reaction of entrepreneurs to an 'inducement' to invest. The 'animal spirits' of entrepreneurs imply that the existence of an incentive to invest does not guarantee the investment will be made in the short or medium term. This is especially the case in underdeveloped regions owing to lack of supporting infrastructure and political instability (Hirschman 1987, p.206). The younger Hirschman failed to justify the mechanical link between demand and investment. As Paul Streeten wittily noted, Hirschman's model 'points only to possibilities, not to necessities or even probabilities. But how illuminating is this? If my aunt had wheels she would be an omnibus. Is this a useful maxim for a minister of transportation?' (Streeten 1984, p.117). Supporting Hirschman's scepticism towards his early mechanistic model are econometric studies of the determinants of investment. Whilst these studies consistently find demand is the dominant explanatory variable, other factors may be of considerable importance (Toner 1988).[10] In addition, Hirschman ignores the central role of skilled labour supply and the cumulative experience with production processes that are an essential precondition for the introduction of modern production techniques into underdeveloped regions. It will be recalled that Rosenstein-Rodan gave particular prominence to these aspects of the development process, and advised that state plans specifically address these factors. Hirschman ignores the possibility that a shortage of skilled labour, insufficient experience with particular industrial processes and the absence of a broad range of industrial inputs may mean it is simply not feasible to construct and run a large-scale modern plant, even though the level of demand for its output may validate the investment. Stigler, in his classic paper on the division of labour, bemoaned the 'widespread imitation of American production methods abroad,...[whereby] "backward" countries are presumably being supplied with our latest machines and methods.' This imitation is 'seriously inappropriate for industrialization on a small scale. Our processes will be too specialized to be economical on this basis. The vast network of auxiliary industries which we can take for granted here will not be available in small economies' (Stigler 1951, p.193). In other words, whilst the size of the market may justify the introduction of a particular plant in terms of being able to absorb its output, the market may be too small to justify the establishment of those suppliers of specialized inputs or services that are essential to the operation of a particular plant and to ensure that the plant's costs are competitive against imports. As Young emphasized, either several similar plants may be required to justify the establishment of specialist suppliers or these specialists may need to supply a variety of different industries.[11]

4.9.2   Input–Output Multipliers and Externalities

Hirschman used backward and forward input–output multipliers, derived from the Leontief inverse as an empirical analogue for backward and forward linkages which, in turn, are related to complementarities in production and consumption.[12] Hirschman undoubtedly made a breakthrough in suggesting the use of input–output techniques to quantify some externalities. Backward and forward multipliers are a precise way of quantifying the inter-industry effects of pecuniary externalities for producers arising from an expansion in general or industry-specific final demand. Input–output is ideally suited to capturing what Hirschman called 'technical complementarities' or the direct and indirect effects of inter-industry purchases and sales.

However, the technique does have major limitations. For example, the identification and exploitation of plant scale economies in Hirschman's model is the principal source of productivity growth, but standard input–output techniques assume a linear production technology, or constant returns to scale. Without this knowledge, the planning of a vertically integrated economy exploiting ongoing reductions in input costs is problematic. Also, input–output does not capture technological externalities, such as benefits arising from training of skilled labour, diffusion of technology or knowledge generated through research and development. In other words, input–output technique is static and assumes fixed coefficients in production, whereas the process of growth and transformation that is the foundation of CC is inherently dynamic.[13] In addition, the technique cannot capture the 'loose kind of complementarity in use' emphasized by Hirschman, where the increased availability of one commodity creates 'entrained wants' or results in an 'upward shift in the demand schedule' for other commodities (Hirschman 1958, p.68). To use his earlier example, input–output cannot show the effect of new office buildings on the demand for restaurants, 'stylish secretaries', or additional new office buildings. This is because additional new office buildings and restaurants are not inputs into the production of office buildings and thus they are not evident in backward linkage calculations. Nor do office buildings appear as inputs into the production of restaurants, etc., and thus they are not evident in forward linkage calculations. In addition, although standard input–output techniques can demonstrate the compounding effects of a rise in production on employment, output and income for an economy, they cannot identify changes in the composition of final demand due to rising per capita income and changes in the income elasticity of demand for different commodities. It will be recalled that changing consumption patterns arising from increases in per capita income, especially an increase in the variety of commodities demanded, are an essential part of development in CC growth theory.[14]

The older Hirschman viewed the use of input–output multipliers in a strategy for development very circumspectly, even finding that the use of input–output analysis to measure linkages 'was largely an illusion' (Hirschman 1987, p.206). It is significant that in this later definitive account of the linkage concept (in the New Palgrave), externalities receive no mention whatsoever, and the role of input–output is relatively minor (Hirschman 1987, pp.206–211). Following the 1958 work, the concept of linkage was taken up by development economists as a generic term for any sort of economic interdependence, though it must be noted that Hirschman (1987) apparently endorsed this wider (and looser) usage. The resulting 'proliferation of linkages' includes, 'lateral, fiscal, financial, procurement, locational, managerial, pricing', etc. (Streeten 1984, p.117). Given the proliferation of meanings and 'the difficulties of measurement', Hirschman concluded that 'the linkage concept has been more influential as a general way of thinking about development strategy than as a precise, practical tool in project analysis or planning' (Hirschman, 1987 p.207).

4.9.3   Balanced and Unbalanced Growth as Competing Development Strategies

Finally, Hirschman's insistence on a profound distinction between the balanced and unbalanced growth theories is not well-founded. By arguing that an optimal growth strategy entails the joint exploitation of backward and forward linkages where capital goods, intermediate, and final demand industries are either established simultaneously or in close temporal relation, has not Hirschman provided an excellent case for a form of balanced growth? At various points in his work, Hirschman recognizes this possible interpretation but seems to recoil from the conclusion. He rejects this conclusion by recourse to the argument (or device) that such simultaneous projects are not possible because of the shortage of managerial expertise to competently co-ordinate these investments. He notes for example, that the

> joint linkage effects of two industries . . . considered as a unit are likely to be larger than the sum of their individual linkage effects . . . Here we have an argument in favour of multiple development that we would consider convincing were it not that our principal argument against it is concerned with its feasibility rather than with its desirability.   (Hirschman 1958, p.104)

Paradoxically, Hirschman maintains that whilst such balanced growth strategies should not be pursued by governments, these same joint linkage effects 'help to account for the cumulative character of development . . . This mechanism may go far towards explaining the *acceleration* of industrial growth which is so conspicuous during the early stages of a country's development' (Hirschman 1958, p.104).

Nath has argued that the only real difference between balanced and unbalanced Growth strategies is the scale or magnitude of investments that each considers feasible at any point in time, with unbalanced growth favouring smaller-scale industrial development over a more limited range of industries. Nath concludes: 'in spite of Hirschman's loud and bitter denunciations of balanced growth, it is difficult to see he has any real quarrel with the concept' (Nath 1962, p.303). Certainly there is considerable agreement with R-R on the goals of development policy; creating a modern industrialized economy based on complementary capital-intensive industries subject to scale economies. There is also considerable agreement on the instruments of planning. 'The way in which investment leads to other investment through *complementarities* and *external economies* is an invaluable 'aid' to development that must be consciously utilized in the course of the development process' (Hirschman 1958, p.73, my italics). Nevertheless, there is one key difference: this is the concentration of Balanced Growth solely on the exploitation of complementarities in consumption with very little consideration given to the vertical integration of industry.

4.10 CONCLUSION

Hirschman's major contributions to the development of CC thought were, firstly, to focus on the detailed industrial structure of an economy and the mechanisms whereby this structure determines the rate of income and productivity growth. 'To look at unbalanced growth means...to look at the dynamics of the development process *in the small*' (Hirschman 1958, p.ix). The extent of backward and forward linkage within a given industry or group of industries determines the size of the stimulus to an economy by a given expansion in final demand. In other words, for a given expansion in final demand, the extent of economic interdependence determines growth in the size of the market. Growth in the size of the market allows for the overcoming of indivisibilities ('minimum economic size' of plants), and exploitation of increasing returns, which in turn improves productivity and facilitates continued growth in the size of the market. Like Young, Hirschman focuses on the intermediate and capital goods sectors in the growth of productivity. In addition, by dwelling on the relation between the producer and consumer goods sectors, Hirschman is much closer to the spirit of Young than R-R or Nurkse, who focused solely on productivity growth in the consumer goods sector. Unlike Young, Hirschman's focus, at least in the first instance, is not on the continuing division of labour that occurs within a mature producer and intermediate goods sector; rather, it is on the processes for creating such a sector.

Hirschman proposed the use of input–output techniques to both rigorously define and quantify complementarities in production and consumption, and to demonstrate the process of inter-industry division of labour, broadly defined. Young also gave prominence to complementarities in production and consumption, but lacked the analytical means to precisely express these economic relations. In Chapter 2 it was suggested that Young was proposing an elementary input–output conception of the economy, whereby goods and services embodying the benefits of increasing returns are traded, and positively affect directly and indirectly virtually all productive activity. Inter-industry trade is the means whereby pecuniary economies, decreasing costs and increasing demand in one sector are transmitted to other sectors. In comparison with Hirschman, R-R provided only a small advance on Young in terms of quantifying the inter-industry flow of external economies that are central to CC growth theory. R-R also furnished the most elementary tools for what Young termed an 'industrial dictator' to introduce virtuous growth circles to an underdeveloped economy. The primary tools were the notion of complementary demand for basic wage goods and ensuring that the supply of commodities is consistent with their respective income elasticities of demand.

Hirschman was one of his own best critics and correctly observed that the principal fault in his early work was that the variety of external economies and the sources of these economies could not be adequately captured on the Procrustean bed of the Leontief inverse matrix. Equally, the model of capital accumulation, where investment is automatically induced by demand, is excessively mechanistic. However, it is arguable that whilst the young Hirschman 'over-sold' the linkage concept, the older Hirschman sold the concept 'short'. The older Hirschman regarded the use of input–output to measure linkages as 'largely an illusion', and dismissed linkages as an operational tool in development planning. Surely, input–output techniques do capture vitally important aspects of economic interdependence; backward and forward multipliers do represent some important pecuniary externalities, especially those arising from complementarities in consumption and production. Additional techniques, either quantitative or qualitative, such as industry case studies or examining historical patterns of development, are required for the identification of these other externalities.[15] These externalities include those arising from co-operation between industries in the training of labour, economies of agglomeration or the recognition of industries that are particularly important in the generation and/or diffusion of new technologies.[16]

Finally, Hirschman's analysis of development through detailed examination of the transformation of the industrial structure using input–output techniques and his findings regarding the central role of manufacturing, and especially the intermediate and capital goods industries and the incremental growth of 'roundabout' production methods and division of labour in the growth of per capita income, has received very impressive empirical support over the last three decades, particularly in the work of Professor Hollis Chenery and his colleagues.[17] Unfortunately, Hirschman's methods and findings have not been accorded the prominence they deserve among contemporary CC theorists. In Chapter 7 this issue is taken up in criticism of contemporary theorists in the CC School and discussion of the future research programme for CC theory.

Chapter 5
Gunnar Myrdal (1898–1987): Circular and Cumulative Causation as the Methodology of the Social Sciences

> The hypothesis of circular and cumulative causation, which tends to be the doctrine of despair for the poorer countries as long as they leave things to take their natural course, holds out glittering prizes for a policy of purposive interferences.
>
> (Myrdal 1958, p.85)

5.1 INTRODUCTION

Any account of the theory of circular and cumulative causation must include Gunnar Myrdal. It was Myrdal who first used the term 'circular causation of a cumulative process', and in the history of economic thought he is the one (other than Kaldor) most identified with the concept. In his methodological work especially, Myrdal made the vital contribution of clearly stating the logic or abstract principles of the CC model. An exposition and analysis of these principles is the primary focus of this chapter.

Myrdal introduced three important innovations into CC theory. Firstly, he regarded the concept as applicable to both underdeveloped and developed regions. R-R and Hirschman maintained that external economies are much less important in the growth of developed regions, given their assumption that the larger the economy the more it would approximate to competitive conditions. The second innovation was to emphasize the effect of trade, capital flows and migration between rich and poor regions as an active cause of underdevelopment. Both R-R and Hirschman regarded the cause of underdevelopment as largely endogenous to underdeveloped regions. Myrdal highlights the development of underdevelopment through free trade, for example, whereby more competitive imports may inhibit the expansion of domestic manufacturing in underdeveloped regions. The third innovation was to give equal prominence to economic and non-economic factors – that is, social, cultural and political influences – in the explanation of growth and decline. The account provided here of Myrdal's explanation of circular and cumulative causation is drawn primarily from his methodological writings. These writings greatly illuminate the general principles or logic of CC and provide an insight into the way Myrdal sought to develop circular and cumulative causation as the appropriate methodology for the social sciences.[1]

5.2 EQUILIBRIUM VERSUS CIRCULAR AND CUMULATIVE CAUSATION

For Myrdal the fundamental problems of what he terms 'conventional economics', which equates primarily but not exclusively with the neoclassical doctrine, are its adherence to the logico-deductive method and the notion of 'stable equilibrium'. Conventional economics also admits only a single cause, the 'economic factor', into the explanation of events (Myrdal 1958, p.22). The method of conventional economics consists largely of the creation of *a priori* premises and the construction of theories based on logical inferences from these premises. Myrdal does not object to abstraction per se; indeed, he recognizes that theory 'must always be *a priori* to the empirical observation of facts. Facts come to mean something only as ascertained and organised in the frame of theory' (Myrdal 1958, p.160). Such theories, however, must be 'realistic' and 'relevant', and this can only be determined by the empirical testing of hypotheses. Myrdal describes the CC approach as concerned primarily with the realism of assumptions from which are constructed 'bold simplifications' or empirically falsifiable theories. Such theories are always tentative or 'makeshift', subject to revision in the light of new experience (Myrdal 1958, p.163).

In Myrdal's methodology we come full-circle back to Clapham who, it will be recalled, was equally critical of Marshallian and neoclassical 'empty economic boxes' fashioned by *a priori* reasoning.

'In our present situation the task is not, as is sometimes assumed, the relatively easy one of filling "empty boxes" of theory with a content of empirical knowledge about reality. For our theoretical boxes are empty primarily because they are not built in such a way that they can hold reality. We need new theories which, however abstract, are more realistic in the sense that they are in a higher degree adequate to the facts'.

(Myrdal 1958, p.163)

Myrdal is particularly critical of adherence by economists to the *a priori* assumption of stable equilibrium. The idea of stable equilibrium has permeated almost all economic and social theory over the last 200 years. The origins of the idea are in the philosophy of 'natural law' and utilitarianism, which were based on the view that there exists or may exist, subject to the removal of certain interferences, a natural harmony of interests between people. Modern social and economic theory has also drawn on equilibrium concepts from physics and mechanics (Myrdal 1953, p.32; 1944, p.1065; 1958, p.142). Stable equilibrium involves two key assumptions: firstly, in any social and economic system there are equal and opposite forces in operation; secondly, these forces operate to provide automatic adjustment in the event of a de-stabilizing endogenous or exogenous force. Consequently, any disequilibrium is only temporary: 'a change will regularly call forth a reaction in the system in the form of changes which on the whole go in the opposite direction to the first change' (Myrdal 1958, p.13). The consequence of this obsession with equilibrium is that 'economic theory in general' has not been 'developed to comprehend the reality of great and growing economic inequalities and of the dynamic processes of underdevelopment and development' (Myrdal 1958, p.157). Although rejecting the specific idea of 'stable equilibrium', Myrdal proposes 'the utilization of other equilibrium notions besides this simplest one' (Myrdal 1944 p.1065). Drawing directly from physics, he notes a number of other forms of equilibrium. These forms are:

(i) the motion of an object in a frictionless universe will continue until acted upon by an outside force;
(ii) the apparently indeterminate final resting position of an object in motion, for example, 'when a pencil is rolling on a plane surface it may come to rest anywhere', and;
(iii) a 'labile equilibrium' such as a falling body subject to 'an accelerated movement away from the original state of balance'.

Myrdal asserts that for 'dynamic analysis of the process of change in social relations [these]... types of equilibrium notions are better descriptions of social reality than the stable one' (Myrdal 1944, p.1065). This basic proposition is to be found unchanged from Myrdal's earliest methodological writings, such as the Appendix to *An American Dilemma*, 1944, through *Economic Theory and Under-Developed Regions*, 1958, to his 1972 work *Against the Stream: Critical Essays on Economics*.[2] Myrdal's methodological work is important in clearly stating the key methodological differences between CC theory and equilibrium modes of reasoning. It is also arguable that Myrdal's work established a foundation for Kaldor's later critique of the logico-deductive method of neoclassical economics and formulating his own approach based on the notion of 'stylized facts'. This is discussed in more detail in Chapter 6. From this rejection of static equilibrium and the logico-deductive method, Myrdal postulated an alternative method based on the principles of circular and cumulative causation. This alternative method is examined below.

5.3   THE PRINCIPLES OF CIRCULAR AND CUMULATIVE CAUSATION

The appropriate method for study of the general dynamics of underdevelopment and development is what Myrdal termed 'the circular causation of a cumulative process'. The secondary literature is in general surprisingly vague as to the meaning of Myrdal's notion of circular causation. Moreover, Myrdal's own accounts are discursive. To provide a precise and concise summary, the theory has been reduced to seven propositions. These fundamental propositions are:

(i) *A change in an economic and social system induces further self-supporting or reinforcing changes.*

'[I]n the normal case there is no... tendency towards automatic self-stabilisation in the social system... a change does not call forth countervailing changes but, instead, supporting changes, which move the system in the same direction as the first change but much further. Because of such circular causation a social process tends to become cumulative and often to gather speed at an accelerating rate'. Consequently, 'the cumulative process, if not regulated, will cause increasing inequalities'.

(Myrdal 1958, p.13; p.12)

(ii) *The time-rate of change of a system and the variables which compose it are not constant.*

'The time element is of paramount importance, as the effects of a shock on different variables of the system will be spread very differently along the time axis. A rise in employment, for instance, will almost immediately raise some levels of living, but a change in levels of education or health is achieved more slowly, and its effects on the other factors are delayed, so that there is a lag in the whole process of cumulation'.

(Myrdal 1958, p.18)

(iii) *Both social and economic factors are responsible for development and under-development and these factors cannot be arbitrarily separated.*

'[I]t is useless to look for one predominant factor, a "basic factor" such as the "economic factor"... it becomes indeed, difficult to perceive what precisely should be meant by the "economic factor" as distinct from the others, and still less understandable how it can be "basic", as everything is cause to everything else in an interconnected circular manner'. 'Economic theory has disregarded... so-called non-economic factors and kept them outside the analysis. As they are among the main vehicles for the circular causation in the cumulative processes of economic change, this represents one of the principal short comings of economic theory'. The 'application' of circular and cumulative causation 'moves any realistic study of under-development and development, in a country or a region... far outside the boundaries of traditional economic theory'.

(Myrdal 1958, p.19; p.30; p.19)

(iv) *Circular and cumulative forces can be consciously controlled.*

Left uncontrolled, the 'free' market will accelerate the simultaneous ten-dency towards development and underdevelopment within a nation and across nations. 'The more we know about the way in which the different factors are inter-related... the better we shall be able to establish how to maximize the effects of a given policy effort designed to move and change the social system'. The circular and cumulative approach provides 'argu-ments for state planning of economic development in an underdeveloped country and large-scale state interferences'. 'The hypothesis of circular and cumulative causation, which tends to be the doctrine of despair for the poorer countries as long as they leave things to take their natural course, holds out glittering prizes for a policy of purposive interferences'.

(Myrdal 1958, p.20; p.156; p.85)

(v) *The theory of circular and cumulative causation applies equally to the explanation of economic growth as to decline, and to underdeveloped nations as to developed ones.*

The theory 'of the circular causation of a cumulative process [provides] a vision of the general theory of underdevelopment and development'. CC is 'the principle by which an underdeveloped country can hope to "lift itself by its shoe strings"'. (Myrdal 1958, p.20)

(vi) *Circular and cumulative processes are caused primarily by industrialization.*

The differential development of manufacturing within regions and nations accounts for differences in per capita income across regions and nations. Explaining the higher per capita income of Northern Europe relative to that of Southern Europe, Myrdal notes that 'industrialization is the dynamic force in this development'. He argues in favour of development policies promoting manufacturing industry, 'industrialisation is intended to rectify an economy in imbalance and to give a dynamic momentum' (Myr-dal 1958, p.29; p.29n). The specific mechanisms of circular and cumulative causation arising from manufacturing are detailed in Section 5.4.

(vii) *Rates of growth or decline may be self limiting.*

For a number of reasons, circular and cumulative processes can give rise to 'countervailing changes' which limit or even reverse the direction of change. In other words, there may be endogenous limits to the operation of virtuous or vicious circles. In regional analysis, for example, Myrdal identified restraints on regional growth arising from external diseconomies, such as congested transportation and the fact that 'wages and the remuneration of other factors of production will be driven up to such a high level that other regions can get a real chance to compete'. In addition, what are termed 'spread effects', emanating from growth centres, may exercise a positive economic effect on poorer regions (Myrdal 1958, pp.35–36; p.31). These spread effects include, for example, increased demand for agricultural produce arising from increased per capita income in industrial centres.

Rather than acknowledging 'countervailing changes' as a contradiction to proposition (i), Myrdal simply regards it as 'a complication of the main hypothesis'. Thus if the 'spread effects' are sufficiently strong and well distributed, 'the problem of inequalities becomes a problem of the different rates of progress between regions'. In the most likely instance, however, 'even in a rapidly developing country, many regions will be lagging behind, stagnating or even becoming poorer'.   (Myrdal 1958, p.32)[3]

5.4   THE MECHANISMS OF CIRCULAR AND CUMULATIVE CAUSATION

Unlike other authors considered in this essay, Myrdal identified a diverse range of dynamic mechanisms that produce circular and cumulative processes. Again, unlike the other authors, he did not develop a 'new' or novel mechanism, such as Young's circular and cumulative relation between increasing returns and growth in the size of the market, Rosenstein-Rodan's complementarity of basic final demand goods, or Hirschman's linkages. Nor did he give priority to any particular mechanism in his methodological work. Different mechanisms should be selected that best explain a particular circumstance. Nevertheless, in common with others in the CC school, it is manufacturing that is capable of generating the increasing returns, external economies, productivity and investment which are the source of per capita income growth.

Myrdal was of the opinion that the mechanisms underlying the theory of circular and cumulative causation did not represent a radical break with conventional economics. He explained his position thus:

The system of thought I have criticized [ie. conventional economics], is actually a matrix of a large number of special theorems, most of which can be reshaped and fitted to other systems founded upon other assumptions... [Moreover] 'many of these theorems which do not fit too well in the present [conventional] structure... fit excellently into the new one. The development of the "infant industry" argument, and many other special considerations by classical economists... contained *in nuce* the hints of a much more realistic approach to the problems of the underdeveloped countries. (Myrdal 1958, pp.156–157)

Since Myrdal considered the mechanisms to be well ensconced in general economic theory, this probably explains the fact that he did not intensively analyse any of them. Where they are used in empirical or methodological accounts, they are referred to as if their workings in a particular situation would be self-evident to the reader. Myrdal's discussion of these mechanisms is generally discursive, so for the purpose of simplicity in exposition the mechanisms have been divided into two major elements.

5.4.1 Increasing Returns and External Economies

The first set of mechanisms that account for growth and/or decline regionally, nationally and internationally are increasing returns and external economies. These are generated through the 'interrelated economic quantities: demand, earning power, and incomes, investment and production' (Myrdal 1958, p.26). Myrdal proposes a form of multiplier–accelerator mechanism order-laid on an increasing returns technology in which a region's initial economic advantage becomes progressively larger.

Within a regional economy,

[t]he establishment of a new business or the enlargement of an old one widens the market for others, as does generally the increase of incomes and demand. Rising profits increase savings, but at the same time investments go up still more, which again pushes up demand and the level of profits. And the expansion process creates external economies favourable for sustaining its continuation. (Myrdal 1958, p.25)

The growth of the market creates 'ever increasing internal and external economies', most notably scale economies in manufacturing, ready supply of skilled labour, 'easy communications and the feeling of growth and elbow room and the spirit of new enterprise' (Myrdal 1958, pp.27–28, and pp.87–88). These economies comprise 'the value of expanding markets, the value of increasing the number of trained workers and... the productive value of higher levels of consumption in general... and higher standards of health, education and culture' (Myrdal 1958, p.87–88). According to proposition (iv), virtuous circles of growth can be planned and created in underdeveloped regions. 'A national plan should be a blueprint of a cumulative process of economic development in a country', the chief mechanism of which is the exploitation of external economies (Myrdal 1958, p.85). Echoing the thoughts of R-R and Hirschman regarding indivisibilities and co-ordination failures, the market if left to itself is incapable of exploiting those external economies essential to the growth process. The 'national plan cannot rationally be made in terms of the costs and profits of individual enterprises. Most of the investments to be planned are not profitable from the market point of view'. A national plan is required to maximize 'the value of the external economies which almost every new enterprise bestows upon other enterprises, now or in the future which might be distant' (Myrdal 1958, p.86–87).

Myrdal's argument that the mechanisms of CC are equally relevant to developed and underdeveloped regions is a critical point of departure from R-R and Hirschman. For R-R and Hirschman, it will be recalled, inchoate factor and product markets, poor information flows and inefficiencies resulting from the small size of the market in poor regions mean that 'markets in underdeveloped countries are even more imperfect than in developed countries. The price mechanism in such imperfect markets cannot therefore be relied upon to provide the signals that guide a perfectly competitive economy toward the optimum position' (R-R 1984, p.211). In contrast, for Myrdal external economies do not diminish in significance in developed economies. 'The principle of interlocking, circular interdependence within a process of cumulative causation... should be the main hypothesis when studying underdevelopment and development' (Myrdal 1958, p.23).

Myrdal does not directly address this important difference in opinion with other CC theorists, though it is arguable that like Young he simply regards the scope for increasing returns as virtually inexhaustible. Growth in the size of the market continually creates demand for new products and opportunities for new more efficient techniques of production. Growth in the size of the market is not necessarily associated (as it is for R-R, Scitovsky and Hirschman) with an approximation to more competitive conditions. Myrdal's views on this matter are very significant, as Kaldor in his mature work regarded the notion of CC as the intellectual foundation for understanding advanced capitalist development. For Kaldor, the typical industrial structure of advanced capitalist nations is an oligopoly. This view is discussed in Chapter 6.

5.4.2   Trade, Capital Movements and Migration

The second set of mechanisms act not only to reinforce the circular relation between growth in income and investment, they are also the means through which the impulses leading to growth or decline are transmitted regionally, nationally and internationally. These are trade, capital movements and migration. This can be illustrated by examining the operation of circular and cumulative processes at the international level. Trade between poor and rich nations may produce increased inequality or widen the gap of per capita income. The high productivity and technological base of advanced manufacturing countries leads to the destruction of traditional handicrafts in poor nations, such as textiles and simple metalwork, and inhibits the development of manufactures generally. The theoretical basis for the potentially immiserating effects of trade rests on a rejection of neoclassical accounts of international trade. Myrdal totally rejects Heckscher-Ohlin-Samuelson assumptions, such as identical production functions across nations, internationally homogeneous factors and the movement towards factor price equalization. These assumptions are rejected because they are 'unrealistic' and founded on notions of 'stable equilibrium' (Myrdal 1958, pp.147–149). The 'role of international trade becomes... one of the media through which market forces tend to result in increased inequalities' (Myrdal 1958, pp.147–153).

> The freeing and widening of the markets will often confer such competitive advantages on the industries in already established centres of expansion, which usually work under conditions of increasing returns, that even the handicrafts and industries existing earlier in the other regions are thwarted. As industrialization is the dynamic force in this development, it is almost tautological to state the poorer regions remain mainly agricultural; the perfection of the national markets even, as I have just mentioned, tend to frustrate earlier beginnings of industrial diversification in agricultural regions.   (Myrdal 1958, p.28)

The uncompetitiveness of domestic manufactures reinforces the tendency of many poor nations to specialize in commodities. Such specialization will not promote economic development, and a manufacturing base will not be generated. Using arguments similar to R-R, Nurkse and Hirschman, Myrdal notes that, historically, demand for commodities is inelastic with respect to price; there are wide fluctuations in commodity prices over time; and productivity improvement in the production of commodities tends to be fully reflected in price reductions (commodities being homogeneous and sold into concentrated markets which exercise some monopsonist powers. Myrdal 1958, p.52).[4] In an argument similar to Hirschman's, Myrdal notes that much of this commodity investment is in the form of 'enclaves... cut out and isolated from the surrounding economy but tied to the economy of the home country'. This pattern of development severely limits the potentially beneficial 'spread effects' of commodity investments arising, for example, from domestic supply of parts and equipment to mines and plantations, transfer of technology, and managerial expertise (Myrdal 1958, p.58). Government intervention is generally required to realize these potentially beneficial spread effects. The absence of these spread effects not only increases international inequalities but magnifies regional inequalities within poor nations (Myrdal 1958, p.55). The effect of trade in goods is reinforced by capital movements. Capital flows from rich to poor nations are directed mostly to commodity activities, and there is a net outflow of capital from poor nations due to the repatriation of profits and the preference of domestic savers to invest in rich nations (Myrdal 1958, p.53). Finally, migration, or more particularly the barriers to large-scale immigration from poor to rich countries, means that population flows cannot be used 'as a factor of importance for international economic adjustment as between underdeveloped and developed countries' (Myrdal 1958, p.54). In addition, where such flows do occur, they often represent a loss of skilled labour to First World nations that poor countries can ill afford. The loss of a younger (and more entrepreneurial) age cohort through migration can lead to a change in regional or national demography which is adverse to development.

Myrdal's arguments regarding trade, capital flows and migration are significant since they identify external economic relations as central in the operation of circular and cumulative growth or decline. Subsequently, Kaldor would argue that the role of foreign trade was central to the explanation of differences in national growth rates.

5.4.3 Non-Economic Factors

Conventional economic and social theory is mono-causal, with only 'economic' factors accepted in the explanation of social life. Such explanations involve a rigid distinction between 'economic' and 'non-economic factors'. The latter category encompasses historical, institutional, cultural and ideological elements. For Myrdal, non-economic factors are central to the initiation and continuity of circular and cumulative processes. 'Economic theory has disregarded these so-called non-economic factors and kept them outside the analysis. As they are among the main vehicles for circular causation in the cumulative processes of economic change, this represents one of the principal shortcomings of economic theory' (Myrdal 1958, p.30).

Myrdal assumed that economic and non-economic factors reinforce each other and augment any tendency a system may have to development or underdevelopment. The selection of and the importance attributed to particular non-economic factors and their interaction with economic factors are entirely contingent on the particular circumstance under study. For example, the set of non-economic factors used to account for the 'Negro problem' in America – race discrimination, reinforced by the 'low plane of living' evident in poor education, health, and housing (Myrdal 1944) – are different from those used to explain Asian underdevelopment. For India especially, Myrdal highlighted problems arising from the 'soft state', the caste system, the semi-feudal social order and dependence of peasants on the landlord (Myrdal 1968). Myrdal's insistence on the central role of social, political and institutional factors in the explanation of development and underdevelopment marks an important extension of the application of CC concepts. R-R and Hirschman located co-ordination failure, or the inability to exploit external economies and increasing returns, squarely in the economic phenomena of market failure. The remedy was simply for the state to properly proportion and synchronise investment and demand. Myrdal, by contrast, locates the failure of virtuous growth circles to arise in underdeveloped regions in large measure in social and institutional relations which are inimical to industrial development.[5] For example, advancement of the American black population and the economically depressed regions of the South in which they were concentrated required the abolition of racial ideology and political repression (Myrdal 1944).[6] Kaldor was also to use political and institutional effects in the study of development, though they do not have the same prominence as in Myrdal's work.[7]

5.5 CONCLUSION

By stating the theory of CC at a high level of abstraction in his methodological writings Myrdal has greatly clarified the type of process suggested by Young, R-R and Hirschman. Myrdal contrasts the notion of self-adjusting neoclassical equilibrium to a self-reinforcing model of social and economic change. These methodological works also express strong antagonism to the logico-deductive method of neoclassical economics. Myrdal introduced three important innovations. Firstly, CC is equally applicable to the study of development in rich and poor lands. Secondly, Myrdal highlights the development of underdevelopment, especially the way international economic relations through trade, capital flows and migration can engender vicious or virtuous economic circles. The third innovation was to give equal prominence to economic and non-economic factors in the explanation of growth and decline.

It can be argued that the theory of circular and cumulative causation reached its apotheosis in Kaldor's 'mature' works. It is also arguable that a large part of the acclaim accorded to Kaldor was due to the fact that he absorbed and elaborated several key elements of Myrdal's work. This intellectual debt to Myrdal has been insufficiently acknowledged both in the secondary literature and by Kaldor himself. Kaldor greatly clarified the theoretical foundations of Myrdal's innovations, formulating them in a rigorous manner and providing strong empirical evidence for their operation. These mature works can be dated from 1966 when Kaldor publicly embraced the notion of circular and cumulative causation and expounded the Verdoorn Law. The principal elements taken over from Myrdal by Kaldor include the idea that CC could be applied equally to the study of underdeveloped nations or advanced capitalist economies. He also adapted through the 'balance of payments constraint to growth' Myrdal's suggestion that international economic relations in addition to domestic economic conditions could be critical to engendering either vicious or virtuous growth circles. Kaldor also adopted a nearly identical methodological critique of general equilibrium reasoning, and his inductive economic method based on the notion of 'stylized facts' owes much to Myrdal. On the other hand, Kaldor and contemporary CC theorists have unfortunately given insufficient priority to those non-economic factors in their methodology or researches which Myrdal regarded as especially important in the understanding of growth and decline. The general failure of contemporary CC theorists to adopt Myrdal's work in this regard is examined in more detail in Chapter 7. It is to Kaldor's contribution to CC theory we now turn.

Chapter 6
Nicholas Kaldor (1908–1986) 'The Marriage of Young and Keynes'

Economic growth is the result of a complex process of interaction between increases of demand induced by increases in supply and of increases in supply generated in response to increases in demand. Since in the market as a whole commodities are exchanged against commodities, the increase in demand for any commodity, or group of commodities, reflects the increase in supply of other commodities, and vice versa.   (Kaldor 1966[a], p.19)

6.1 INTRODUCTION

It is generally accepted that the theory of circular and cumulative causation reached its apotheosis in the work of Lord Kaldor. There are however, considerable difficulties confronting the student of Kaldor. Foremost amongst these is that Kaldor never wrote a *magnum opus*, a grand unified theory of growth and distribution based on CC principles. Recourse must therefore be had to his immensely prolific output of books and articles to assemble both his model of CC and its application to key topics such as regional economics and international trade.[1] There are also several crucial topics, such as his synthesis of Young and Keynes, which demanded intensive analysis, but received only modest attention from Kaldor. Further, there is an excellent and steadily growing secondary literature, particularly on the balance of payments constraint to growth and the Verdoorn Law, though much of this secondary literature is written by avowedly Kaldorian scholars. Several aspects of Kaldor's work have not received sufficient critical attention in the literature. These include Kaldor's two sector-two stage model of development and failure to fully acknowledge his considerable debt to other CC writers.

Kaldor's contribution to economics was, of course, soundly established by the time he embraced disequilibrium growth theory.[2] In the mid-1930s, Kaldor made substantial contributions to neoclassical economics, naming the 'cobweb' theorem, developing the notion of compensation tests in welfare economics, and contributing to the theory of imperfect competition.

117

From the late 1930s and 1940s, as a convert to Keynes, he broke with the neoclassical mainstream in a series of papers on the nature of the firm, entrepreneurial expectations, the trade cycle, and interest rates. Over ten years from the mid-1950s he focused on technological change and income distribution. Kaldor rejected the neoclassical distinction between a movement along a production function (due to relative price changes) and shifts in the production function (due to exogenous technological change). Given the assumption that technical progress is embodied in new capital goods, the rate of growth of output per worker is determined by the rate of growth of capital per worker. Kaldor also developed novel views on income distribution. Drawing on the Keynesian idea that investment determines savings, and assuming that the propensity to save out of profits is much greater than out of wages, 'there will be a unique equilibrium distribution of income between wages and profits associated with that level of investment' (Thirlwall 1991, pp.32–33).

By the mid-1960s, Kaldor came to reject the efficacy of formal macro-economic modelling and equilibrium notions, turning full circle to draw inspiration from his under-graduate teacher at the London School of Economics, Professor Allyn Young.[3] This last phase, which continued to his death in 1986, can be dated from 'The Frank W. Pierce Memorial Lecture' at Cornell University (October 1966) and his Cambridge Inaugural Lecture (November 1966). In these lectures he fully embraced the principle of circular and cumulative causation and formulated his Growth Laws. Kaldor regarded this principle as essentially expressing the notion of the self-reinforcing interdependence between the rate of growth of manufacturing output and increasing returns, which, he argued, received empirical support in the Verdoorn Law. The focus of this chapter is on this last period, and is limited in particular to those aspects that illuminate Kaldor's use of, and contribution to, CC thought.

6.1.1   Structure of the Chapter

Section 2 begins with a brief account of Kaldor's methodological critique of equilibrium reasoning and his alternative approach based on induction and the generation of 'stylized facts'. The critique of neoclassical methodology and his own alternative inductive approach based on 'stylized facts' underpins his theory of the production process and growth. In the simplest terms, this critique inverts the major assumptions of neoclassical production theory. Kaldor argues the economic system generates increasing returns, endogenous technological change, factor creation, and complementarity in production and consumption. Whilst there are considerable similarities between Kaldor's critique of neoclassical economics and that proffered by earlier writers in the CC School, Kaldor was also highly critical of Allyn Young's formulation of the

CC doctrine. Section 3 provides a brief analysis of Kaldor's critique of his former teacher, Allyn Young. Kaldor was critical of Young (and by inference R-R, and Hirschman) for failing to consider effective demand and specifically the mechanism for translating an improvement in aggregate supply into growth of aggregate income. Kaldor also rejected the view explicit in Young and implicit in other CC theorists, that there are virtually no limits to the process of endogenous self-sustained growth in the industrial sector. Within a 'closed economy', Kaldor contends, the limit to growth is sectoral imbalance between the 'processing' or manufacturing sector subject to increasing returns, and 'land-based' agriculture and mining which are subject to decreasing returns. It is the rate of productivity growth in land-based activities which is the ultimate determinant of the rate of growth of manufacturing output. Sections 4 and 5 provide an analysis of Kaldor's cumulative causation model based on the pervasiveness of increasing returns, endogenous technical change and the role of complementarity in dynamic systems. These sections highlight the unique contribution of Kaldor's Growth Laws and the notion of 'balance of payments constraint to growth' in rigorously defining the process of cumulative growth and framing the theory in a way that is amenable to empirical testing. This section also critically analyses how Kaldor attempted to apply the theory of circular and cumulative growth to explain the principal features or 'stylized facts' of an advanced industrial economy. These features include, for example, an oligopoly industry structure in manufacturing, large income disparities between regions and nations, and certain long-run trends in capital–output and capital–labour ratios. Kaldor also applied his growth model to the study of underdevelopment and evolved an export-oriented strategy for raising per capita income.

A number of criticisms of Kaldor are advanced in Section 6. These include objections to the two sector-two stage model of development, and especially the view that diminishing returns in land-based economic activity are the principal constraint on manufacturing growth in a 'closed' economy. Criticisms are also made of Kaldor's attempted synthesis of Young and Keynes. This section also highlights the conflict between Kaldor's export-led development strategy and the domestic-led growth strategies of earlier CC theorists. The Conclusion to this chapter critically evaluates Kaldor's contribution to the development of circular and cumulative growth theory. This section identifies the vital contributions of Kaldor to CC theory, but also highlights his failure to adapt many important insights of earlier contributors to the CC School. A major theme introduced in this section is that the contemporary research programme of CC has in general continued many of the deficiencies evident in Kaldor's work. This theme is pursued in more detail in Chapter 7, where it is argued that contemporary CC research would greatly benefit by adapting many of the research interests and analytical methods of earlier theorists in this tradition.

6.2   THE CRITIQUE OF EQUILIBRIUM ECONOMICS

6.2.1   Critique of Equilibrium Methodology

Like many of the key figures in the CC tradition, Kaldor as a young economist made important contributions to the neoclassical canon, but through a long period of critical analysis came to utterly reject this mode of thinking. This rejection is most evident in his methodological writings. However, whilst Kaldor's principal methodological writings (1972[c], 1985) are justly famous, they are also largely derivative. In particular, his writings on the *a priori* deductive reasoning and unrealistic assumptions of neoclassical economics are notable for their failure to recognize the very large debt to Myrdal's (or R-R's) methodological writings.[4] Notwithstanding this assessment, a brief exposition of Kaldor's methodology and the major principles underlying his thinking is essential to understand Kaldor's Growth Laws.

Like Myrdal, Kaldor is critical of the unrealistic assumptions underlying general equilibrium analysis. These assumptions are either unfalsifiable, such as the utility maximisation hypothesis, or 'directly contradicted by observation' (Kaldor 1972[c], p.1238). The latter include linearly homogeneous and continuously differentiable production functions which assume readily substitutable factors, constant returns to scale and diminishing returns to a factor. These unrealistic assumptions are, in turn, the outcome of a deductive and *a priori* methodology. The purpose of economic theory is to identify a set of universal axioms and logically deduce an internally coherent theory or theories. The alliance of economic theory and mathematics found in general equilibrium theory is explained, according to Kaldor, by the fact that both disciplines employ the same logico-deductive and *a priori* methodology. The requirement for tractable mathematically determinate solutions necessitates assumptions such as homogeneous linear production functions and optimizing consumer and producer behaviour (Kaldor 1972[c], p.1240; 1985, pp.55–57).

Kaldor's principal contribution to the methodological critique of neoclassical economics was not, as most commentators suggest, to demonstrate the incompatibility of increasing returns and general equilibrium (Thirlwall 1991, p.42). Both Young and Myrdal (to say nothing of Marshall, Sraffa and Hicks) explicitly demonstrated the incompatibility of continuously declining marginal cost and competitive equilibrium. Rather, his principal contribution was to propose that economics should proceed by identifying and explaining 'stylized facts'.[5] This concept is derived from Kaldor's analysis of the essential difference between social reality and the natural world. In the former case 'it is impossible to distinguish facts that are precise and at the same time suggestive and intriguing in their implications, and that admit of no exception' (Kaldor 1985, pp.8–9). Research should proceed inductively, to identify 'empirical regularities' which are however, historically contingent, changing over time with transformations in the economic system. It is not necessarily the goal of economics to develop a grand unified theory accounting for all empirical regularities; separate theories may be required for each 'stylized fact' (Kaldor 1985, p.8). Kaldor was as good as his word. The last period of his work from 1966, which focused on the growth process in industrial economies, was 'never developed into anything approaching that level of synthesis' which characterized his earlier work in the 1950s on income distribution and technical change (Thirlwall 1991, p.33).[6] In this last period Kaldor also abjured the formal model-building employed in his earlier work; mathematics was restricted to elementary regression analysis (as in the Verdoorn Law), or the expression in symbols of what could also be readily explained in words.[7] Kaldor identified several 'stylized facts' of dynamic advanced industrial economies, and it is their explanation which dominated the last twenty years of his life. The principal stylized facts are: an oligopolistic industry structure within manufacturing; sustained differences in the rate of output and productivity growth across industrial nations; spatial concentration of industrial activity; a steady increase in the capital–labour ratio, and 'the fact that although the capital-labour ratio differs between countries, the capital-output ratios of countries are similar' (Thirlwall 1991, p.33, p.43). It was Kaldor's contention that these facts could be largely explained through the phenomena of increasing returns. These stylized facts are examined in Section 6.6.

6.2.2 Increasing Returns

Like all of the contributors to CC theory examined above, Kaldor argued for a major distinction between manufacturing or 'processing' activities subject to increasing returns, and 'land-based activities' – agriculture or mining – which are subject to decreasing returns to scale. Kaldor regarded services as subject to constant returns (Kaldor 1966[a]). The assumption of diminishing returns in land-based activities is central to Kaldor's explanation of the ultimate limits to growth within the system (See Section 6.3). His argument regarding agriculture and mining is based on the classical premise that natural resources have finite limits, and that the marginal cost of utilisation or extraction increases with the exploitation of new or additional resources. In addition, technical progress in land-based activity is independent of increases in the scale of output.

> [E]conomies of scale do not extend to all forms of economic activity... They have no equivalent in agriculture even though technical progress is equally the joint result of experience and the progress of scientific knowledge, but their realization does not depend, or only to a minor extent, on the size of the market, and they do not really extend to services.
>
> (Kaldor 1985, p.70)

Earlier theorists had a partial view of the sources of increasing returns, in that each of these theorists gave priority to particular sources of increasing returns and did not emphasise or apply the broad range of such returns.[8] For example, Young emphasized overcoming indivisibilities in the employment of capital and inter-industry specialization, whilst R-R's focused on increasing the scale of individual plants. By contrast, Kaldor integrated the various sources. Kaldor is unique among CC theorists in arguing that increasing returns arise within the plant and enterprise, can be static or dynamic, and internal or external in origin. Kaldor also took considerable theoretical interest in the mechanisms of increasing returns and the empirical detail of their operation.[9] Secondary accounts of Kaldor's growth theory note the importance he attributed to increasing returns, though they do not systematically identify the variety of returns in his model, nor do they provide an analytical account of these returns. As emphasized in earlier chapters, the differing conception that theorists have of the sources and scope of increasing returns has a profound effect on key features of their respective growth models. The following briefly describes the sources of increasing returns to be found in Kaldor's work, as well as indicating some of their more important implications for his growth model.

Plant costs 'per unit of output necessarily decrease with size in any integrated process of operation... simply on account of the three-dimensional nature of space' (Kaldor 1972[c], p.1242). In process-flow technologies utilizing cylindrical containers – such as oil refining and steel making, or even transport and storage – a doubling of the surface area of a vessel results in a more than proportionate increase in the volume.[10] This has important cost savings in construction, operation and maintenance. Moreover, in the exploitation of these plant-based static scale economies, 'there appears to be no reason why this process should come to a halt' (Kaldor 1972[c], p.1242).[11] It will be recalled that R-R and Hirschman argued for definite limits to the exploitation of scale economies, so that the optimum size plant (in terms of technical efficiency) is the same in both developed and underdeveloped regions. Such reasoning also underpins their claim that as the size of the market increases more competitive conditions will obtain. This is due to the fact that increasing output does not result in an unlimited increase in the size of individual plants, but in a replication of plants of the same size. By arguing that there are no practical limits to the exploitation of plant scale economies, Kaldor provided an important foundation for his claim that a stylized fact of advanced industrial economies is the existence of pervasive oligopolistic markets.

Firm- or enterprise-scale economies are also significant. The development of 'large multi-product corporations – the conglomerates' in the twentieth century arose from their capacity to capture a large share of a growing market, in part through the use of trade marks and 'large-scale advertising'

(Kaldor 1985, pp.27–28). The conglomerate can also exploit advantages of risk reduction through diversification, and advantages of vertical and horizontal integration.

Those economies traditionally associated with the division of labour, as emphasized by Young, are also given a central place in Kaldor's account of increasing returns. An increase in the level of aggregate output permits an increase in the division of labour within firms and across industries, as well as the adoption of more roundabout or capital-intensive production methods. Kaldor argues that the principal insight of Young was that 'the capital – labour ratio in production is a function of the extent of the market rather than of relative factor prices' (Kaldor 1972[c], p.1242). The circular and cumulative relation between increasing returns (or productivity growth) and growth of output is a foundation for Kaldor's explanation of persistent differences in regional and international per capita income disparities.

In addition, 'there are the inventions and innovations induced by experience to which Adam Smith paid the main emphasis – what we now call "learning by doing" or "dynamic scale economies"' (Kaldor 1972[c], p.1243). Kaldor's conception of learning by doing encompasses both incremental improvement in efficiency flowing from the repetition of a given manufacturing process and the generation of new technologies. Rather than being exogenous to the system, technological change is largely a by-product of the production process. Again, learning by doing is another reason for the continued importance of increasing returns in advanced industrial economies. Kaldor harks back to his work in the 1950s on the 'technical progress function', with technological change conceived primarily as the result of

> innumerable design improvements that result from the repeated application of particular engineering principles. The optimum design for the steam engine or for the diesel engine or the sewing machine has only been achieved after many years or decades of experience... The gain in design through experience is even more important in the making of plant and equipment; hence the *annual* gain in productivity due to "embodied technical progress" will tend to be all the greater the larger the number of plants constructed per year. (Kaldor 1972[c], p.1243)

Productivity improvements in the capital goods sector, arising from experience in the use of these goods in production or 'learning by using', has been extensively investigated by Nathan Rosenberg' (Rosenberg 1982, pp.121–122). Productivity improvements due to the continuous flow of information from the users of capital goods to the manufacturers of capital goods provides an invaluable source of design improvement. One might also add that such information flows are an important external economy provided by purchasers to manufacturers.

Another source of increasing returns arises from the spatial concentration of manufacturing activity. Allyn Young had emphasized the crucial role of industry and inter-industry specialization in the growth of productivity, and how this was positively linked in a circular and cumulative manner to growth in total output. Young also identified – although he did not subject the claim to detailed analysis – that such specialization has a crucial spatial dimension which must be regarded not just as an important effect or result of the growth of total output, but as a discrete cause or source of increasing returns. These arguments are central to Kaldor's application of the CC principle to the study of differences in the industry structure of regions and income disparities across regions. (A discussion of these economies of agglomeration is provided in Section 6.6.1.)

6.2.3   Complementarity versus Substitution

The notion of complementarity in production and consumption is central to CC theory. For Kaldor, given his concern with growth and dynamics as opposed to the allocation of fixed resources, complementarity in production and consumption is far more pervasive and significant than the neoclassical principle of substitution. The neoclassical focus on substitution

> ignores the essential complementarity between different factors of produc-
> tion (such as capital and labour) or different types of activities (such as that
> between primary, secondary, and tertiary sectors) which is far more import-
> ant for an understanding of the laws of change and development of the
> economy than the substitution aspect. Indeed, it is, I think, the concentra-
> tion on substitution, which makes "pure" equilibrium theory so lifeless and
> motionless.   (Kaldor 1975, p.348)

As with previous CC theorists, complementarity in production also arises from the existence of indivisibilities, which in turn give rise to fixed factor coefficients. In addition, given endogenous factor creation and increasing returns, and excluding the very short run, the supply of one product does not have to be at the expense of another (Kaldor 1985, pp.61–62). There is another meaning of complementarity introduced by Young, and taken up by all CC theorists. Kaldor accepts, although with important qualifications, a key element of Young's notion of reciprocal demand. Kaldor accepts the view that '[t]he rate at which one industry grows is conditioned by the rate at which other industries grow, but since the elasticities of demand and of supply will differ for different products, some industries will grow faster than others' (Young 1928, p.534, p.537). In other words, 'the demand for any particular product or group of products is a reflection of the level of production of other products' (Kaldor 1972[c] p.1255). Kaldor qualifies the use of Say's Law in the growth model of Young and R-R by arguing that increases in supply will not necessarily result in increases in demand. Kaldor introduces Keynes's notion of 'effective demand' to argue that increases in supply may not automatically induce increased demand. (This is discussed below in Section 6.3.) Nevertheless, Kaldor accepts Young's central insight that the level of output and rate of growth of a particular commodity is a function of the level of output and rate of growth of all other commodities.

The expansion of output and investment creates external economies, especially opportunities for additional investments. This is due not simply to growth of final demand for an existing range of commodities, but the growth of the market allows for the production of a whole new set of commodities. Expansion in the size of the market permits production of a new set of commodities, firstly, by overcoming indivisibilities in production which may have precluded their supply and, secondly, the growth of per capita income is associated with an increasing diversity in the demand for goods and services. The various roles of complementarity are central to the model of self-reinforcing growth.

6.2.4 Endogenous Technological Change and Factor Creation

Using this inclusive view of increasing returns, Kaldor crafted a comprehensive critique of equilibrium economics. This critique provides an important background to his other substantive contributions to CC theory, such as the relation between increasing returns and oligopoly, and the particular role of prices in concentrated markets. Underlying or reinforcing increasing returns is the fact that technological change and factor supply are largely endogenous to the system. This contrasts with general equilibrium theory which assumes 'that the operation of economic forces is constrained by a set of "exogenous" variables which are "given" from the outside and stable over time' (Kaldor 1972[c], p.1244). It will be recalled from Chapter 2 that Young's analysis of technological change (through the application of science to industry) and steady improvement in the efficiency of capital goods and intermediate inputs provided a foundation for Kaldor's views on endogenous technical progress as they evolved from the 1950s. With respect to factor supply, labour is not a constraint on output, since labour is available from international or internal migration; the latter mainly involving the transfer of workers from low-productivity agriculture or services to high-productivity manufacturing (Kaldor 1970, p.338; 1972[c], p.1251; 1975, p.356). In the famous 1966[a] article Kaldor argued that labour supply could in fact be a major constraint to growth, though he soon recanted this position. (This is discussed in Section 6.4.) Capital is not a constraint on growth, since it 'is as sensible – perhaps more sensible to say – that capital accumulation results from economic development as that it is a cause of development. Anyhow, the two proceed side by side' (Kaldor 1970, p.339; 1975, p.355).

Kaldor drew two important conclusions from the existence of endogenous technical change, factor creation and increasing returns. The first is a rejection of one of the central notions of equilibrium: that the function of an economic system is the optimum allocation of given scarce resources. Each new investment creates external economies, 'or opportunities for further change *which would not have existed otherwise*'. Within a dynamic system, the idea 'of an "optimum" allocation of resources... becomes a meaningless and contradictory notion' (Kaldor 1972[c], p.1245). The contrast between the neoclassical 'choice of technique' and the CC approach is well articulated by Kaldor.

> [I]f at any actual level of output the "best" available technique for that output is less efficient than that available for a somewhat larger output – if, in other words, there is a whole hierarchy of activities not all of which are feasible or attainable at any one point in time – the choice among "activities" becomes primarily a matter not of prices but of scale of production. With every enlargement of production, new "activities" become profitable which would not have been employed earlier, whilst the introduction of such new "activities" leads to the invention of further "activities" which have not been "known" earlier... The problem then becomes not just one of "solving the mathematical difficulties" resulting from discontinuities [in production functions] but the much broader one of replacing the "equilibrium approach" with some, as yet unexplored, alternative that makes use of a different conceptual framework.   (Kaldor 1972[c] p.1255)

The second key conclusion was that given endogenous technical change, factor creation and increasing returns, growth in the system is not governed by supply, as equilibrium theory argues, but is basically demand-determined.[12] Within equilibrium theory, growth in aggregate output is basically determined by the growth in factor supply.[13]

6.3   KALDOR'S CRITIQUE OF YOUNG

It can be said without too great an exaggeration that the last twenty years of Kaldor's life were spent in the investigation and extension of Allyn Young's cumulative growth model. In a constant stream of published work until his death in 1986, Kaldor sang a paean to Young, rounding on the economics profession for failing to appreciate the 'full revolutionary implications' of Young's disequilibrium growth model (Kaldor 1972[c], p.1243). Nevertheless, in formulating his own growth model Kaldor did develop a number of important criticisms of Young. Kaldor was critical of Young's acceptance of Say's Law, and rejected the claim of earlier CC theorists that manufacturing growth within an 'closed' economy could be self-sustaining.

6.3.1 Effective Demand

Kaldor correctly characterizes Young's growth model as a combination of J.B. Say and Adam Smith: supply creates its own demand, and the continuing expansion of manufacturing output is stimulated by the presence of increasing returns. Growth in the system is ensured by the operation of 'reciprocal demand', or elastic demand for goods produced under conditions of increasing returns (Kaldor 1972 [c], p.1246). As an acolyte of J.M. Keynes, Kaldor criticized Young's classically inspired model of growth with its presumption that supply creates its own demand and goods exchange for goods. Such a model ignores the implications of effective demand.[14] Whilst Kaldor agreed with Young that demand generates its own supply, he rejected Young's view that supply automatically generates its own demand.[15] To explain the effect of an increase in aggregate supply or increased productivity on aggregate demand Kaldor introduced three key Keynesian concepts: these are the role of money, entrepreneurial expectations and the notion of induced investment. Kaldor's efforts on this topic may be interpreted as an attempt to integrate Young's long-run theory of growth based on increasing returns in an industrial economy with Keynes's account of short-run fluctuations in income and output. It must be emphasized that Kaldor did not attempt a detailed synthesis of Young and Keynes, and his comments on effective demand in this context were cursory. When Kaldor did address the topic of integrating Young and Keynes, he used it mainly as a platform to expound his own ideas on effective demand (such as the role of merchants' inventory holding activities) rather than introduce a textbook treatment of effective demand into disequilibrium growth. Indeed, Kaldor was highly critical of Keynes for retaining too many neoclassical assumptions which expedited the conservative interpretation of the *General Theory* (such as Samuelson's 'neoclassical synthesis'). Many of Kaldor's post-1966 articles and books contain brief comments on the inadequacies of Keynes's system. The only sustained commentaries are the 1982 Keynes Lecture on Economics, *Limitations of the 'General Theory'*, and the 1983 essay *Keynesian Economics After Fifty Years*. Kaldor argues Keynes's failure to properly break with neoclassical economics is evident in his acceptance of diminishing marginal productivity, marginalist theory of price formation and failure to unambiguously reject the quantity theory of money. Kaldor is also critical of Keynes's failure to recognize Harrod's claim that exports are the principal source of autonomous demand.

Kaldor rejects Young's acceptance of Say's Law of Markets primarily because the 'existence of durable money which can be stored... destroys

the necessary equivalence between demand and supply in the aggregate'
(Kaldor 1983, p.48). With the introduction of money 'in the real world...
there are or can be persistent differences between production and consumption' (Kaldor 1972[c], p.1247). Money and entrepreneurial expectations
regarding future demand establish the conditions for such differences. Secondly, Kaldor argues that Young's model of reciprocal demand is incapable of
explaining how increased demand for, or supply of, a particular commodity
can lead to an increase in the demand for other commodities.

> Clearly what Young intuitively perceived was that the pre-condition of
> cumulative change is that the rise in production of any one commodity *a*,
> should be associated with an increase in the demand for all other commod-
> ities. He thought that this condition will be satisfied when the elasticity of
> demand for commodity *a* will be greater than unity... A little reflection
> will show however that if by "elasticity of demand" we mean something
> which is a reflection of the elasticity of substitution of consumers... the
> increase in purchasing power of the producers of commodity *a* following
> upon the rise in the production of *a* must have been the result of a *diversion*
> of expenditure in favour of *a* against other commodities. The rise in
> incomes of the *a* producers must therefore be offset by reduced incomes
> of the producers of other commodities.   (Kaldor 1972[c], p.1247)[16]

In other words, Young does not adequately explain the mechanism for
absorbing a continually rising volume of production. A theory of 'income
generation' is essential to explain reciprocal demand or the phenomena of
'rising demand, followed by rising production, followed by rising demand'
(Kaldor 1972[c], p.1247). Kaldor sums up his critique of Young's failure to
supply a theory of income generation. 'The essential element missing from
Young's presentation, and which can only be supplied on the basis of Keynesian economics; is the additional incomes resulting from the accumulation
of capital (in other words, from investment expenditure) combined with the
induced character of such investment' (Kaldor 1972[c], p.1249). An adequate
theory of income generation requires the mechanisms of the income multiplier and the investment accelerator. In addition to these mechanisms, an
accommodating 'monetary or banking system [is required] which allows the
money supply to grow in automatic response to an increased demand for
credit' (Kaldor 1972[c], p.1252).[17] A responsive money supply 'enables capital
investment to increase in response to inducements so as to generate the
savings required to finance additional investment out of the *addition* to
production and incomes. This is the real significance of the invention of
paper money and of credit creation through the banking system' (Kaldor
1972[c], p.1250). Kaldor's criticism of Young's adaptation of Say's Law and
his synthesis of Young and Keynes was criticized by another leading CC

theorist and contemporary of Kaldor's, Lauchlin Currie. Currie's defence of Young's classical model is critically examined in Section 6.7. This section also attempts to reconcile the conflicting interpretations of Currie and Kaldor.

Rather than focus exclusively on the state to fill the deflationary gap which expectations may induce, Kaldor ascribed a key role to merchants, and especially their stock- or inventory-holding activities to reduce the potential gap between production and consumption.[18] Generally, 'merchants absorb stocks in the face of excess supplies and... release stocks in the face of excess demand. The merchants' function in other words is to create and preserve an orderly market' (Kaldor 1972[c], p.1248). The inventory activity of merchants reduces price instability for both commodities and manufactures, and this is important in 'inducing' investment. Price stability implies that the response to changes in demand is made primarily through quantity adjustments, and that the response to an increase in demand will be additional investment in capacity:

> [T]he process of endogenous self-sustained growth requires both a certain *elasticity* of expectations concerning the *volume* of sales (in regard to manufactures) and *inelasticity* of expectations concerning *prices* (in respect to primary products)... Induced investment reflecting the "acceleration principle" is a property of the latter; induced investment reflecting the price-stabilizing effect of the operation of traders is a property of the former. (Kaldor 1972[c], p.1250)

The price-stabilising effect of traders acts both to encourage investment in commodity production and indirectly to encourage investment in manufactures. Kaldor regarded volatile commodity prices as a major source of instability in manufacturing output, through the effect on manufacturers' input costs and demand for manufactures from commodity producers. Over many decades Kaldor proposed a series of commodity price stabilization schemes. Kaldor's interest in commodities reflects Keynes's own concerns regarding the adverse effects of volatile commodity prices.[19] It also reflects Kaldor's two sector-two stage model, in which the rate of productivity growth in agriculture and mining is the ultimate determinant of the rate of manufacturing growth. It is to this model we now turn.

6.3.2 Manufacturing Growth is Not Self-Sustaining

Kaldor accepted Keynes's argument that Say's Law does not apply at the aggregate level, as evidenced by his introduction of 'effective demand' into CC theory. Kaldor extends this by claiming it is also invalid at the sectoral level. 'Say's law does not apply to the processing [manufacturing] part of economic activities looked at in isolation'. In other words, the manufacturing sector 'cannot grow on its own, lifting itself by its own bootstraps' (Kaldor 1972[a], pp.162–163). Young explicitly argued, it will be recalled, that the manufacturing sector is capable of self-sustained growth, subject only to the constraints that increasing returns and high income elasticity of demand for manufactures are not exhausted. Kaldor uses the Keynesian concept of endogenous and exogenous demand to explain how the long-run rate of growth of manufacturing output is determined by demand from outside this sector. Endogenous demand 'reflects (i.e. is automatically generated by) production' though in a money economy demand can be a function of supply without the two being equal. 'To make the two equal requires the addition of an exogenous component' (Kaldor 1983, p.49). Keynes emphasized the role of domestic investment as the source of exogenous demand. Kaldor accepted this, but also gave particular importance to exports.

> Although the expansion of industrial production itself provides an element of this growth of demand, since part of the incomes generated by industrial activities is spent on goods produced by the industrial sector, this self-generated component of demand cannot alone be sufficient to make an increase in production profitable. The growth in demand, which has a determining influence on the pace of expansion–both of the growth of production and employment and of the growth of productive capacity – must be external to the industrial sector.   (Kaldor 1972[b], pp.141–42)

6.3.3   Two Sector-Two Stage Model of Development

Kaldor applied the argument regarding autonomous and exogenous sources of demand for manufactures to a simple two sector-two stage model of development.[20] The two 'stages' respectively refer to a 'closed' economy at an early stage of industrialization and an 'open' economy at an advanced stage of industrialization. The two sectors refer to manufacturing and agriculture/mining. The first sector is characterized by increasing returns to scale and oligopolistic industry structure with price-setting behaviour. Land-based activities are characterized by diminishing returns to scale and competitive pricing for commodities. The assertion that land-based activities are subject to diminishing returns is based on two premises. Firstly, natural resources are finite, so that the continued application of additional units of capital and labour will result in declining marginal productivity to these factors. Secondly, continuing technological change is required to offset this effect. However, this technological change is independent of the scale or rate of output growth of land-based activities (Kaldor 1985, p.70). Further, much of this technological change is not endogenous to the land-based sector, but is embodied in more efficient inputs sourced primarily from the manufacturing sector. Kaldor is not explicit on this point, but presumably if technological change is endogenous and linked to increases in output in much the same way as the Verdoorn law applies to manufacturing, there would be a built-in countervailing force to diminishing returns arising from the finiteness of natural resources.

For a country at an early stage of industrialization operating as a closed economic system with no foreign trade or capital flows, the principal source of exogenous demand for manufactures is the 'increase in the supply of other goods (mainly food and raw materials) for which the products of industry can be exchanged... industrialization and the growth of agricultural productivity go hand in hand, and are complementary to one another' (Kaldor 1972[b], p.142). At this early stage of industrialization the growing agricultural surplus is the principal source of demand for manufactures as well as supplies of capital and labour for industry. Consequently, it is the rate of technical progress in land-based activities which determines the rate of growth of manufacturing output (Kaldor 1972[a], pp.155–157, p.165; Thirlwall 1987, p.204). At a second or 'open' stage of development, export demand for industrial goods grows more rapidly than domestic demand from the agricultural sector. This is due mainly to the higher income elasticity of demand for manufactured products (Thirlwall 1987, p.220). It is the growth of exports, through the Harrod foreign-trade multiplier, which determines the rate of manufacturing output growth for a particular country. (This is examined in more detail in Section 6.5.) The rate of growth of manufacturing output for a particular country depends on the rate of growth of world income and the share of world demand captured by the country's exports.

However, considering the global economy as a closed economic system, it is Kaldor's contention that the rate of growth of world income is determined by the rate of technical innovation or productivity growth in land-based economic activities. '[I]f you regard the world as a whole and not just any single region or country trading with others, it is surely true to say that it is the growth in the output of primary products (of fuel, food, and raw materials) which governs the rate of economic growth generally, and not the rate of capital accumulation or some exogenous growth rate in the labour force' (Kaldor 1975, p.611). Kaldor's view on the ultimate determinant of the growth of industrial output is based on the interaction of two economic forces. The first, already outlined, is the rate of technical progress in land-based activities offsetting diminishing returns. Secondly, Kaldor rejects the claim that price adjustments and the ready mobility of factors between land-based activities and manufacturing will result in an equilibrium of supply and demand between these sectors. According to Kaldor, the classical economists claimed diminishing returns in agriculture cannot constrain the growth of industrial output, since

the operation of competitive markets would...ensure that equilibrium between market demand and supply in individual *sectors* is restored through the movement in prices. If agricultural goods are scarce, relative to industrial goods, agricultural prices will rise in terms of industrial prices: this will mean a transfer of "real" purchasing power from industry to agriculture; and the process will go on until the producers in the agricultural sector are able (and willing) to buy all the goods which industry is capable of producing.   (Kaldor 1972[a], p.161)

In other words, 'there must be *some* price... at which the excess supply of *B* (or excess demand for *A*) disappears: to suppose otherwise is to assume that industrial goods remain in excess supply even at zero price' (Kaldor 1975, p.351). However, demand and supply will not equilibrate across sectors because there is a limit to the transfer of purchasing power from the manufacturing to agriculture sector. This is due to 'the peculiar character of labour as a commodity... [the] *price* of labour in terms of food cannot fall below a certain minimum determined by the cost of subsistence, whether that cost is determined by custom or convention or by sheer biological needs' (Kaldor 1975, pp.351–352). It is for this reason that Say's Law does not apply in exchange between agricultural and industrial sectors (Kaldor 1972[a], p.162).[21] Since the terms of trade between industry and agriculture cannot be reduced or compressed beyond some minimum subsistence level, this is 'the equivalent of a "fixed price" situation (as Hicks named it), where production is determined by demand, or rather by the exogenous components of demand, which in turn determine, through the usual multiplier and accelerator effects, the endogenous components of demand... [Hence] it is the income of the agricultural sector... that determines the level and rate of growth of industrial production' (Kaldor 1975, pp.353–354). Within a closed two-sector economy, the rate of growth of industrial output is given by the function

$$Q = I_a/k,$$

where Q is industrial output, I_a is the land-based sector's demand for industrial goods, and k is the industrial sectors propensity to import the land-based sector's raw materials (Kaldor 1975, p.354; Thirlwall 1987, p.206).

6.4 KALDOR'S GROWTH LAWS

6.4.1 Background

Kaldor's critique of both equilibrium economics and existing CC theory provided the foundation for a series of 'laws' regarding the development of industrial economies. The basis of these laws is the view that manufacturing is the 'engine of growth' (Kaldor 1985, p.70). Kaldor enunciated these laws in a series of lectures during 1966 at Cornell and Cambridge Universities, though he modified and extended a number of the Laws' assumptions over the following twenty years. These laws have been the subject of considerable debate over their theoretical and empirical validity. Given that the singular purpose of this chapter is to highlight Kaldor's contribution to CC theory, these debates receive only limited attention. Kaldor's Growth Laws are a very important contribution to the development of CC thought. Firstly, they state precisely the significance and role of the manufacturing sector in economic growth. Secondly, the laws are formulated so as to permit empirical testing of two key theses, that is, the existence of increasing returns within manufacturing, and the central role of manufacturing in aggregate growth.

6.4.2   The Three Growth Laws

First Growth Law[22]

Kaldor's first law states there is a strong positive (causal) relation between the rate of growth of manufacturing output (g_m) and the rate of growth of aggregate output (gGDP):

$$[g_{GDP} = 1.153 + 0.614(g_m), r^2 = 0.959]$$
$$(0.040) \; s.e.$$

A one per cent increase in GDP is associated with a 0.6 per cent increase in manufacturing output. Kaldor argued the direction of causation runs from manufacturing to GDP. This relation is not simply a tautology reflecting the fact that manufacturing represents a large share of GDP. Rather it is based on the view that manufacturing is the 'engine of growth'. This view is based on three premises. Firstly, manufacturing is a unique economic activity as it alone is subject to increasing returns. Secondly, manufacturing products embody continually improving technologies, which – for example as inputs into agriculture and mining – are a significant source of technology diffusion and productivity growth within the economy.[23] Lastly, the growth of manufacturing output results in the expansion of manufacturing employment, which in turn, involves the transfer of labour from lower-productivity land-based activities.[24] The beneficial effects on aggregate productivity and aggregate output from inter-industry labour transfer were first introduced into CC literature and development economics more generally by Rosenstein-Rodan (1943). Owing to agrarian underemployment, R-R argued, there is virtually unlimited labour supply in a developing country. The bulk of the agricultural labour force has very low or zero marginal productivity. The planned establishment of manufacturing industry would not be labour supply-constrained, and the higher output per person in manufacturing would raise aggregate productivity. Neither Kaldor nor his commentators acknowledge this direct lineage.

Second Growth Law

Kaldor's second law states there is a strong positive (causal) relation between the rate of growth of manufacturing output (g_m) and the rate of growth of manufacturing productivity (p_m).

$$[(p_m) = 1.035 + 0.484(g_m), r^2 = 0.826]$$
$$(0.070) \; s.e.$$

A one per cent increase in manufacturing output is associated with a 0.5 per cent increase in manufacturing productivity. The constant term reflects an 'autonomous' rate of productivity growth of around one per cent per annum (Kaldor 1966[a], p.11). This empirical relation was first identified by P.J. Verdoorn (1949) and Kaldor drew on Verdoorn's work in the formulation of the second growth law.[25] Before Kaldor, Verdoorn's work had been used by Colin Clark (1957), and Kenneth Arrow (1962), though it was Kaldor who coined the term 'Verdoorn's Law'.[26] Although Kaldor gave some prominence to plant scale economies, it is clear that by endorsing an industry-wide measure of increasing returns Kaldor accepted the view of Young that increasing returns were not to be adequately discerned by examining variations in the output of a single plant, enterprise or branch of industry. In Kaldor's oft-quoted phrase, 'increasing returns is a "macro-phenomenon"'' (Kaldor 1966[a], p.9).[27]

   Agriculture and mining are subject to diminishing returns. The regression results for agriculture and mining respectively are

$$p_{(a)} = 2.700 + 1.041(g_a), r^2 = 0.812$$
$$(0.155) \; s.e$$
$$p_{(mi)} = 4.071 + 0.671(g_{mi}), r^2 = 0.705$$
$$(0.153) \; s.e$$

where $P_{(a)}$, $P_{(mi)}$ are the annual rate of productivity growth for agriculture and mining respectively, and (g_a), (g_{mi}) are the rates of output growth for each sector. For both sectors, 'the growth in productivity owed nothing to scale ... [since] productivity growth shows a large trend factor which is independent of the growth in total output' (Kaldor 1966[a], p.37). The constant term indicates this large trend factor. Kaldor's interpretation of these results is critically discussed in Section 6.7.

Third Growth Law

The third law, which is simply an amplification of laws 1 and 2, states that aggregate productivity is positively associated with the growth of employment in manufacturing and negatively associated with the growth of non-manufacturing employment:

$$[\,g_{GDP} = 2.899 + 0.821(e_m) - 1.183(e_{nm}), r^2 = 0.842\,]$$
$$(0.169)\text{ s.e.}(0.367)\text{ s.e.}$$

Owing to the presence of increasing returns in manufacturing, Kaldor found a strong positive relation between the rate of GDP growth and manufacturing employment growth (e_m). Conversely, diminishing returns in non-manufacturing (e_{nm}) industries give rise to a strong negative coefficient for the relation between the rate of employment growth in these sectors and aggregate output growth.[28]

6.5 EXPORT-LED GROWTH

If, as Kaldor argues, the rate of growth of manufacturing productivity is determined by the rate of growth of manufacturing output and the rate of growth of a national economy is determined by manufacturing increasing its share of total output, what determines the rate of growth of demand for manufactures? Within an 'open' economy at a fully developed stage of industrialization the primary determinant of manufacturing output growth is the growth of industrial exports (Kaldor 1972[b], p.142). The faster the rate of growth of manufacturing exports, the faster the rate of manufacturing output, the greater the scope for exploiting increasing returns, and thus the faster the growth of manufacturing productivity, output and exports. This creates a virtuous circle of increases in output and productivity, which leads to an expanding share of export markets.

Kaldor was critical of Keynes (1936) for assuming essentially

> a closed economy and one which consisted only of industrial enterprises with financial resources (or borrowing powers) which were in excess of their projected capital expenditure – otherwise he could not have treated decisions concerning investment as the main autonomous component of demand depending only on long-term expectations. The result of this was that exports as the *main* source of autonomous demand tended to be ignored. (Kaldor 1982, p.9)

The primary inference Kaldor drew from this claim was that investment in manufacturing 'in part at any rate, [is] not a truly autonomous factor; it [is] *induced* by variations in export demand' (Kaldor 1982, p.11). The faster the growth rate of exports, given the usual multiplier and accelerator effects, the faster the rate of growth of investment and demand. The rate of growth of manufacturing, 'both absolutely and relatively to GDP as a whole' and differential rates of growth of countries, can be explained by the operation of the Harrod foreign-trade multiplier. 'Harrod's theory was a simple application of Kahn's multiplier, taking exports as the exogenous variable and imports as a function of income' (Kaldor 1982, p.10). This can be summarized in the formula

$$Y = E/m$$

where the rate of growth of output Y is a function of the rate of growth of the volume of exports (E) over the income elasticity of demand for imports (m).[29] It will be observed that this is the counterpart to the equation for the growth of industrial output in a closed economy. The Harrod foreign-trade multiplier also expresses Kaldor's scepticism to the equilibrating role of prices and exchange rates, since 'import variations are mainly governed by *real* income variations rather than price variations' (Kaldor 1981, p.603).

Recognition of the primary role of exports in autonomous demand implies that traditional Keynesian attention on internal demand management may have the perverse effect of gradually reducing sustainable growth rates. For example, Kaldor was critical of economic policy as practised in post-war Britain because it directed demand primarily into consumption rather than investment, and into services rather than manufactures. Kaldor reasoned that because Britain's merchandise exports were primarily manufactures, and especially engineering products, export-led growth would result in a higher share of manufactures in output and a higher investment ratio per unit of output, compared with an equivalent level of stimulus to GDP directed across all sectors of the economy. In the latter case, only a small proportion of demand is directed to manufactures (Kaldor 1971, p.13). Aside from the role of exports as a primary source of autonomous growth, exports are essential for a healthy balance of payments. An excess of imports over exports will result in domestic demand being curtailed, and if a balance of payments crisis results in an extended period of under-utilized capacity, this can result in a vicious circle of discouraged investment, reduced technological progress, and reduced ability to afford imports – especially intermediate and capital goods.[30] In such a situation the competitiveness of the country may be in continuous decline. This 'balance of payments constraint to growth', which has been extensively investigated by Professor A.P. Thirlwall and others, has received impressive empirical support for advanced industrial nations over the period from the 1950s to the early 1980s (Thirlwall 1979, Kaldor 1981, McCombie and Thirlwall 1994). The structure of advanced industrial economies is such that a large share of manufactured output is exported, though the faster-growing economies generally have a low income elasticity of demand for imports (Kaldor 1981, p.603). This structure allows them to maintain high growth rates and avoid balance of payments crises. Kaldor's prime example of a balance of payments-constrained economy was post-war Britain. Periodic expansions in domestic output were continually cut short by balance of payments crises. The resulting stop–go policies, in which domestic output was necessarily constrained, caught Britain in a vicious cycle where low output growth impeded productivity growth. The necessary investments were not undertaken to either raise or lower export or import propensies, respectively (Kaldor 1971).

The primary solution to overcoming a balance of payments constraint is offered by industry policies designed to enhance the competitiveness of manufacturing industries and thereby lower and/or raise import and export propensies, respectively (Kaldor 1982, p.14, McCombie and Thirlwall 1994, p.456). Although Kaldor placed considerable emphasis on the role of fiscal deficits for the maintenance of growth in a slowing economy, he also recognized the limits to such action if an economy is balance of payments-constrained. In addition, Kaldor advocated incomes policies in recognition of the fact that fiscal stimulus could lead to inflation rather than output growth, given strong union power and/or price-setting behaviour in the oligopoly sector (Wood 1987, p.8).

6.5.1 Kaldor's Cumulative Causation Model

There are a number of graphical representations of the Kaldor cumulative causation model (Petit and Boyer 1991, Cornwall 1977, Ch.9). The most comprehensive is that of Dixon and Thirlwall (1975, p.207), and its adaptation by Whiteman (1990).[31] This is reproduced as Figure 4. The figure is especially useful in highlighting the crucial role Kaldor ascribed to the external sector in his growth model.

The first step in the divergent 'cobweb' model starts in the upper right quadrant, which illustrates the Verdoorn effect or positive relation between the growth of output q and productivity y. The upper left quadrant indicates the improvement in international competitiveness following a rise in productivity. It is assumed that the ratio of foreign to domestic prices (the function CD) is inversely related to the level of domestic productivity. The export demand function (EF) in the bottom left quadrant translates these relative prices into export demand growth. It is assumed the growth of exports is determined by the ratio of foreign prices to domestic prices. The final step is the positive relationship between the rate of growth of exports and the rate of growth of output. This reflects, firstly, that an increase in

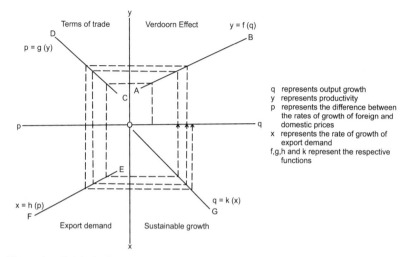

Figure 4:   Kaldor's Cumulative Causation Model
(*Source*: Whiteman 1990, p.42).

exports entails an increase in aggregate output (assuming no substitution of output from domestic consumption to export supply). Secondly, the relation OG captures the lifting of the balance of payments constraint to growth, which makes an increase in output sustainable over the long term.

It is evident that the outward spiralling virtuous growth path is very sensitive to the assumptions. For example, if the Verdoorn relation (AB) is relatively modest (the line being nearly horizontal to the x-axis) then this will yield a low and stable growth rate. Currency appreciation due to export success may reduce the ratio of foreign to domestic prices. A high income elasticity of demand for imports, (OG parallel to the Y axis) will result in an inwardly spiralling 'vicious' circle of declining output.

6.5.2   Exports and Development Strategy

Having described Kaldor's growth model and highlighted its important and original contributions to CC thought, this section briefly analyses the strategy for under-developed regions that Kaldor drew from this growth model. The principal purpose of this section is to compare and contrast Kaldor's development strategy with that of earlier CC theorists. To anticipate the findings of this analysis, Kaldor's advocacy of an export-oriented growth strategy and promotion of the benefits of specialization in the production of a limited range of commodities conflicts with the diversified domestic growth strategies of R-R, Hirschman and Myrdal.

It will be recalled that Kaldor's two sector-two stage model of industrial development posits that, in a 'closed' economy with no foreign trade, it is the rate of growth of productivity within the agricultural sector that determines the rate of growth of the industrial sector. Within the 'open' model exports are essential to raise the growth rate of manufacturing output. This follows from his premise that 'exports [are]... the main source of autonomous demand' (Kaldor 1982, p.9). In contrast, earlier CC theorists regarded the manufacturing sector as capable of self-sustained growth.[32] Drawing on the examples of Latin America, Pakistan and India, Kaldor argued their development plans

> failed to bring about any significant improvement in living standards. The single common characteristic of all these countries is that they failed to develop a significant volume of exports in manufactured goods. The stimulus to industrial production came from high tariffs or severe quantitative restrictions on imports. This made it profitable to develop home industries in substitution for imports, but since the exogenous component of demand for the products of industry was confined to the purchasing power of the agricultural sector, which was limited, and improved only slowly, the basis for a sustained growth of industrial production was lacking.
>
> (Kaldor 1972[a], p.172)

Earlier CC theorists advocated a diversified industrial structure based on import-substitution. The growth of per capita income depended on rapid industrialization, the driving force of which was assumed to be complementary demand between an ever-growing number of manufacturing industries. Given their assumption that optimal plant scale economies could be achieved at comparatively low levels of output (such as those in a developing country), there was little or no incompatibility between efficiency and import-substitution. A diversified or vertically integrated economy was advocated by Hirschman in particular as the means of generating cumulative increases in supply capacity and demand and to prevent the leakage of demand into imports. Reinforcing these arguments was a general 'export pessimism' amongst structuralist development writers of the 1940s and 1950s (Meier 1984, pp.15–22).

In contrast, Kaldor regarded plant scale economies as very elastic, and other forms of increasing return as having no practical limit (e.g. dynamic scale economies). The historical experience of countries engaged in large-scale import-substitution is that 'the hoped for improvements in productivity failed to materialize (or did so only to a moderate extent). With so many industries established more or less simultaneously, none of them could reach a sufficient size to become efficient; the economics of specialization and large-scale production tended to get lost' (Kaldor 1972, p.146). In addition, 'industrialization fostered through high tariffs itself militates against the development of exports... [Under high tariffs] the internal price structure is adapted to the internal cost structure – not the internal cost structure to the external price structure... and the higher the protection, the greater the deviation between the system of internal prices and world prices will tend to be' (Kaldor 1972, p.145). Kaldor therefore advocated a development strategy based on industrial specialisation and export expansion. Such a strategy would

> give maximum scope for obtaining the advantage of economies of scale through international specialisation. Protection on the other hand tends to reduce international specialisation, and forces each region to spread its industrial activities over a wider range of activities on a smaller scale, instead of a narrower range on a larger scale. The effects of protection in inhibiting the growth of industrial efficiency is likely to be the greater the smaller the G.N.P (or rather the gross industrial product) of the protected area.   (Kaldor 1970, p.346)[33]

The difference of opinion between Kaldor and earlier CC theorists regarding the long-term sustainability of industrialization founded on import-substitution and the growth of domestic demand is not absolute, but is one of degree. For example, Kaldor did acknowledge a role for import-substitution and infant industry arguments, though with very strict conditions. Nevertheless, the degree of difference is sufficient to identify this as an important bifurcation in the history of CC thought. Kaldor's two sector-two stage development model and arguments regarding an export-oriented development approach are critically evaluated in Section 6.7.

6.6   INCREASING RETURNS AND THE STYLIZED FACTS OF INDUSTRIAL ECONOMIES

In addition to the empirical support for the disequilibrium growth model provided by the Verdoorn Law, Kaldor argued the growth model received strong empirical support in several key features or 'stylized facts' of mature industrial economies. These 'facts' are important not only because they contradict the predictions of equilibrium theory; they can also only be explained by the presence of external economies and increasing returns.

6.6.1   Industrial Agglomeration

Drawing on Marshall's account of 'localization' or the growth of 'industrial districts', Kaldor argues that one of the most remarkable features of industrial development is the spatial concentration of manufacturing activity.

The spatial concentration of industrial activity is to be explained largely by the fact that agglomeration confers a variety of benefits or externalities on firms. Kaldor is not correct in arguing that Young did not adequately emphasize the spatial concentration of industrial activity (Kaldor 1985, p.69). Growth in the size of the market 'lends itself to a better geographical distribution of industrial operations, and this advantage is both real and important' (Young 1928, p.538).

The advantages arising from agglomeration 'go well beyond the economies of large-scale operations', such as plant and enterprise scale economies (Kaldor 1972[b], p.147). 'The advantages of geographical concentration' arise from the availability of specialized skills and ready communication of trade and managerial know-how (Kaldor 1972[b], p.148). Important also is the 'joint production between small specialized firms which involves frequent transfer of an unfinished product between numerous specialized firms' (Kaldor 1985, p.69). The latter is important and novel, since it links Young's emphasis on the advantages of specialization across firms and industries to the advantages of spatial concentration.[34] Kaldor also notes that the growth of manufacturing and the growth of great cities has gone hand in hand and is an important influence on the spatial concentration of industrial activity. 'The fact that in all known historical cases the development of manufacturing industries was closely associated with urbanization must have deep-seated causes which are unlikely to be rendered inoperative by the invention of some new technology' (Kaldor 1972[b], p.147). The strong historical relation between mass urbanization and manufacturing industry can be explained in large part by various advantages arising from close proximity to a final-demand market (Kaldor 1970, p.340). These include, for example, a ready identification of market opportunities for one's product or related products and monitoring of changing market trends and competitors' behaviour. Finally, spatial concentration can also be explained by the capacity of the market to ignore external diseconomies, such as transport congestion and pollution because these costs are 'external to the individual producer and therefore may not be adequately reflected in money costs and prices' (Kaldor 1970, p.344).[35]

6.6.2   Regional Income Disparities

The spatial concentration of industrial activity largely explains regional and international disparities in per capita income growth. Employing arguments identical to those of Myrdal (although not acknowledging the antecedents), Kaldor argues that unfettered market forces will lead to growing income disparities. The predictions of orthodox trade theory, especially the Heckscher–Ohlin–Samuelson (HOS) variant regarding the welfare enhancing effects of free trade, are dismissed by Kaldor. As a result of factor price equalization HOS predicts that free 'trade must necessarily *reduce* the differences in real earnings per head between the different trading areas and in favourable circumstances... eliminate them altogether' (Kaldor 1981, p.594). These predictions rely on very strong – and, in the assessment of Kaldor (and Myrdal), unrealistic and unverifiable – assumptions (Kaldor 1981, p.594). Not only do external economies of agglomeration mean that industrial development and urbanization are spatially concentrated, but the presence of increasing returns results in competitiveness becoming self-reinforcing. Growth in productivity and growth in output and market share interact in a cumulative manner. As with Myrdal, free trade has asymmetrical results: 'relatively fast-growing areas tend to acquire a cumulative competitive advantage over relatively slow-growing areas' (Kaldor 1970, p.343). A region with an initial advantage is able to increase its market share through exports, which by increasing output expands the scope for increasing returns or productivity growth. In turn, this creates additional cost and quality advantages for the exporting region (Dixon and Thirlwall 1975). The concentration of manufacturing in certain regions is largely due to the 'inhibiting effect of superior competitive power of the industrially more efficient and dynamic economies, as compared to others' (Kaldor, 1981, p.597). The most dramatic result of this 'inhibiting effect of superior competitive power' is what Kaldor termed the 'de-industrialization' of advanced economies (Kaldor 1972[a] p.166; 1981 p.600).[36]

Whereas the scope for differences in industrial development and, therefore, per capita income disparities across countries is largely unconstrained, within a nation these processes are subject to significant constraints. Firstly, interregional labour mobility is much greater within than between nations. This, combined with the action of national trades union and industry wide collective bargaining, tends to 'equalize earnings per head'. Secondly, there are 'built-in stabilizers' arising from income transfers such as unemployment benefits or public works (Kaldor 1970, pp.344–345).

Like all previous CC theorists (except Young), Kaldor was of the view that market forces were subject to a variety of co-ordination failures. One of the most important forms of such co-ordination failure was in the field of international (and interregional) trade. As a consequence of processes such as the de-industrialization of existing advanced economies, it is possible that international trade may produce a zero-sum game without any growth in overall global output. In other words, the international economy may be constituted of chronic 'balance of payments-constrained' nations unable to sustain even low rates of growth and nations with high growth rates and persistent and growing external surpluses. The growth of the latter nations occurs effectively at the expense of the former, who experience growing imports and declining domestic production. 'It does not follow... that free trade leads to the maximum development of trade; if it involves chronic imbalances it might lead to a situation in which the world economy is in a state of continued recession, which cannot be effectively counterbalanced by national policies of economic management' (Kaldor 1981, p.607). Consequently, Kaldor advocated 'a system of *planned trade* between the industrially developed countries on a multilateral basis. This means an agreed pattern of surpluses and deficits, so as to remove the balance of payments constraint on their internal expansion' (Kaldor 1981, p.608).

6.6.3 Trends in Capital–Labour and Capital–Output Ratios

The stylized facts Kaldor regarded as the most incongruent with neoclassical economics are the long-run increase in the capital–labour ratio in industrial economies and large differences in the capital–labour ratio of rich and poor countries but similarities in their capital–output ratios (Kaldor 1975, p.356).[37] Kaldor regarded these facts as more destructive of the neoclassical canon than the Cambridge critique of neoclassical capital theory – more corrosive 'than the possibility of "double switching" of techniques' (Kaldor 1975, p.356). Kaldor rejected the neoclassical parable relating the capital–labour ratio to the rate of interest. The long-run increase in the capital–labour ratio is largely explained as an effect of increasing returns. Increasing returns take their most important form in the introduction of more roundabout or more capital-intensive production methods. '[A]s Young emphasized, it is the increase in the scale of activities that makes it profitable to increase the capital–labour ratio: the larger the scale of operations, the more varied and more specialized the machinery that can be profitably used to aid labour' (Kaldor 1975, pp.355–356).

Secondly, 'higher capital–labour ratios... are *not* associated with higher capital–output ratios' (Kaldor 1975, p.356).[38] However, Kaldor's explanation for the similarity of capital–output ratios between rich and poor nations is problematic.

'The form that increasing returns normally takes is that *the productivity of labour rises with the scale of production, while that of capital remains constant*. The best proof of this resides in the fact that, while the capital–labour ratio increases dramatically in the course of progress... these differences arise without corresponding changes in the capital–output ratio.... Paul Samuelson emphasized as the central proposition of neoclassical value theory "Capital–labour up: interest or profit rate down: wage rate up: capital–output up." These propositions are *only* true in a world of homogeneous and linear production functions, where an increase in capital relative to labour increases output less than proportionately. In reality this is not so: higher wage rates in terms of products are associated with higher capital–labour ratios but are not associated with higher capital–output ratios. (Kaldor 1975, p.356. my italics)

The view that the productivity of capital is constant over the long run is inconsistent with Kaldor's view that technological change is largely embodied in new, more efficient productive vintages of capital equipment. Furthermore, the notion that the productivity of 'capital' and 'labour' can be readily differentiated is dangerously close to acceptance of an aggregate production function. This is indeed ironic, since Kaldor was one of the principal protagonists in the Cambridge capital controversy (Kaldor 1966[b]).

6.6.4   Oligopoly

It will be recalled that R-R and Hirschman accepted the view of Young that the size of the market in mature economies was sufficient to overcome indivisibilities, exploit increasing returns and create a competitive industrial structure. In contrast, for Kaldor, the effect of increasing returns in a mature industrial economy is to promote an increased concentration of output in fewer firms. The forces leading to increased concentration of industry arising from static, dynamic, plant, and enterprise scale economies, outweigh Young's forces of 'industrial differentiation' arising from the growth of specialized firms, increased division of labour across industries, and growth in the variety of commodities. Not only did Kaldor have a much broader view of the sources of increasing returns than Young, R-R and Hirschman, but Kaldor assumed that static and plant scale economies in particular were very elastic with respect to the size of the market. Consequently, for Kaldor the typical pattern in most manufacturing industries is that 'not more than three large firms account for the great majority of sales (perhaps 70 or 80 per cent) while the remainder is divided among a large number of firms' (Kaldor 1985, p.53).

The prevalence of oligopoly and general absence of monopoly is not explicitly addressed by Kaldor. Nonetheless, a number of reasons for the absence of monopoly can be inferred from his writings. Foremost is the importance of non-price factors in imperfect competition, such as technological innovation, design, quality of service, timeliness of supply and customer loyalty. These factors suggest that the lowest-cost producer will not necessarily be able to capture all of a market (Kaldor 1985, p.48).

6.6.5   Price Formation and Role of Prices

Allyn Young was content to assume that prices were set by the force of competition within atomistic markets. Such competition ensured a reduction in the real price of manufactures, which is essential to induce a greater than proportionate increase in demand for such goods. Neither R-R, nor Hirschman addressed the issue of price formation – even though for all CC theorists, real price reductions were essential to the circular process of growth in the size of the market and capital accumulation.

Kaldor emphasized the indeterminacy of pricing and the forms and outcomes of competition within an oligopoly. '[N]obody really knows the answers to the most important questions [regarding]... how competition works in a modern industrial economy' (Kaldor 1985, p.48). Nevertheless, he did venture the view that prices are set by producers on normal costs of production, assuming normal capacity utilization. Generally, producers do not adjust prices to changes in demand but adjust the quantity produced, since quantity adjustments are a much better indication of changes in market demand. Moreover, price stability not only aids corporate planning, but is essential to the maintenance of customer goodwill (Kaldor 1985, pp.23–28). Profits are set by a mark-up on costs of production, with the level of this mark-up designed to maximize *'the attainable rate of growth of profits'* (Kaldor 1985, p.50). However, the rate of growth of profits is the outcome of two conflicting objectives. First, given increasing returns, profits will be maximized by increasing the rate of growth of market share. Following this criterion, a mark-up as low as possible would be selected. Secondly, for a number of reasons, such as risk reduction by lessening reliance on external sources of funds, firms seek to finance expansion via retained earnings.[39] Following this criterion, the mark-up will be set as high as possible (Kaldor 1985, pp.50–52). How these conflicting objectives are resolved is not explained, but the answer presumably depends on a great many market-specific factors, such as number of competitors, rate of technological change, and scope for non-price competition, etc. It would seem however, that the balance of these forces is such as to produce steady real-price reductions for manufactures.[40]

Kaldor agreed with Young's claim that the fundamental role of prices is to transmit reductions in the real cost of manufactures produced under conditions of increasing returns. For example, in developing nations the major obstacles to continued growth of the manufacturing sector are 'the monopolistic character of manufacturing industries of underdeveloped countries' and the relatively high growth of money wages for manufacturing workers. Consequently,

> a reduction in costs is not normally passed on in prices [with the result that] the growth of productivity is prevented from having its normal effect in lowering the prices of industrial goods... it does not therefore lead to any increase in the purchasing power of the rest of the community for industrial goods. (Kaldor 1970, p.150)

As noted above, Kaldor does not indicate how these distributional problems are resolved in concentrated product and factor markets in developed nations. In this light, Kaldor's persistent advocacy of incomes policies may be interpreted as reflecting not only concern over inflationary pressures, but also the possibility of co-ordination failure or imbalance between sufficient profits for continued capital accumulation and the necessary real-price reductions for continued growth in the size of the market (Kaldor 1985, p.79). Given the critical dependence of his growth model on a particular pattern of distribution of income, the fact that Kaldor did not address these issues at length in his later work is one of the most important gaps in his CC model.[41] This criticism is taken up below.

6.7 CRITICISMS OF KALDOR

The following criticisms of Kaldor are focused on his synthesis of Young and Keynes and the two sector-two stage growth model. One source of these criticisms is the late CC theorist Lauchlin Currie, who strongly endorsed Young's original classical or 'Sayian' approach. The conflicting views of Currie and Kaldor are outlined and evaluated. The key criticisms of the two sector-two stage model are that it is inconsistent with the evidence Kaldor adduced to support it and a number of prominent examples of successful industrialization.

6.7.1 Synthesis of Young and Keynes

The development economist Lauchlin Currie (1901–1993) staunchly defended the adaptation of Say's Law by Young (and R-R) and was highly critical of Kaldor's Keynesian reinterpretation of the CC model. Both Currie and Kaldor were students of Young, the former at Harvard and the latter at the LSE, and in later years they corresponded on the subject of their conflicting interpretations of their intellectual mentor (Sandilands 1990, Ch.12).

Currie defended Young's model of 'self-perpetuating growth' based on the adaptation of Smith and Say, and lamented its displacement by monetary (Keynesian) and supply-side (neoclassical) growth models. (Currie 1981, p.53). 'The basic idea of the product of one man's work furnishing the demand for the product of others was presumed to have been a victim of Keynes's "burial" of Say, and "demand management", in which demand became purely monetary demand, took the centre of the stage' (Currie 1981, p.54). Currie argues that Young identified a number of mechanisms to ensure an equality of supply and demand. Firstly, Young emphasized the 'insatiability of overall wants that ensured that over time (though not always in the short-run) all income is spent. The income elasticity of demand for goods in general is unity (Sandilands 1990, p.310). Secondly, Currie argues that Young's view of demand and increasing returns was based on Smith's notion that goods exchange for goods and the 'physical quantity of output' determines the scope for use of roundabout production methods.

[D]emand is used in the sense of real output. In Smith's famous pin-making illustration, the "market" was the physical quantity of pins that could be disposed of for other things at a profit. The size of the market in this sense determines the extent to which it pays to use special skills and machinery in the production of pins. Young used the term "market" in the same traditional sense, which appears to me to be the proper sense for this purpose. Purely monetary demand, unaccompanied by any increase in physical production, provides no incentive to use more costly but more efficient techniques.   (Currie 1981, p.53)

Thirdly, Currie argued that 'Kaldor did not fully understand or accept the Sayian type of reciprocal demand to which Young [was]... referring' (Sandilands 1990, p.304). In particular, Kaldor interpreted Young's notion of 'elasticity of demand' as implying that an increase in the demand for commodity A following an increase in supply of A can only occur through a substitution of demand from other commodities. (This aspect of Kaldor's interpretation of Young was detailed earlier in Section 6.3.1). Because of this substitution or diversion of demand, aggregate output remains unchanged. In a letter to Currie in 1977, Kaldor explained that '[t]he Keynesian element which was missing from Young is the fact that for total demand to increase [following increased supply of A] either exports or home investment must increase' (Sandilands 1990, p.297). Currie responded to Kaldor by noting, firstly, that investment was a central element in Young's account of the division of labour and reiterated his view that 'Keynes's treatment... runs too exclusively in monetary terms to furnish an adequate theory of growth' (Sandilands 1990, p.302). Currie is correct in highlighting Kaldor's misinterpretation of Young's notion of reciprocal demand and his refusal to accept the mechanisms that ensured an equality of supply and demand. On the other hand, by emphasizing the 'self-generating and self-perpetuating' nature of growth, Currie heavily discounted the contradictions and countervailing forces to continual expansion identified by Kaldor (and Myrdal). Currie discounts effects such as the balance of payments constraint to growth and persistent and growing regional and international per capita income inequalities (Sandilands 1990, p.316). It will be recalled that in Kaldor's view these effects may imply that growth of one region occurs at the expense of another, so that taking the world as a whole there may be no net growth. Again in contrast to Kaldor, Currie saw no inherent tendency to income inequality arising from trade between industrial and commodity-based regions (Sandilands 1990, p.317).

An assessment of the strength of Currie's criticisms of Kaldor may be made by brief reference to a number of well-established empirical findings. There is not sufficient space here for a detailed empirical assessment of the two competing interpretations of Young's growth model, though a number of 'stylized facts' strongly support Kaldor's model. Firstly, the evidence in favour of the balance of payments constraint to growth highlights persistent differences in growth rates across regions and the contradictions inherent in the growth process (McCombie and Thirlwall 1994). Secondly, the potentially immiserating effect of trade as evidenced by 'de-industrialization' and the long-run adverse movement in the net barter terms of trade for commodity producers does not support Currie's view of the relatively benign effects of trade and the strongly equilibrating impact of international factor mobility (Sandilands 1990, pp.317–318). Another factor undercutting Currie's criticism of Kaldor is the ambiguity in Currie's attempt to defend a rigorous classical interpretation of Young, but at the same time to account for deviations from trend growth rates by acknowledging the importance of monetary phenomena and expectations. '[T]here appears to be nothing to lose and much to gain by conceding that an increase in monetary demand *pari passu* with real output eases or facilitates the growth process and, if there is slack in the system, may actually tend to increase aggregate output. There is, in other words, no necessary conflict between Sayian and Keynesian demand' (Currie 1981, p.55). The difficulty confronting Currie is that the assumptions required for Sayian growth (such as overall unitary elasticity of demand and automatic reinvestment of savings or surplus) are inconsistent with the factors Currie introduces to explain deviations from trend growth rates. These factors include expectations or uncertainty resulting in a non-equality of production and consumption and the potential gap between savings and investment. In other words, Currie attempts to reconcile two irreconcilable world-views: that in the long run Sayian equality holds, but in the short run 'factors causing departures from trend' may be significant (Currie 1981, p.58). Finally, Currie is correct to emphasize that for Young the basis for increasing returns was an increase in the 'physical quantity' of production, but it is illicit to contrast this with Keynesian 'monetary demand'. Excluding the effects of inflation or supply constraints, an increase in monetary demand will lead to an increase in the output of real goods and services (even allowing for a partial diversion into savings and imports). Nevertheless, Currie has provided a very important service in highlighting the different assumptions between the classically inspired growth model of Young and the Keynesian foundations of Kaldor's model of CC.

6.7.2   Kaldor's Constraint to Growth

Prior to Kaldor, CC theorists emphasized the self-perpetuating nature of growth and generally did not reflect on impediments or constraints to continued growth. In the two sector-two stage model of development the overall rate of economic growth is determined by 'autonomous' demand. In a closed newly industrializing economy and the world as a whole, the determinant of manufacturing output growth is productivity growth in agriculture and mining

(Kaldor 1981, pp.611–612). For an open economy, exports are the key source of autonomous demand. Kaldor's model has the merit of introducing limits to the rate of output growth, though the formulation of these limits is arguably one of the least satisfactory aspects of his overall model.

Kaldor presents two statistical findings for the claim that agriculture and mining are subject to diminishing returns. Firstly, in these industries 'productivity growth shows a large trend factor which is independent of the growth in total output' (Kaldor 1966[a], p.39). This trend factor is the comparatively large constant term in the Verdoorn 'equation' for the two industries. Secondly, in these industries 'productivity growth and employment growth tend to be negatively related, not positively' (Kaldor 1966[a], p.16). The Verdoorn equation for manufacturing found a positive relation between productivity growth and employment growth, where a one per cent increase in output was associated with a half a per cent increase in employment. The latter, apparently, is consistent with the view that increasing returns obtain when an increase in inputs (in this case labour) is associated with a more than proportionate increase in output. This evidence supports 'the classical contention that [agriculture and mining]... are "diminishing returns" industries: the fact that this is overlaid by technological progress or the adoption of more capital-intensive methods may statistically conceal this, but it does not eliminate its significance' (Kaldor 1966[a], pp.16–17).

Kaldor's evidence for the claim that agriculture and mining are subject to diminishing returns is deficient on several grounds. Firstly, Kaldor's attempt to invoke the name of Young, amongst others, to support the claim of diminishing returns in agriculture runs up against the difficulty that Young's pronouncements on this subjects was exceedingly ambiguous. The contemporary CC theorist Roger Sandilands has not only highlighted statements by Young downplaying the significance of diminishing returns in agriculture but also argued that Young's account of productivity growth should be viewed from the level of the aggregate economy and not focused exclusively on manufacturing.[42] (The latter aspect of Sandilands' critique is examined in the next section.)

Secondly, Kaldor's regression results are certainly consistent with the claim that the most important source of productivity growth in the primary sector is largely unrelated to output growth – given the large constant terms for agriculture and mining. The constant terms for agriculture and mining are 2.7 and 4.1, respectively. (These results were reported in Section 6.4.2.) But the regression results do not support the claim that the primary sector is subject to diminishing returns. If anything, the coefficients suggest that both agriculture and mining are subject to greater increasing returns than manufacturing. Kaldor found that a one per cent increase in manufacturing output was associated with a 0.5 per cent increase in manufacturing productivity. For agriculture and mining, a one per cent increase in output for these industries results in a one per cent and 0.7 per cent increase in productivity, respectively. (A similar interpretation of Kaldor's regression results is to be found in Sandilands 1990, p.311.)

Thirdly, growth of productivity in agriculture is attributed to 'the effects of technological progress and capital investment in raising *yield per acre*' (Kaldor 1966[a], p.39n). Kaldor claims that new technology and investment have 'overlaid' or prevented diminishing returns from being evident in statistical examination of productivity growth in the primary sector. If diminishing returns are not evident in the statistical data it is not at all clear on what basis, other than on a reassertion of the claims of classical political economy, Kaldor argues that increasing returns do not extend to the primary sector. One could equally claim that given the central role of 'technological progress and capital investment' in the CC explanation of productivity growth in manufacturing, if these factors were absent, manufacturing as well would not be subject to increasing returns.

Finally, Kaldor's constraint to growth is inconsistent with the 'stylized facts'. Long-run real global commodity prices (excluding oil) have declined, or at best remained stable, at the same time as their output has increased dramatically (Spraos 1980).[43] On the basis of these empirical results it is illicit to infer that the primary sector is subject to diminishing returns. Leading Kaldorian scholars, such as Thirlwall (1987), and McCombie and Thirlwall (1994), apparently accept the principle of diminishing returns in agriculture–mining, and this sector's role as both the source of 'autonomous' demand in the development of a 'closed' economy and effect of this sector in determining the rate of world output.[44] Interestingly, however, the overwhelming focus in their works is on the 'open' model, and the role of exports and the balance of payments constraint to growth in determining the rate of growth of regions and nations. Moreover, in accounts of circular and cumulative causation which focus almost exclusively on Kaldor's contribution, such as Ricoy (1987) and Eatwell (1982), the closed model is ignored entirely. It is surely a conundrum that the closed model should have received such minimal attention when the model purports to be the Holy Grail of the economics profession in explaining the long-run growth of world output.[45]

6.7.3   Identification of Industries Subject to Increasing Returns

The previous section propounded that Kaldor's interpretation of the evidence regarding the presence of diminishing returns in agriculture–mining was invalid. In the following, it is argued that Kaldor did not give sufficient weight to his own empirical findings that certain industries other than manufacturing are subject to increasing returns. Further, the view is put forward that the division of labour across industries or Young's 'industrial differentiation' of

production makes the task of identifying the type of returns to which industries or activities are subject extremely problematic.

Kaldor was inconsistent in the identification of industries other than manufacturing that are subject to increasing returns. Kaldor claimed that increasing returns 'do not really extend to services – at least the part of services
connected with transport and distribution of goods' (Kaldor 1985 p.70). This
claim contradicts his view expressed elsewhere that plant scale economies are
significant and pervasive (Kaldor 1972[c]). It is precisely in the field of
transport services that those advantages (much emphasized by Kaldor) arising from the non-linear relation between surface area and volumetric capacity
have been most extensively exploited. In fact, Kaldor specifically cited oil
tankers as an example of this principle in action (Kaldor 1972[c], p.1242). In
addition, Kaldor identified that some very important non-manufacturing
industries, notably construction and public utilities (electricity generation,
water, and gas distribution) exhibit increasing returns, as evidenced by a
statistically significant relation between output growth and productivity
growth.[46] 'One can thus conclude that the effects of economies of scale on
the growth of productivity are significant not only for manufacturing industry
but for the industrial sector generally' (Kaldor 1966[a], pp.38–39). Whilst
Kaldor recognized that the Verdoorn relation held for some industries
other than manufacturing, it is notable that neither he nor later CC scholars
emphasized this fact, nor did they study the sources of increasing returns
within these industries. This is an important lacuna in CC theory, especially
since these industries represent a large share of GDP. For Australia, construction; electricity, gas and water; and transport and distribution represent
6 per cent, 3 per cent and 6 per cent of GDP respectively (ABS Cat. No.
5204.0 Current Prices 1994–95). To put this in perspective, manufacturing
industry represents about 15 per cent of GDP.

A related difficulty in the identification of industries subject to increasing
returns arises from the process of 'vertical disintegration' of industry. Allyn
Young and subsequent CC theorists emphasized that the division of labour
takes one of its most important forms in the 'vertical disintegration' of
industry, whereby growth in the size of the market leads to established
firms 'throwing off' existing functions to be taken up by new specialized
firms with these new firms constituting whole new branches of industry.
This process of vertical disintegration has important implications for the
role of manufacturing in productivity growth. With the progressive division
of labour, activities previously undertaken within a manufacturing firm or
enterprise are, for the purposes of national statistical collections, conducted
in other industries. An important example of this is the growth of the business
services industry which provides, for example, scientific research, engineering
and computer consultancy services to industry. Moreover, a considerable
share of national research and development expenditures occur in this

industry.[47] It is arguable that an important source of technological innovation and/or diffusion is provided by these service industries. In other words, whilst Kaldor and other prominent CC theorists such as John Cornwall recognize the key role of manufacturing as the source of inputs embodying important technological innovations for other industries, they do not adequately acknowledge the possibly significant technology flows from the service sector to manufacturing and other industries.

Currie and Sandilands have a related criticism of Kaldor's 'sectoral' view of increasing returns which identifies manufacturing as the exclusive or at least dominant source of growth. In contrast to this sectoral view Sandilands proposes a 'global' or economy-wide view of the growth process. Not only may other sectors be subject to increasing returns, but the rate of growth of a particular industry is dependent on the rate of growth of all other industries. Kaldor's 'sectoral' approach is criticized 'because it fails to analyse increasing returns in Young's inclusive sense in which *all* sectors can benefit from the endogenous spread of cost-reducing methods made worthwhile and feasible as the overall market expands' (Sandilands 1990, pp.316–317). From this point of view, Kaldor's Verdoorn equation for agriculture, for example, can be interpreted as the sum of benefits or external economies accorded to agriculture by other industries, as reflected in the constant term, and economies internal to agriculture which are reflected in the regression coefficient (Sandilands 1990, p.314).

To conclude this section, the combined effect of the following factors – difficulties in the identification and definition of diminishing returns industries; inconsistencies in the treatment of increasing returns in services; recognition of industries other than manufacturing as being subject to increasing returns and as important sources of technological innovation – is to challenge the exclusive position of manufacturing in Kaldor's explanation of per capita income growth. Two inferences may be drawn from these findings. The first is a rejection of the view that diminishing returns in primary industries are the principal constraint to growth, either within a newly industrializing 'closed' economy or the global economy as a whole. Secondly, the findings support the inclusive view of growth as proposed by Currie and Sandilands. Nevertheless, it is arguable that manufacturing should still be regarded as the primary motive force, if not the singular 'engine' of growth. This is due to the congruence within this industry of the following factors. Manufacturing is subject to significant increasing returns; there is a high income elasticity of demand for manufactures; given the scope for 'factor creation' and the fact that a high proportion of inputs to manufacturing are themselves manufactures, the industry has a high long-run elasticity of supply; manufactures have higher long-run real prices compared to commodities; manufactures have a key role in overcoming the balance of payments constraint to growth; and manufacturing has a continuing importance in technological innovation and diffusion.

6.7.4   Criticisms of Kaldor's Strategy for Economic Development

The two sector-two stage model of development was outlined in Section 6.3.3. The conflict was highlighted between the strategy for development Kaldor derived from this model and the strategies of earlier CC theorists which focused on the growth of domestic demand and on broadening the industrial base. The purpose of this section is to demonstrate that in his very early work on cumulative causation Kaldor employed an analysis of development that was not based on the two sector-two stage model but was much more in sympathy with the development strategies of earlier CC theorists. In other words, there is an ambiguity in Kaldor's oeuvre regarding the optimal strategy for underdeveloped regions. Secondly, it is argued that the two sector-two stage model is inconsistent both with a number of crucial historical patterns of development and the circular and cumulative growth process it is intended to explain.

6.7.4.1   Ambiguity in the Strategy for Economic Development

The earlier discussion of Kaldor's strategy for development concentrated on the two sector-two stage model. This is because this model is the one he employed almost exclusively in his analysis of and prescriptions for development. This is also the model most prominent in the secondary literature on Kaldor. However, it is argued here, Kaldor enunciated two competing and contradictory strategies for development. The second model (perhaps more adequately described as a typology) is a four-stage analysis of development drawn from historical patterns of industrialization. The four-stage model was outlined in the 1966 Cambridge Inaugural Lecture. Kaldor never returned to this formulation of his growth model but instead consistently propounded the two sector-two stage model. The four-stage model is notable for its unqualified adoption of Young's account of growth and the relative absence of those Keynesian elements, such as autonomous demand, the effects of money, expectations and inventory investment, which Kaldor subsequently argued were essential to improve the explanatory power of Young's model.[48] A crucial aspect of the four-stage model is the assumption that import-substitution and the growth of domestic demand provide a long-run sustainable pattern of national development. Moreover, a key element in explaining this pattern of development is the growth of a broad-based or integrated industrial structure. Kaldor gave particular emphasis in this model to the cumulative effects on growth consequent upon the establishment of a capital goods sector:

> It is a peculiarity of a highly developed industrial sector that it largely provides the goods on which capital expenditure is spent, and thereby generates a demand for its own products in the very process of supplying

them... the very establishment of an investment goods sector makes for a built – in element of acceleration in the rate of growth of manufacturing output that could – theoretically – go on until technological constraints – the input–output relationships *within* the investment goods sector – impose a limit on further acceleration.   (Kaldor 1966[a], pp.20–21)

In this case, the determinant of the rate of manufacturing output growth is located within this sector (with the constraint identified as supply elasticity within the capital goods industries). This contrasts with the two sector-two stage model where the respective constraints to growth in closed and open economies are productivity growth within the primary sector and the rate of growth of manufactured exports. Exports certainly play an important role in the four stage model, but they are largely restricted to accelerating the rate of growth by increasing the size of the market to which a nation's industries have access. The export phase is not associated with a fundamental change in the industry composition or structure of the economy (Kaldor 1966[a], pp.21–22). Exports are only one of 'the three sources' of demand for manufactures: 'consumption, domestic investment, and net exports'. The historical pattern of industrialization is that each of these sources in turn is dominant during a specific phase of development (Kaldor 1966, pp.19–22). The first stage of industrialization entailing import substitution of consumer goods 'invari-ably involves reduced imports of manufactured consumer goods and increased imports of machinery and equipment'. The second phase involves a shift from import-substitution to the net export of consumer goods, espe-cially textiles. Import-substitution of capital goods is the primary source of demand growth in the third stage. Once an economy attains the level of domestic demand and technical competence to supply a large proportion of its capital needs, it is capable of lifting itself by its own bootstraps.

The expansion of capacity in the investment goods sector feeds upon itself, by increasing the growth rate of demand for its own output, thereby providing both the incentives and the means for its own further expansion. The establishment of an investment goods sector thus provides for a built-in element of acceleration in the rate of growth of demand for manufac-tured goods.   (Kaldor 1967, p.30)

The fourth and final phase arises when a country becomes a net exporter of capital goods. During this phase an economy experiences 'explosive growth' when a fast rate of growth of external demand is combined with rising demand within the capital goods sector to satisfy this external demand. It was entry into this fourth phase which Kaldor says explains the phenomenal post-war growth of Japan. This fast growth rate is not sustainable, because 'once a country has acquired a reasonably large share of world trade in investment goods, the growth of demand is bound to slow down, as the broad historical experience of older industrial countries has shown' (Kaldor 1966[a], p.20).

The two sector-two stage development model denied the possibility of long-run growth founded substantially on endogenous or domestic demand and prescribed a narrowly based industrial structure as the optimum strategy to exploit scale economies for developing nations. The two sector-two stage model of growth denied the capacity of a domestic industrial sector to 'lift itself by its own bootstraps'.[49] The significance of the four-stage model is that it is much closer to the type of analysis of growth and development proposed by Young, R-R, Hirschman and Myrdal.

6.7.4.2 Criticisms of the Two Sector-Two Stage Model

Earlier it was shown how the assumption of diminishing returns in the primary sector was inconsistent both with Kaldor's own regression results (for the primary sector) and the stylized facts of long-run movements in commodity prices and volumes. A number of other criticisms may also be adduced against the two sector-two stage model. These criticisms are that the model is inconsistent with historical patterns of development and the circular and cumulative growth process it is intended to explain.

The factors underlying historical patterns of industrialization are enormously complex and the variations within this pattern across countries are numerous (Syrquin 1988). It is obviously well beyond the scope of this book to test Kaldor's two sector-two stage development model against these historical patterns. Consequently, the following comments simply indicate the broad directions that such an analysis might follow. The evidence provided in a number of important case studies, especially those of post-war Japan and Taiwan, would seem to be inconsistent with this model. In particular, the argument against import-substitution and domestic-led growth as a sustainable model of development has been challenged by the leading Kaldorian scholar, Professor John Cornwall. In summary, Cornwall concludes that the question as to 'whether growth is export-led or homespun is a somewhat secondary, peripheral matter... [since] the factors leading to a rapid growth of both exports and domestic sales are one and the same' (Cornwall 1977, p.175). Cornwall's evidence for this position is a detailed comparison of rates of growth of production for domestic consumption and export in 50 manufacturing industries in post-war Japan. The study concluded that 'growth in exports seldom exceeds growth in the home market, even in a country considered to be the most oriented towards realizing and exploiting foreign markets... growth would have to be characterized as homespun' (Cornwall 1977, p.193). Moreover, Cornwall contends that success in the home market is in most cases a precondition for success overseas. Cornwall does not explicitly confront Kaldor's argument; his analysis is directed generally to opponents of long-term import-substitution strategies. Like other leading contemporary CC theorists, Cornwall has not directly confronted either the conflicts between Kaldor's two models of growth nor Kaldor's theoretical opposition to national development strategies founded on long-term import-substitution and domestic growth. In fact, it is something of a common-place for contemporary CC theorists actually to cite Kaldor to explain the success of some long-term import-substitution strategies. Eatwell, for example, claims

> the Japanese case suggests that the traditional dichotomy between import substitution and export-led growth is invalid. Whilst Japanese industry was developed within a rapidly growing and protected home market, that growth proved to be a springboard for expansion into world markets. Exports were domestic growth-led. The performance of the successful Japanese (and French) examples of import substitution, and the problems encountered in Latin America, cannot be evaluated using static conceptions of allocative efficiency... Nicholas Kaldor's version of the Verdoorn Law... provides a framework within which trade strategies may be evaluated. (Eatwell 1987, p.738)

One can only concur with Eatwell and others, that the Kaldor–Verdoorn model (and CC growth theory more generally) provides a framework to explain such strategies. It is however, first necessary to explicitly abandon Kaldor's two-sector two-stage model of development.[50] This, of course, is not to deny the crucial role exports play in overcoming the balance of payments constraint to a newly industrializing economy, especially one which has yet to develop its own capital goods sector or is heavily reliant on imported raw materials. Nor is it to deny the very significant gains to be obtained in exploiting scale economies by expanding the size of the market through exports. The benefits of exports and the validity of the balance of payments constraint to growth are not in question. These important aspects of Kaldor's theory are not logically dependent on the two sector-two stage model, and the abandonment of this model in no way diminishes their importance in explaining development and differences in cross-country growth rates. Import-substitution and export growth are not necessarily competing strategies, in which the former is simply a stage an economy must go through before it becomes a mature and independent nation able to trade openly with other nations. Rather, they may be complementary strategies, with the relative balance between them depending on the stage of industrial development and particular requirements of particular manufacturing industries.[51] The case against Kaldor is that he did not follow his own inductive precepts, but imposed an abstract two sector-two stage model on to the study of industrialization. He thereby ignored the great diversity in historical patterns of development and denied the scope for endogenous self-sustained growth through import-substitution and domestic output growth.

It is also arguable that Kaldor's endorsement of specialization, or restricting the range of industries as a development strategy for newly industrializing nations and mature economies, is inconsistent both with the historical pattern of industrial development and the CC growth model. Let us recall Young and Hirschman's arguments that increases in per capita manufacturing output are causally associated with an increased complexity of inter-industry and intra-industry transactions and increase in the variety of goods produced. These arguments are strongly supported by econometric and historical studies of development patterns. These studies find that the process of development is virtually defined by an 'increase in the overall density of the input–output matrix' (Syrquin 1988, p.252). Increases in per capita manufacturing output are strongly associated with an increase in the ratio of intermediate and capital goods to total output and increasing diversity of manufactured final demand goods (Syrquin 1988, pp.231–232; Chenery 1986). The rise in the diversity of manufacturing industries is due, firstly, to increases in the division of labour as the size of the market increases. The division of labour within and across industries is evident in the significant increase in the growth of intermediate and capital goods industries. Secondly, industrialization and rising per capita income widens the range of consumer wants and gives rise to an increased diversity of final demand manufactured products. Beyond a certain point, too narrow an industrial base is incompatible with realizing further increasing returns, and especially those benefits of specialization much emphasized by Young flowing from the division of labour within and across industries.[52] For many firms the

> degree in which it can secure economies by making its own operations more roundabout is limited. But certain roundabout methods are fairly sure to become feasible and economical when their advantages can be spread over the output of the whole industry. These potential economies, then, are segregated and achieved by the operations of specialized undertakings which, taken together, constitute a new industry.   (Young 1928, p.539)

The growth of new specialized undertakings may require a level of output greater than that from a single industry, so that the joint demand from several industries requiring similar components or processing is necessary to ensure the profitability of such an undertaking. (Even a cursory examination of a disaggregated input–output transaction table for an advanced industrial economy will reveal the very large number of industries which are the customers of a typical intermediate goods supplier.) In this way, a large diversified industrial structure and specialization in production are mutually reinforcing or interdependent.[53]

The circular and cumulative relation between specialization, productivity growth and growth in the size of the market is expressed in Young's famous aphorism, 'the division of labour depends upon the extent of the market, but the extent of the market also depends upon the division of labour' (Young 1928, p.539). A concrete example may illuminate the point. A specialized metallurgical firm involved in the heat treatment of steel products can service a very wide range of industries, such as case hardening of components for the automotive, machine tool, railway rolling stock and building products industries. Taken separately, each of these industries may not have a level of output sufficient to justify an entrepreneur's investment in a specialized metallurgical plant. Conversely, the establishment of this specialized firm encourages growth in the size of the market by import-replacement (of heat treated components) and stimulation of new firms which use the services of this local specialist enterprise.

It is arguable, therefore, that Kaldor's 'goal' of development through expansion of manufacturing is inconsistent with his preferred 'means', that is, specialization in production. In terms of the development of CC thought, there is a conflict between Kaldor's claim (repeating similar arguments to those of Sheahan) that national development is best promoted through specialization, and the analysis of Young and Hirschman with their optimal strategy for raising per capita income through the construction of a diversified and integrated industrial structure. It will be recalled, that Sheahan (1958) argued against R-R and Hirschman, in favour of an export strategy based on international specialization to exploit increasing returns.

6.7.5   Income Distribution

Kaldor described his model of CC as a 'marriage of the Smith–Young doctrine on increasing returns with the Keynesian doctrine of effective demand' (Kaldor 1972[c], pp.1245–6). However, as noted earlier, Kaldor did not address all of the complex issues entailed in combining Young's growth theory with Keynes's system. One of the most important of these issues is Kaldor's failure to consider the determination of income distribution within the CC model.[54] Kaldor was critical of Keynes for accepting the marginal productivity theory of income distribution (Kaldor 1982). Similarly, Young's reliance on a competitive industry structure to ensure the passing-on to producers, wage earners and consumers of the benefits of lower intermediate and final demand prices is incompatible with Kaldor's argument that the market structure of advanced industrial economies is oligopolistic. Other than some brief, though highly important, comments on price determination in the oligopoly sector (Kaldor 1985), Kaldor did not propose an alternative theory of distribution. Boyer and Petit (1991) have also been critical of Kaldor's failure to adequately address these issues. There are 'a variety of complex transmission mechanisms' between changes in productivity and changes in demand and income distribution which remain poorly examined in Kaldor's model (Boyer and Petit 1991, p.497). For example, how does the economy adjust its wage indexation system in the transition from an import-substitution phase of development to an export-driven phase? In the former, high levels of domestic consumption are necessary, whereas the latter phase may require productivity gains not to be passed on to workers, so as to lower the ratio of domestic to foreign prices (Boyer and Petit, 1991 p.498). Boyer and Petit do not provide answers to these difficult questions, but argue that these 'transmission mechanisms' must be specified in future development of the CC model.

6.8 CONCLUSION

This chapter began by noting the formidable difficulties confronting the student of Kaldor. One of these difficulties is that most of the secondary literature on Kaldor has been written by advocates (or in some cases disciples) of the Cambridge don. Further, this literature is largely silent on the lineage of CC thought, on what Kaldor took from this tradition, and what he added to it. Kaldor himself was also spare in acknowledging his debt to earlier theorists. For example, he acknowledged Myrdal only as the inventor of the term 'circular and cumulative causation', without outlining his more substantive contributions to the concept (Kaldor 1972[c]; 1985). Kaldor's explanation of the geographic concentration of economic activity, for instance, is very similar to Myrdal's work on the causes of regional specialization of activity and income inequality (Kaldor 1970, 1981, 1985). Similarly, Kaldor's (1981) critique of Heckscher–Ohlin–Samuelson trade theory, especially of its unrealistic assumptions, is largely a repetition of Myrdal's work on the inadequacy of international trade theory (Myrdal 1958). Most importantly, Kaldor repeated Myrdal's view that CC growth theory was equally applicable to advanced and underdeveloped nations. Of greater concern is that Kaldor's substantial debt to Myrdal is also largely ignored in the secondary literature.

Nevertheless, Kaldor's contributions to the development of the CC concept are vitally important. These contributions are of two types. The first are extensions of earlier CC theorists, where he formulated more precisely – or in terms that were empirically tractable – the arguments of those theorists. The second are what may be regarded as genuinely original additions to the concept. As to the first category, the most important of these was the adoption of a very broad view of the sources of increasing returns and a concentration on the empirical workings of some of these sources. Kaldor was also the only CC theorist (other than Myrdal) to argue that increasing returns give rise to a pervasive oligopolistic structure within advanced industrial economies. Kaldor also provided a coherent account of the role of markets and prices in such concentrated markets. The unique character of manufacturing as an economic activity subject to increasing returns, and the significance of manufacturing for the aggregate economy, were rigorously formulated by Kaldor in his famous Growth Laws. These laws were also expressed so as to be amenable to empirical study. Lastly, Kaldor rigorously defined for the CC model the role of the external sector in the Harrod foreign-trade multiplier and the balance of payments constraint to growth. As to the second category, Kaldor's original contributions included the integration of Young's model of growth with Keynes's theory of 'effective demand'. By introducing expectations and monetary influences into the CC analyses of demand and fluctuations in output, Kaldor greatly enhanced the realism of CC growth theory. (Earlier CC theory relied on Say's Law to explain the absorption of increased supply). Kaldor also introduced limits to growth to explain why a system subject to increasing returns does not experience unbounded expansion. However, the latter contribution is subject to significant limitations.

Kaldor's contribution to the development of CC thought is second only to that of his former teacher, Professor Allyn Young. Moreover, Kaldor's contribution has dominated the research interests of most other CC theorists over the last twenty-five years. The effect of Kaldor's legacy, both for good and ill, on the current research programme of CC theorists is examined in the following and final chapter.

Chapter 7
Conclusion

This essay has critically examined the logical structure of the concept of circular and cumulative causation and the evolution of this structure over time. The study has identified the central propositions of this theory and critically evaluated the principal contributions of the chief contributors to this theory. The evolution of these propositions were demonstrated primarily through the works of Allyn Young, Paul Rosenstein-Rodan, Albert Hirschman, Gunnar Myrdal and Nicholas Kaldor. This study has also demonstrated that the theory of circular and cumulative causation, as it has evolved over the past seventy years, constitutes a distinct and coherent model of growth and development.

Three reasons have been advanced for undertaking this task. Firstly, there is the failure in histories of economic thought either to recognize CC theory or to acknowledge the existence of a coherent school founded on CC principles. Moreover, this deficiency has not been addressed by modern proponents of the theory, who, from Kaldor onwards, have shown little interest in the origins or evolution of the theory over the twentieth century. This essay has been concerned primarily with charting these main currents in the development of CC thought. Secondly, it is claimed that the present study has important implications for contemporary economic studies, such as recent empirical studies of East Asian development and endogenous growth theory, which employ similar or related analytical tools to the CC doctrine. These detailed empirical studies strongly support the validity of CC growth theory. The authors of these detailed empirical studies decline to propose a coherent and overarching theory of industrial development to explain these empirical results or to account for the success of national industry policies. It is argued below that the theory of cumulative causation can provide such an overarching and coherent theoretical understanding. The present study is also significant for endogenous growth theory. Although notions of increasing returns and external economies are central to endogenous growth theory, key proponents of this theory have adopted a critical (and indeed dismissive) attitude towards the earlier CC tradition. Such an approach effectively abandons many insights of the earlier CC tradition into the process of industrial development. Thirdly, it is suggested that an improved understanding of the origins and intellectual foundations of CC may assist further development of the CC research programme. In particular, it is argued that many of the key contributions of earlier theorists in the CC tradition have been subsequently ignored or downplayed, and contemporary CC theory can benefit substantially from the rehabilitation of these concepts and methods. The last two of these reasons for undertaking this study are the primary focus of this final chapter.

Before embarking on these implications, a brief overview and synthesis of the cumulative causation doctrine is warranted. Having presented and critically assessed the main currents flowing into the theory, what are the essential elements which constitute the theory of cumulative causation?

7.1   CIRCULAR AND CUMULATIVE CAUSATION: A SYNTHESIS

The theory of circular and cumulative causation posits a circular relation between growth in productivity and growth in total output. The growth in output causes growth in productivity and the growth in productivity stimulates growth in total output. Growth in productivity and growth in output are interdependent and self-reinforcing. Growth in productivity and total output is cumulative and inherent to a market-based industrial economy. The primary source of productivity growth is increasing returns. Within an industrial economy increasing returns are pervasive and significant. CC adopts a very catholic view of the sources of increasing returns. They encompass economies of the plant and firm, static and dynamic economies (the latter include learning by doing and using) and Marshallian and Youngian increasing returns arising from the division of labour within an industry and economy-wide, respectively. The division of labour is intimately connected with increases in capital per worker, as increases in the size of the market permit not only finer specialization in labour tasks and skills but also overcome indivisibilities in the use of capital equipment. As produced means of production and so themselves subject to increasing returns, capital goods are also subject to real price reductions. CC theory views increments to the capital stock as essentially complementary to this stock, enhancing increasing returns (and not competitive as in the neoclassical framework and subject to diminishing returns). The division of labour also has a crucial spatial dimension. Industrial development has historically been linked to the growth of cities, not only due to proximity to the principal source of demand for manufactures, but also due to a variety of economies of agglomeration, such as transport networks, reduced information transaction costs and skilled labour markets. These economies may best be viewed as a subset of the concept of externalities. Externalities such as those resulting from learning by doing and using are important in explaining the spatial concentration of production with a given region. (The spatial dimension is also discussed below.) Technological change is also regarded as an aspect of increasing returns. Technological change is positively related to growth in the size of the market due to a number of factors, such as learning by doing and using, and the over-coming of indivisibilities and sunk costs in research and innovation activities. Technological change is embodied in new capital goods and intermediate products and thus investment in new vintages of capital equipment is a key transmission mechanism for new technology.

The assumptions of CC theory – including the existence of pervasive and significant increasing returns; complementarities in investment, production and consumption; endogenous technical change and factor creation; imper-fect information; and the capital–labour ratio dependent on the size of the market – contradict the conditions for general equilibrium. Accordingly, the notion of externalities, both pecuniary and technological, is an essential apparatus for understanding the operation of 'market forces' within this disequilibrium framework. The corollary of externalities, that is, the diver-gence of private and social costs and benefits, implies the existence of 'co-ordination failures' in the timing, volume and industry composition of invest-ments. Externalities and co-ordination failures provide a rationale for wide-ranging policy interventions by the state.

Growth in total output is a function of the growth of demand, and is not determined exogenously by the growth of factor supplies (and a residual such as an unexplained rate of technical progress which is sufficient to maintain equilibrium and full employment of all resources). Factor supplies, including savings, capital equipment and labour, do not over the medium term con-strain the growth of output; rather the growth of factor supplies is determined by the growth of output. Even many raw materials may be displaced by synthetic substitutes. During the early stages of industrial development labour shifts from low per-person productivity sectors such as agriculture to manu-facturing, and at higher stages of development immigration is an important source of skilled and unskilled labour. Kaldor emphasized the Keynesian dynamic of savings as a function of the growth of income, and both Kaldor and Currie highlighted the central role of retained earnings in the corporate sector, where current sales fund future investment.

Unlike the neoclassical approach, which does not distinguish between industries in terms of their differential effects on growth, CC identifies manufacturing as the primary motive force in per capita income growth. Neoclassical analysis, for example, assumes constant returns in production, elevates price effects over income effects, emphasises substitution over com-plementarity and regards technical change and 'factor endowment' as exogen-ous. In contrast, CC identifies manufacturing industry as the primary motive force, if not the singular 'engine' of growth. This is due to the congruence within this industry of the following factors. Manufacturing is subject to significant increasing returns; there is a high income elasticity of demand for manufactures; given the scope for 'factor creation' and the fact that most inputs to manufacturing are themselves manufactures, the industry has a high long-run elasticity of supply; manufactures have higher long-run real prices compared to agricultural and mining commodities; manufactures have a key role in overcoming the balance of payments constraint to growth; and manufacturing has a continuing importance in technological innovation and diffusion. Other industries may also be subject to increasing returns or at very high income levels their income elasticity of demand may exceed that of manufacturing. It is the concentration of all the factors listed above within manufacturing which make it a unique economic activity.

As emphasized by Young and Kaldor (such as the latter's four-stage model) the pattern of industrial development is incremental This does not imply development is necessarily slow; the growth process can be controlled, planned and accelerated such as in post-war Japan and Taiwan. It does imply, however, that there is a definite order and priority within national economies in the development of particular industries. A regional or national industrial structure is on a developmental trajectory based on the prior acquisition of capital, skilled labour force (including the effects of learning by doing and using), as well as the industrial inputs from a wide range of specialized suppliers. Confirmation of the incremental nature of industrial development is provided by the work of Hollis Chenery, amongst others, who has demonstrated the remarkable regularities in input–output structure at similar per capita income levels. These studies highlight the progressive growth of the intermediate inputs and capital goods sector with increases in per capita income. This stylized fact confirms a key argument of Young and Hirschman that the growth of per capita output is causally associated with a progressive increase in the density of the input–output structure. This progressive increase in capital widening and deepening is a function of the increased division of labour within and across industries, which in turn is both a cause and effect of increases in the size of the market. In other words, the division of labour or increase in intra- and inter-industry purchases and supplies, by definition gives rise to a 'filling in' of the input-output matrix. This specialization occurs especially in the intermediate and capital goods sectors.[1] The second cause of the increased density of the input–output structure is the growth in the diversity of consumer wants at progressively higher levels of per capita income. At low levels of per capita income, consumer demand is concentrated on wage goods – staple foods, simple clothing and shelter. At higher levels of income more complex foods, clothes and shelter are demanded as well as new wants such as private motor vehicles and so forth. An increased diversity of consumer wants will in turn lead to an expansion in the number and range of industries to meet these wants.

Whilst these growth processes are inherent to a market industrial economy, the initiation and continuation of growth are not inevitable. At an early stage of development, with a comparatively small domestic market, indivisibilities in the employment of capital can prevent the introduction of modern production techniques. Competitive imports can also inhibit the creation of a local manufacturing base. Similarly, even at an advanced stage of development, a too rapid decline in manufacturing's share of total output or de-industrialization can lead to balance of payments constraints, which lowers a nation's long-term growth potential. Reduction in manufacturing output and competitiveness within an advanced economy can result from a wide range of factors. These include government policy indifference to the industry, a concentration of national manufactures on products with a lower income elasticity of demand than imports, or a related factor of an inability to innovate products and processes due to the high costs of R&D or new capital equipment. Balance of payments constraints not only affect an individual nation subject to adverse movements in its export or import propensities; without international co-ordination of external balances, total world growth can be lowered. Other factors determining the pattern and pace of growth are the Keynesian (or Myrdalian) influences of expectations, uncertainty and effective demand. Aside from these effects, a slowing in the growth of per capita output within a nation is to be expected at higher stages of development owing to a greater equality of productivity across industries (especially in agriculture) and a gradual reduction in the share of manufactures in total output as the income elasticity of demand for manufactures declines relative to that of services at high per capita income levels.

CC theory predicts uneven and unequal development across and within nations. The processes of cumulative growth and decline across nations and regions are far more significant and pervasive than tendencies towards equilibrium. International trade in manufactures and services is not based on comparative advantage and nor is it necessarily welfare-enhancing. Given the similarities in input–output structures amongst advanced industrial countries, intra-industry trade (often based on quality differences for 'identical' commodities) is the dominant form of trade in manufactures and services. These three stylized facts – no necessary tendency to long-run congruence of per capita income across nations; a predominance of intra-industry trade in world non-commodity exports; and similar input-output structures at the same level of per capita income – are entirely consistent with CC theory.

The analysis of growth and decline must be integrated with historical, social, cultural, institutional and political factors. CC theory is firmly grounded in the traditions of political economy, which recognizes that market economies do not operate within an institutional vacuum. These institutional arrangements may or may not be conducive to development or may promote development up to a certain stage and inhibit further progress. It must be recognized that there are a wide variety of state and institutional structures, each reflecting particular historical experiences, which are consistent with the growth of industrial market economies.

7.2 ENDOGENOUS GROWTH THEORY

External economies are central to endogenous growth theory, which has become very prominent over the last decade.[2] Like neoclassical growth theory, endogenous growth theory identifies technological innovation as the principal source of increase in per capita output. Unlike the neoclassicals, endogenous theorists locate the source of technological change primarily within the economic system. The principal implication of the neoclassical growth model is that the underlying rate of output growth is the sum of exogenous labour force increase and exogenous technical change (Solow 1994, p.48). This implication gives rise to the central paradox in neoclassical growth theory whereby it demonstrated that 'technological change was of fundamental importance for economic growth... but denied the possibility that economic analysis could have anything to say about this process' (Romer 1991, p.85). This theoretical paradox was reinforced by neoclassical 'growth accounting' exercises, which found that the bulk of increase in long-run national output is due to reasons other than increase in the quantity of factor supplies (BIE 1992, p.6).

The solution proffered by endogenous growth theorists to difficulties confronting neoclassical theory is the 'straightforward abandonment of the idea of diminishing returns to capital' (Solow 1994 p.49). This abandonment 'is achieved by invoking some externality that offsets any propensity to diminishing returns' (Pack 1994 p.56). The primary externality invoked is that of knowledge. The particular form of knowledge on which they focus is that which gives rise to technological change or improved productivity. In the various models of endogenous growth, knowledge is generated within the system as the product or by-product of economic activity. The specific sources of knowledge identified by endogenous growth theorists include investments in R&D, 'human capital', physical capital, as well as learning by doing (Grossman and Helpman 1994, p.26, p.31; BIE 1992). The central claim of endogenous growth theory is that knowledge is a unique economic good, since to varying degrees it is non-rivalrous and non-excludable. In the former case, the use of knowledge by one firm does not preclude its use by another. In the latter, much productive knowledge developed by particular individuals or companies enters into the public domain, and even patented information has a finite period of exclusion. The non-excludability of knowledge arises primarily from limits on the efficacy of intellectual property rights.[3]

The economic significance of these attributes is, firstly, that there are no costs (or minimal costs) in the use of the current stock of knowledge to expand output. There is, in other words, no opportunity cost in the use of non-rival inputs (Romer 1994, p.12). A conventional neoclassical production function is linearly homogeneous (constant returns to scale, and diminishing returns to each factor), so that a doubling of output requires a doubling of inputs. The existence of non-rivalrous inputs implies scale economies in production since an increase in output can occur without an increase or less than proportionate increase in the use of these inputs. Secondly, with endogenous technical change diminishing returns to a factor do not apply, as improvements in the 'quality' or productivity of factors (especially capital) offset such tendencies. Such quality improvements reconcile rising productivity and long-run growth in the capital-labour ratio.[4] Finally, the non-excludability of knowledge provides an important externality through the transfer of information to economic agents at no cost. Through 'technological spillover' the social rate of return from technological innovation exceeds the private return (Grossman and Helpmann 1994, p.31).

In the endogenous growth model knowledge and the cumulative expansion of knowledge 'sustains both capital accumulation and growth' (Grossman and Helpmann 1994, p.35). Endogenous learning performs this function 'like the exogenous technological progress of the neoclassical model – [it] prevents the marginal product of capital from falling to the point where investment ceases to be profitable' (Grossman and Helpmann 1994, p.35).

7.2.1 External Economies in Endogenous Growth Theory and Circular and Cumulative Causation

Whilst endogenous growth theorists place externalities at the centre of their analyses, they provide little illumination on the earlier CC School. Endogenous growth theorists generally, and Professor Paul Romer in particular, adopt a very critical and in some respects dismissive attitude to the earlier tradition. 'Nicholas Kaldor and Joan Robinson waged a form of guerilla warfare against the neoclassical model, and they invoked Young's name, among others, in support of their cause. But they offered no tractable alternative model' (Romer 1991, p.89). Romer's primary objection is to the conception of externality in the Marshall–Young tradition, since the growth process in this tradition is not based on a 'true externality'. Romer asserts that only 'technological' externalities resulting from various forms of knowledge spillover are true externalities. 'The problem with the suggestive discussion of specialization offered by Marshall and Young is that it contains nothing resembling a true externality in production. Rather, it seems to be based on an underlying model of differentiated commodities that are used as inputs in the production of final goods' (Romer 1986, p.4). Secondly, citing Frank Knight's (1925) contribution to the 1920s cost controversy, Romer argues that no example of an economy 'external to the firm, but internal to the industry' has been empirically identified.[5]

It is now widely accepted that the inclusion of knowledge as an input to production can lead to increasing returns and that spillovers of knowledge between firms can be treated as externalities because patent protection is incomplete. Yet beyond this, Knight seems to have been largely correct. No convincing examples of external economies have been offered. In particular, the notion emphasized by Young – that there could be improvements in the organization of the industry or the economy as a whole as production is divided between firms producing more specialized outputs – cannot be captured as an externality in the modern sense.

(Romer 1986, p.5; see also 1991, pp.88–89)

The focus on technological externalities in modern endogenous growth theory is driven, in part at least, by methodological concerns to construct the new growth theory in a mathematically tractable equilibrium framework.[6] 'Most of the contributors to the new literature on innovation-based growth have adopted a general equilibrium perspective' (Grossman and Helpmann 1994, p.34). Imperfect competition is assumed in the supply of new technologies given non-appropriability of all profits from innovations, and 'sunk' costs of innovation.[7] However, in most endogenous growth models, the rest of the economy, including markets for labour, final demand goods, capital and assets, is perfectly competitive (Grossman and Helpmann 1994, p.34).

In contrast, the CC School has not adopted a sophisticated mathematical modelling approach, in part at least, since the conditions giving rise to pecuniary economies and the effects of these economies are incompatible with an equilibrium approach. The explicit rejection of equilibrium reasoning has been a feature of the CC tradition from Young through to Kaldor and beyond. A leading modern proponent of CC, Professor John Cornwall, has highlighted two other key differences between endogenous growth theory and CC. Firstly, 'the new growth theory treats the economy as an homogeneous whole' (Cornwall 1994, p.247). The new growth theory carries over from neoclassical economics a highly aggregated view of the economy, as represented, for example, in the use of its own form of the aggregate production function (Romer 1994). The generation of knowledge and technological external economies is treated at a high level of abstraction where it is either a by-product of 'production' or the outcome of R&D activities. 'As in neoclassical growth theory, the focus in endogenous growth is on the behaviour of the economy as a whole. As a result, this work is complementary to, but different from, the study of research and development or productivity at the level of the industry or firm' (Romer 1994, p.3). Within CC theory by comparison, manufacturing is regarded as the engine of per capita output growth and the primary source of pecuniary and technological external economies. Further, within manufacturing certain industries such as machine tool production, chemicals and electronics have been highlighted for their above-average role in the generation and diffusion of technology (Cornwall 1977). Cornwall is also critical of the strong supply-side orientation of endogenous growth theory (Cornwall 1994, p.248). The theory has focused on the positive effects of knowledge spillovers rather than the factors calling forth or underlying productive knowledge and its diffusion. By contrast, CC growth theory assumes that 'demand acts on the sectoral productivity growth rates by generating the incentive to invest and innovate' (Cornwall 1994, p.248).

To conclude this section, endogenous growth theory has made an important contribution in highlighting both the role of technological external economies in growth and the damning impact on the neoclassical canon if knowledge is accepted as a factor in production.[8] Whilst endogenous growth theory has developed some fundamental criticisms of neoclassicism, paradoxically, it has also retained many of the features which impede realism in economic analysis. These include the methodological priority given to the creation of tractable equilibrium models, and the corollary of admitting technological externalities as the only source of increasing returns. 'The significant shortcomings of the new growth theory, which are carried over from neoclassical growth theory' have led Cornwall to conclude that these 'are models of growth, but not of development. They neglect entirely the changes that characterize development, the determinants of these changes and their impact on the aggregate growth rate' (Cornwall 1994, p.248).

7.3 RECENT STUDIES OF EAST ASIAN DEVELOPMENT

There has been a recent revival of interest in the notion of increasing returns, external economies and disequilibrium growth in detailed empirical studies of post-war East Asian economic development. These economic histories seek to provide an alternative to neoclassical explanations of rapid and sustained growth in East Asian countries since WWII.[9] External economies and increasing returns are central to the explanation of rapid and sustained East Asian growth in several influential studies of development, such as those of Taiwan, by Wade (1990), and Japan, by Johnson (1982), and Johnson, Tyson and Zysman (1991), Stein (1993) and Argy and Stein (1997).[10] These historical accounts emphasize the central place of import substitution, increasing returns, pecuniary and technological externalities, and learning by doing in the growth process and as the foundation for state industry policies. These studies also detail the 'co-ordination' function of the state in determining the industrial composition, volume, and sequencing of investments, as well as manipulation of demand to validate these investments through tariffs, government procurement, export assistance and policies on income distribution etc. According to some economic historians, the co-ordination effort required to achieve 'high-speed growth' was very great indeed (Johnson 1982, p.29). In summarizing the experience of post-war Japan, Chalmers Johnson argues 'there are two basic components to industry policy, corresponding to the micro and macro aspects of the economy' (Johnson 1982, p.27). At the micro level it involves

> state intrusion into the detailed operations of individual enterprises with measures intended to improve those operations ... in its simplest terms it is the attempt by the state to discover what it is individual enterprises are already doing to produce the greatest benefits for the least cost, and then ... to cause all enterprises of an industry to adopt these preferred procedures. (Johnson 1982, p.27)

At the macro level, the concept of 'industrial structure' was the key to the Ministry of International Trade and Industry (MITI') planning.[11] This planning

> concerns the proportions of agriculture, mining, manufacturing, and services in the nation's total production; and within manufacturing it concerns the percentages of light and heavy, and of labour-intensive and knowledge-intensive industries. The application of the policy comes in the government's attempts to change these proportions in ways it deems advantageous to the nation. Industrial structure policy is based on such standards as income elasticity of demand, comparative costs of production, labour absorptive power, environmental concerns, investment effects on related industries, and export prospects. (Johnson 1982, p.28)

Moreover, these studies describe how state functions evolved as economic development proceeded. For example, in the early stages of industrialization direct state ownership of key capital intensive inputs to production was a feature of industries such as oil refining, coal, iron and steel and railways. In addition, the state was either the primary source of loan funds to the private sector and/or exercised considerable control over private credit providers. In later stages of industrialization, many state-owned industries were privatized, and direct controls over technology imports, foreign exchange and capital markets were relaxed. An interesting characteristic was the way in which the private sector itself increasingly assumed these co-ordination functions. In Japan, the keiretsu form of industrial organization involves close inter-firm and inter-industry co-operation. Companies within the keiretsu are closely tied through high levels of cross-shareholding, interlocking directorates, and engage in inter-company financing, purchase, supply and joint R&D ventures. High levels of intra-company transactions and co-ordinated investments created a 'partially internalized market in final/intermediate products' (Gerlach 1988, p.142).[12] It is significant that both Rosenstein-Rodan and Hirschman denied capitalists were capable of the extensive inter-industry and inter-firm co-operation exhibited by keiretsu. For these writers, the state is the exclusive agent for the co-ordination of economic activity.[13] However, it will be recalled that both Rosenstein-Rodan and Hirschman focused on the very early stages of industrialization. Nevertheless, from the perspective of CC theory the keiretsu organization is entirely explicable in that such an organization of economic activity creates and internalizes a number of positive externalities. (A more detailed account of state industry policy in Japan and Taiwan and the keiretsu form of industrial organization is provided in the Appendix.)

The empirical support provided to CC theory by these economic histories is especially important, since the theoretical legitimacy of CC has been questioned by claimed implementation failures during various national development episodes in the post-war era. The noted Harvard development economist, Professor Pranab Bardhan, claims that growth theory based on increasing returns and pecuniary external economies, which was

> so central to the development economics of the 1950s, lost much of its intellectual force in subsequent decades, not so much because it lacked, until recently, a firm anchoring in a formal model using tools of imperfect markets equilibrium... but more because at the policy level the difficulties of aggregate co-ordination were underestimated (particularly at the existing levels of administrative capacity and political coherence in the developing countries) and the incentive and organisational issues of micro-management of capital were underappreciated. The resulting government failures diverted the profession's attention from what nevertheless remains an important source of market failure discovered by early development economics'.
> (Bardan 1993, p.134)

It is significant that Bardhan does not cite an actual instance of implementation failure.

These studies of East Asian development are relevant for another reason. Whilst these economic histories provide enormous empirical detail regarding East Asian development, there is an absence of theory to explain the growth process. In the case of Wade (1990), Johnson (1982), and Johnson, Tyson and Zysman (1991), reference is made to aspects of imperfect competition such as externalities, economies of scale and learning by doing, to account for the success of industry policy. However, no overarching or coherent theoretical structure is offered to unify these disparate insights. For example, Dosi, Tyson and Zysman (1991) provide an amalgam of separate theorems from heterodox sources, including Schumpeter, strategic trade theory, and historians of technological innovation. Johnson simply explains that 'Japan's political economy' was derived from non-Anglo-American sources, especially the 'German Historical School – sometimes labelled 'economic nationalism',

Handelspolitik, or neomercantilism' (Johnson 1982, p.17). Johnson does not take up the important task of outlining the key ideas in this tradition or their influence on Japan's policy-makers. The theory of circular and cumulative causation provides a means of integrating the empirical generalizations and insights offered by these economic historians into a coherent structure.

Lastly, from the perspective of modern political economy, there is a notable absence of discussion about the 'role of the state' by the advocates of balanced and unbalanced growth, Kaldor, and among current theorists such as Thirlwall and McCombie.[14] Their implicit assumptions are that it is in the rational self-interest of a nation to support CC policies and the state is simply a vehicle for implementing strategies which private capital is unable to perform. The economic histories cited above provide detailed accounts of the historical development of the bureaucratic and political structures that implemented growth strategies, the ideological underpinning of these strategies and the place of these strategies in the history of a particular nation-state. In addition, political sociologists (such as Hewison, Robison and Rodan, 1993) highlight the way in which the implementation of state policies is constrained by class and ethnic conflict, the competence and probity of the bureaucracy, competing interests among private investors (e.g. agriculture vs manufacturing), and the relative strength of local and international capital.[15] The economic historians and political sociologists highlight the very particular circumstances necessary for the initiation of a 'developmental state'. For example, Wade (1990) highlights the central role of the military in Taiwan in promoting industrialization, as well as considerable direct and indirect assistance from external sources, especially the United States in the context of the Cold War. In other words, these studies emphasize what Myrdal termed 'non-economic' factors in growth and development, and provide an important contemporary example of how these factors could be reincorporated into the CC research programme. Considerable progress may be achieved by a synthesis of disequilibrium growth theory and the type of economic history and political sociology cited above. What is necessary is an integration of a theory of production and growth with economic history and political sociology. This suggestion is amplified below, in a discussion of the future research programme for CC theory.

7.4   FUTURE OF THE CC RESEARCH PROGRAMME

This section draws together and elaborates on a number of areas for additional research identified throughout this essay. These areas for research were derived from valuable ideas of early contributors to CC theory that were downplayed or ignored by later theorists, or arise from unresolved tensions or conflicts between theorists. This section also identifies a number of deficiencies within the broad approach of contemporary CC theory, and recommends further work for their redress. It is argued that contemporary CC theory should reincorporate what Myrdal termed 'non-economic factors' into the explanation of growth and decline. Secondly, although Kaldor's methodology and research interests have proved to be immensely fruitful, they are also subject to significant limitations. As Kaldor's methodology and research interests still dominate most contemporary CC research, these limitations have been continued. Finally, criticisms are advanced of the general failure of CC theorists to provide a detailed empirical or theoretical analysis of several core assumptions underlying CC theory, such as the sources and extent of increasing returns, externalities and complementarity in production and consumption. This lack of attention to these core assumptions is also evident in the neglect of important recent advances in the theory of production and increasing returns which provide important insights into the process of disequilibrium growth.

The importance of reintroducing 'non-economic' factors into the explanation of growth as emphasized by Myrdal was highlighted earlier. Balanced and Unbalanced Growth theory, Kaldor, and current theorists such as McCombie, Thirlwall and Cornwall, have generally failed to incorporate non-economic factors into their work. This lacuna is evident in the failure to examine either the particular historical conditions giving rise either to successful implementation of national growth policies or the inability to correct long-run circles of vicious decline.[16] One of the major well-springs for the currents of CC theory has been the criticism of equilibrium analysis for its lack of 'realism'. This lack of realism takes a number of forms, such as the assumption of linear homogeneous production functions, exogenous technological change, a focus on 'logical' rather than 'historical' time, and separation of economic and non-economic factors. There is the danger that if contemporary CC theory ignores the role of history in the explanation of growth and decline it could be led increasingly into abstract model-making. Current theorists have largely left unexplored the study of those national policies designed, for example, to raise domestic demand for local manufactures or to alter the composition of the industrial structure, the linkages within this structure and the rate of growth of industries and (even particular firms) within this structure. This lacuna is anomalous as these theorists frequently cite rapid and sustained post-war growth in North Asian countries as confirming the efficacy of CC principles generally and interventionist industry policies in particular (Cornwall 1977, Eatwell 1982, 1987; McCombie and Thirlwall 1994, Thirlwall 1994).[17] To date the focus of research has been on the end result, or what are presumed to be the end result or effects of such policies on patterns of development.

Undertaking case studies linking national policies to changes in the industrial structure and their effect on comparative international performance would significantly improve the plausibility and explanatory power of CC theory. A priority should be given firstly to identifying the particular historical conditions that have been conducive to the successful (and possibly unsuccessful) implementation of state policies, where these policies can be demonstrated to be consistent with CC theory. This examination should also determine the efficacy of particular strategies in achieving their stated goals, the way in which these strategies evolve or are adapted to a changing industrial structure or international situation and the extent to which there are commonalities in these strategies across nations at the same stage of development.[18] The failure to undertake such studies partly reflects the downplaying of 'non-economic' factors which has been a long-term feature of CC theory (with the exception of Myrdal), but – equally important – has been the legacy of Kaldor's economic methodology (described in Section 6.2).

In summary, Kaldor's general approach was to identify key empirical 'stylized facts' regarding the process of advanced capitalist development and deduce a simple theory to explain each fact and then to 'test' the theory by applying relatively simple but robust econometric techniques to highly aggregated statistics. Kaldor's growth laws exemplify this approach (Kaldor 1966[a], Thirlwall 1983). This methodology and these research areas have of course proved not only to be remarkably fruitful, but possibly also crucial to the re-invigoration of the CC tradition following declining interest in development economics from the 1970s.[19] Nevertheless, this methodology has had a discernible and it is arguable an 'unbalancing' effect on contemporary CC research, leading to a dis-regard of 'non-economic' factors. Kaldor's methodology and research interests still dominate contemporary CC inquiry. The overwhelming focus of contemporary CC research has been the elaboration of Kaldor's Growth Laws and the balance of payments constraint to growth. This work has been invaluable in clarifying the statistical and econometric foundations of the Growth Laws and in confirming the role of the Harrod foreign-trade multiplier and the balance of payments constraint to growth in the explanation of differences in national growth rates. Yet, it is arguable that after the nearly twenty-five years of massive intellectual effort that has gone into the 'elaboration' and 'confirming' of Kaldor's key findings, a point of diminishing returns has been reached in this research effort and other topics should be given higher priority on the research agenda.

It has been insufficiently recognized by CC theorists and in the secondary literature, that in his methodological writings Allyn Young explicitly recognized the limitations of 'economic theory' and advocated the incorporation of institutional and historical studies into the economics discipline. In an article on the history and method of economics Young highlighted the contribution of the Historical School, which he associated primarily with Friedrich List, Wilhelm Roscher and Karl Knies. He summarized their position thus;

[t]he structure of a nation's economic life... is an "historical category," something peculiar to a given nation at a given time, a product of its past, and to be understood therefore, only by the study of that past. The wisdom of particular economic policies is relative to place and time, and the general or supposedly universal "laws" of abstract economics need to be *supplemented by or even subordinated to* an analysis of the concrete facts of each nation's economic growth. If they had gone no further these critics would have found many to agree with them'.   (Young 1929[b] p.929, my italics)

However, Young was also critical of the Historical School's tendency to make 'something peculiarly arbitrary and doctrinaire' about the 'historical method... [as] they proposed to derive from history universal and binding laws, akin to the laws of the physical sciences'. Nevertheless, Young concludes that

[d]espite the extremes to which they pushed their contentions, the historical economists gave a needed emphasis to what may be called the institutional as contrasted with the free or contractual aspects of economic activities. Their work and that of their successors has made economists more mindful of the way in which *institutions are the masters as well as the servants of men*, and less ready to assume that the particular economic order with which their analysis is mostly concerned is inevitably permanent or final. The historical economists also gave a needed impetus to the study of *economic history – a most valuable complement to the study of economic theory*.   (Young 1929[b] p.929. my italics)

In general, past and contemporary CC theorists have paid insufficient heed to Young's methodological statements.[20]

Another effect of this orientation of contemporary CC theory is that it has concentrated on manufacturing industry in the aggregate. It focuses especially on the relation between growth in aggregate manufacturing output and productivity growth, and the role of manufacturing industry in overall national economic performance. A crucial element in the earlier CC tradition has been largely ignored, that is the detailed study of the industrial structure and its transformation over time. Whilst it is certainly true that contemporary theorists acknowledge the importance of Hirschman's apparatus of backward and forward linkages and input–output methods (Thirlwall 1994, Chapter 11; Cornwall 1977, pp.130–135), there is virtually a complete absence of empirical or theoretical application of these methods. The central role earlier theorists, notably Hirschman and Chenery, gave to national inter-industry structure for the study of development has largely been lost by later CC writers. Chenery's work over the last thirty years has identified the systematic transformations in the input–output structure of economies at different levels of per capita income at successive stages of development. These researches confirm the claim of Young and Hirschman of a causal connection between per capita income growth and increase in the diversity of industries and density of intra- and inter-industry trade.[21] There would be considerable advantage if the two levels of analysis, that is the aggregate study of the significance and role of manufacturing and disaggregated studies of manufacturing industries and structural change, were to be pursued in a complementary manner.

In addition, contemporary CC research has in general failed to study or develop many of the theory's fundamental assumptions – or, what might be better termed the mechanisms of growth identified by Young and elaborated through to Kaldor. The detailed empirical examination of increasing returns, for instance, has largely been the domain of industry economists, such as Blair, Pratten, Scherer, and Gold. Their studies underscore the manifold difficulties in employing econometric methods to identify the sources and extent of scale economies at a plant, firm and industry level.[22] Contemporary theorists have been largely content to accept as given most of the mechanisms of growth identified by earlier CC theorists, and to treat these mechanisms at a high level of generality. These mechanisms include increasing returns in manufacturing; the notion of complementarity in consumption and production; reciprocal demand; technological and pecuniary external economies and endogenous technological change.[23] To express this another way, current theorists have focused on the superstructure of CC or the logical inferences and policy conclusions arising from the existence of increasing returns, externalities and complementarities, and have generally left unexamined the detailed operation of these mechanisms.

In this respect, Alice Amsden's work (cited earlier) on the development of Taiwan's machine tool industry provides an important example of the benefits to be derived from a detailed examination of the operation of increasing returns within a particular industry. Amsden's historical case study approach, focused on long-term changes in the organization of production and technology within the industry and individual firms. Amsden stated that this methodology is essential 'to try to understand the cumulative causation process involving fast economic growth in newly industrializing economies' (Amsden 1985, p.282). Further, her findings explicitly support Kaldor's catholic views on the sources of increasing returns. Amsden also provides an excellent example of the insights to be obtained by reflecting on the principal assumptions of CC theory. Her studies of increasing returns led her to posit an interesting refinement to Smith's dictum that 'the size of the market determines the extent of the division of labour.' Amsden argues that 'the division of labour is limited not only by the size of the market and growth rate of the market but also by its *type*. If two markets are of equal size in terms of income, there are still likely to be different consumption and production patterns if one market contains a small number of high income earners and the other a large number of low income earners' (Amsden 1985, p.275).

Amsden describes the shift in Taiwan's machine tool industry in the 1970s from supplying large southeast Asian markets which had 'modest demands for quality combined with pressing demands for rock bottom prices', to supplying U.S. and European markets in which quality was paramount. This shift to supplying a different market necessitated large changes in the characteristics of the products, which in turn necessitated large-scale changes in the organization of production. The shift to supplying U.S and European markets forced 'machine tool producers to raise quality not so much by developing more sophisticated models as by improving the durability, reliability and precision of traditional products'. The principal changes to the organization of industry required to meet the needs of this new 'type' of market entailed a substantial increase in the division of labour through subcontracting, increased capital investment and growth of management with professional qualifications (Amsden 1985, pp.276–277).

Another example of an important topic on the subject of increasing returns that has not received the warranted attention is the analysis of sectors other than manufacturing that are subject to increasing returns. In Chapter 6, it was noted that certain service activities such as transport, construction and utilities have been identified by CC theorists as subject to increasing returns – i.e. there is a statistically significant Verdoorn relation between productivity growth and output growth in these activities. Whilst Kaldor (1966[a]) and later Thirlwall (1983) reported these results, they did not investigate their potential importance. The importance of these results is that they challenge the privileged position of manufacturing in the growth process by suggesting that other industries are capable of exploiting the benefits of increasing returns. In addition, it was noted that activities other than manufacturing such as the business services industry may be a major source of technical innovation and diffusion. It will be recalled that one of the reasons why CC theorists like Kaldor and Cornwall identified manufacturing as the 'engine of growth' was that manufacturing products, especially intermediate and capital goods, embody technological innovations that are transferred to the rest of the economy through intra- and inter-industry trade. It is important therefore, to determine the extent and significance of these external economies from sectors other than manufacturing.

There have also been a number of very important recent developments in the field of industry economics and production theory that are relevant to the major assumptions of CC theory and which should be evaluated by current CC theorists. Some of these important new ideas include additions to the theory of increasing returns such as learning by using, economies of scope and flexible production systems (BIE 1988[a]). Also, the extensive recent literature on inter-firm and inter-industry 'networks', which involve extensive co-operation between firms, has been largely ignored by CC theorists (with the exception of Whiteman 1991). These networks would seem to address, at least in part, those co-ordination failures which were emphasized by Rosenstein-Rodan and which he claimed are inherent to a decentralized capitalist economy. Other writers, such as Mario Morroni (1992) have taken up the task of integrating many of these new ideas into disequilibrium growth and production theory. Morroni draws on the work of Kaldor, Georgescu-Roegen, Robinson, Pasinetti and Rosenberg. Its analytical foundations are increasing returns, indivisibilities, complementarities, endogenous technical change, and production processes in historical time. This work also incorporates important recent advances in production theory, such as economies of scope, and flexible production systems which have not been examined by past or present CC theorists. These numerous recent developments in the theory and empirical study of increasing returns and production are important as they confirm the key assumptions of dis-equilibrium growth and open up new research areas for the application of this theory.

A necessary area for research is Kaldor's 'marriage' of Keynes's principle of 'effective demand' with Young's classically inspired theory of long-run productivity growth. Kaldor's attempt to integrate the two approaches emphasized the central role of 'autonomous' demand in explaining the rate of growth; the role of demand in 'inducing' investment; the importance of expectations on the part of manufacturers and commodity dealers in determining capital investment and stable input prices, respectively; and the role of money in accounting for fluctuations in output. The principle of effective demand examines the influences governing the short-run determination of the level of aggregate income. The CC model focuses on the causes of long-run growth in per capita income, which are to be found in increasing returns in manufacturing and other industries. In other words, Keynes focused on short-run influences on demand, and CC on long-run structural influences on the long-run rate of per capita output growth. To effect his 'mariage' Kaldor found it necesary to abandon Keynes's assumptions of constant returns to scale and marginal productivity theory of income distribution.

The notion of demand is central to CC theory, with the rate of growth of output determined by the rate of growth of demand – as Kaldor expressed it the economic system is 'demand-constrained', not 'supply-constrained'. However, until Kaldor's work, the notion of demand within CC theory had received very little attention. In Young's analysis the key concepts were Say's Law, income elasticity of demand and complementarity in production and consumption. The introduction of expectations and monetary influences certainly introduce greater complexity into the model, but also more realism. With respect to future research, there are several other important influences on demand, directly or indirectly linked with the work of Keynes, that need to be integrated into the CC framework. These influences include, for instance, the determinants of income distribution and the effect of different distributions on demand and rate of output growth. Income distribution is critical within the CC framework, given the assumption that productivity increases are effectively passed on in the form of lower real prices. Young (and Lauchlin Currie) relied on the force of competition to ensure this outcome; Kaldor suggested prices within an oligopoly were set on 'normal' costs of production given normal capacity utilization. Aside from Kaldor's cursory suggestion, there is no theory of income distribution or the nature and type of 'competition' in concentrated markets within the CC framework.

Finally, one of the important advances of CC was to make technological change endogenous to the economic system. Young asserted that growth in the size of the market and growth of applied scientific knowledge are mutually reinforcing. This claim was accepted by later CC theorists, though it was not subjected to further study. Given the central role of technological change in the model, further work on this topic is essential. It is suggested that the broad direction of these investigations could build on the work of a number of current researchers. The work of historians of technology, such as Nathan Rosenberg (1976, 1982, 1994) is strongly supportive of, and provides important insights into, the disequilibrium understanding of growth. For example, Rosenberg has identified key sectors such as capital goods industries which are a primary source of innovation and has detailed the diffusion or intersectoral flows of technology from these industries. He also noted the importance of specialized firms in the capital goods industries.[24] As noted earlier, Rosenberg's historical studies were also responsible for identifying an important new source of increasing returns, through the notion of 'learning by using' (Rosenberg 1982). A common feature of these studies of technological change is their disaggregated level of analysis. Their focus is on the conditions of production for particular commodities and technologies, as well as the intra- and inter-industry diffusion of these technologies. This disaggregated approach is important, as the focus of Kaldor and most subsequent CC theorists has been on aggregate manufacturing as the 'engine of growth', without examining the 'engine's' components, assembly, and interaction.

Reference must also be made to 'complex systems theory' developed by the Stanford economics professors W. Brian Arthur and Paul David. They draw explicitly on the work of Myrdal and Kaldor to investigate how increasing returns and cumulative processes affect technological development (Arthur 1990, p.81).[25] Using a number of examples of innovation, such as the QWERTY keyboard, computer operating systems (e.g. DOS), and video recorder technology (the struggle between Beta and VHS systems for market share), they demonstrate how chance events, like early entry into the market or adoption of an innovation as an industry standard, can 'lock-in' an innovation and exclude potentially superior innovations. This lock-in is due to a number of factors, such as the training investment in a technology like the

QWERTY keyboard. A major role is also given to increasing returns in production or 'positive feedbacks' flowing especially from the overcoming of indivisibilities and learning by doing. Early entry to a market and growth in market share can lead to increasing returns in production and lower prices to consumers which may exclude potentially superior technologies. The major implication of technological 'lock-in' is abandonment of the notion of a determinate equilibrium, given the role of increasing returns and chance events in the market selection of new technologies. Secondly, the notion that markets optimally allocate resources must be jettisoned. 'There is no guarantee that a particular economic outcome selected from among the many [technological] alternatives will be the "best" one. Furthermore, once random economic events select a particular path, the choice may become locked-in regardless of the advantages of the alternatives' (Arthur 1990, p.81). The work of Professors Arthur and David provides a complementary set of arguments and evidence in favour of a disequilibrium growth model.

If the theory of circular and cumulative causation is to continue to be relevant and vital, it is essential that contemporary members of this School reflect on the theory's origins and development. As has been demonstrated, there is much to be gained by adapting the ideas and methods of earlier contributors. Whilst progress arises from 'standing on the shoulders of past giants' it is equally important that current members of the School also remain open to new ideas and developments from the broad field of economic and social science research.

APPENDIX

Post-War Taiwan

In Wade's (1990) account of post-war Taiwan, the state had an active role in directing the volume and sectoral composition of investment and in manipulating demand to support these investments. Investment or supply capacity was created through high levels of public ownership of 'basic' industries, direct and indirect control of lending authorities to target financial support for particular industries, and rigid controls over firms' access to foreign exchange, technology imports and foreign investment. On the demand side, markets were created and/or channelled through tariffs, quotas, government procurement, and local content requirements. Support was provided to selected export industries through rebates on duties on imported inputs and reduced company tax on export earnings. In Taiwan, state support and/or direction occurred sequentially in strategic industries, building on the incremental expansion in demand, supply and technological capacity. The industries assisted (in order) included 'cotton textiles, synthetic fibres, petrochemicals, basic metals, shipbuilding, machine tools, automobiles, and electronics' (Wade 1990, p.303). In Wade's analysis the state 'governed the market', acting not to override market mechanisms but to accelerate cumulative growth processes inherent in a market economy. Thus, the explanation for the existence and conduct of industry policy, or 'government efforts to concentrate investment in selected industries', is the creation and exploitation of increasing returns and pecuniary and technological externalities. According to Wade, the growth processes exploited by the state included:

(i) *Economies of scale and learning*: 'Whereas neoclassical analysis normally assumes rising cost curves, in many manufacturing processes a doubling of production volume per unit of time gives rise to a substantial fall in unit cost, commonly on the order of 20 per cent... Producers who expand production can have falling unit costs. They can therefore race down these falling costs curves and capture market share from existing producers' (Wade 1990, pp.351–52). Wade combines the effects of static scale economies (arising, for example, from increases in plant size) and dynamic scale economies such as learning by doing. Scale economies, such as the overcoming of indivisibilities in the employment of capital were achieved by policies of import-substitution and export promotion (Wade 1990, pp.303–04);

(ii) *Government co-ordination of investment decisions*: Using concepts and language clearly taken from Rosenstein-Rodan Wade argues that '[a] big push, involving simultaneous expansion of several industries, can insure the profitability of each investment, even though each would be unprofitable on its own... such simultaneous expansion helps to overcome the constraint of a small domestic market' (Wade 1990, p.353).[26] Wade notes there is a 'second kind of externality', in this instance taken directly from A.O. Hirschman: 'Sequential externalities occur where a large upstream plant would, if built induce the entry of downstream firms to make use of the new profit opportunities created by the upstream firm, but not appropriable by it' (Wade 1990, p.353)[27].

(iii) *Capital market imperfections* that require public investments or subsidized loans to business (Wade 1990, p.353);

(iv) *Market instabilities*: 'Another justification for governing the market has to do with the adverse effects of market instabilities on long-term investment' (Wade 1990, p.354).

Post-War Japan

Authors such as Stein (1993), Yamamura (1986, 1990) Johnson (1982), and Johnson, Tyson and Zysman (1991) argue that from the beginning of the post-war period the key Japanese economic agencies – the Bank of Japan, the Ministry of Finance and the Ministry of International Trade and Industry

(MITI) – had a clear 'vision' of Japan as a modern industrialized nation. The objective was to create an integrated industrial structure to maximize backward and forward linkages in a virtuous circle of increasing output, incomes, investment, productivity, and demand. 'Japanese policy-makers overrode notions of comparative advantage in favour of such ill-defined criteria as the dynamic or technological potential of a particular economic activity... [entailing] flagrant and self-aware violations of the nostrums of traditional economic thinking' (Tyson and Zysman 1991, p.4). Foremost amongst these violations was the policy of comprehensive import-substitution. 'Over the long run, developmental policies that promoted exports and discouraged imports in Japan contributed to domestic expansion that fuelled both savings and investment... *Japan's performance is consistent with the cumulative effects of import-substitution strategy*' (Johnson, Tyson, Zysman 1991 p.107, my italics).

The second key policy was promotion of an oligopoly industry structure, to exploit increasing returns to scale and eradicate what MITI termed 'wasteful competition' arising from atomistic industry structures. The post-war economic planners 'feared that excessive competition would be associated with excess plant capacity, predatory pricing policies and low profit margins... the government believed it had a duty to shape the country's industrial structure along lines similar to those of its leading competitors' (Stein 1993, p.15). Under conditions of falling average costs with market prices given, an individual firm can increase total profit by increasing output. 'Additional market share pushes a firm down its cost curve, setting off a continuing cycle. As the firm increases volume, it takes additional market share, which lowers its costs, making it able to increase sales, thus starting the cycle over' (Tyson, Zysman 1991, p.84). Policies to foster concentration were, however, tempered by strategies to promote competition between large firms, and large groups of firms (keiretsu). In other words, 'competition was bounded and orchestrated' (Johnson, Tyson, Zysman 1991, p.77). Within the domestic market, rivalry between several large firms in each industry such as steel, automobiles, and electronics, etc. was intense (Stein 1993, p.15; Murakami 1988, p.54; Hart N. 1992, p.78).

In addition to the overall oligopolistic industry structure promoted by MITI, several authors emphasize the unique role of vertical and horizontal keiretsu within this structure (Johnson, 1982). Vertical keiretsu are formed by long-term commercial relations between manufacturers and subcontractors. The best known vertical keiretsu are in the automobile and electronics industries, such as Toyota, Matsushita, and Sony. These vertical keiretsu are a 'balance between vertical integration and independence', where the principal manufacturer provides financial and technical support to suppliers for the purpose of improving the quality and timeliness of component supplies (Yamamura, 1990 p.32). 'Close links between assemblers and suppliers economize on transaction costs, enhance the transfer of technology, and increase incentives to make specific investments' (Lawrence 1993, p.12). Horizontal keiretsu, of which the major ones are Mitsui, Mitsubishi, Sumitomo, Fuyo, Dai-ichi Kangyo, and Sanwa, are each comprised of a few dozen firms including a bank, manufacturers and distribution companies. These companies are closely tied through high levels of cross-shareholding and interlocking directorates and engage in inter-company financing, purchase and supply and joint R&D ventures. High levels of intra-company transactions and co-ordinated investments created a 'partially internalized market in final/intermediate products' (Gerlach 1988, p.142). One of the major benefits of these forms of industry organization is that by providing stable shareholdings management can plan for long-term growth. Long-term investment strategies can be implemented without the need for high short-term dividends to shareholders. Evidence for this effect is in the comparatively very low levels of dividends but very high rates of capital gains accruing to shareholders in public companies over the high growth period 1950–1980 (Aoki 1988, p.277).

From the perspective of the circular and cumulative School, the keiretsu organization is entirely explicable in that such an organization of economic activity creates and internalizes a number of positive externalities. Firstly, as emphasized by Rosenstein-Rodan (1943), the joint planning or close integration of investment projects provides a major stimulus to development in that co-ordination simultaneously secures an expansion in supply and/or demand. Co-ordination of economic activity may convert marginal investment projects to profitability and generally increase the scale of such projects. Secondly, the role of distribution or trading companies in providing exclusive wholesale and retail outlets to keiretsu members and inhibiting the marketing of competitive imports facilitates industry concentration and the exploitation of increasing returns (Yamamura 1990, p.45). Thirdly, linked investment projects and the very close commercial oversighting of these projects by the particular keiretsu bank reduces the risk of default or malfeasance and should therefore reduce the cost of funds (Hamada and Horiuchi 1988, p.232). It is significant that both Rosenstein-Rodan and Hirschman denied that capitalists were capable of the extensive inter-industry and inter-firm co-operation exhibited by keiretsu. For these writers in particular, the state is the exclusive agent for the co-ordination of economic activity.

Notes

1 INTRODUCTION

1. Representative of these accounts is Stern's (1989) substantial review article on Development Economics for the Economic Journal. Stern notes only the connection between Young and Rosenstein-Rodan in terms of linking increasing returns to the 'size of the market', and neglects the continuity of these and other concepts amongst a small but influential group of development economists.
2. These neoclassical accounts include, for example, the World Bank (1993).
3. This revival of interest also occurred in debates about and programmes for industry policy in Australia and overseas. Many of these debates and programmes have drawn explicitly on CC theory to make a case for state assistance and co-ordination of manufacturing industry. The outstanding contribution in Australia has been the Metal Trades' Union *Policy for Industry Development and More Jobs*, (1984). More recently Sheehan, Pappas and Cheng (1994) evaluated the effect of the Federal Government's sectoral policies from a broadly Kaldorian perspective.
4. The most complete statement of 'disequilibrium growth' production theory of which the author is aware is Mario Morroni, *Production Process and Technical Change* (1992).
5. The treatment of increasing returns in many textbooks and even specialized publications is generally unsatisfactory. Definitions in one text frequently conflict with those in another, and there is a tendency for authors to develop their own terminology. For example, many texts (e.g. Lipsey, Langley, and Mahoney, 1982) equate increasing returns solely with 'plant'-based scale economies, and ignore other sources of increasing returns, such as economies of the firm, external economies arising from the growth of the industry or industries, and 'dynamic' economies such as learning by doing or learning by using.
6. 'We may divide the economies arising from an increase in the scale of any kind of goods, into two classes: firstly, those dependent on the general development of industry; and secondly, those dependent on the resources of the individual houses of business engaged in it, on their organization and the efficiency of their management. We may call the former *external economies* and the latter *internal economies*' (Marshall 8th Ed, 1920, p.221)
7. Chamberlin explains that constant proportions are necessary given the assumption of 'homogeneity as part of the problem of distribution... The firm will be in equilibrium under pure competition at the minimum point of the *envelope* curve; Euler's theorem will apply approximately at the minimum point of the *constant proportions* curve; and it is because these two points coincide that Euler's theorem applies to equilibrium conditions' (Chamberlin 1948, p.143, quoted in Gold 1981, p.10).
8. As noted, the distinction between some forms of economies of scale for plants and firms/enterprises is not that clear in the literature. Pratten (1971, p.8) for example, includes economies of vertical integration as a plant scale economy, whereas Devine et al. (1976) specifically include it as a scale economy enjoyed by firms.

9. Pratten, quite correctly, objects to use of the term 'long-run' average cost curve to describe the effects of scale. All the LRAC actually shows, is the 'effect of scale ... on the average costs of production of a series of alternative plants built at a point in time, each perfectly adapted to the required scale and operated at that scale.' Pratten uses the term 'scale curve' to describe such effects (Pratten 1971, p.4).

10. Subsequent discussion has helped to identify these 'technical' indivisibilities and to broaden the sources of indivisibility. The former arise '(a) where a given amount of a commodity cannot be physically divided into fractional parts in any meaningful sense; (b) when fractional parts of a commodity cannot be physically combined in a meaningful sense; ... (c) when for any reason, institutional or otherwise, a decision unit cannot purchase fractional parts of an input; (d) when for any reason a decision unit cannot sell fractional parts of an output' (Frank 1969, p.32). Morroni distinguishes between economic and technical indivisibility. 'The former is present when it is impossible to exchange less than a given unit of a particular commodity (a length of cloth or bushel of corn). The second refers to the impossibility of dividing a particular commodity, once it is exchanged, into amounts useable for production or consumption (in this case the length of cloth or bushel of corn are technically divisible, while a refrigerator or a loom is not)' Morroni 1992, p.26. Morroni argues that economic and technical indivisibility have very different effects on the level of utilization of fixed capital. 'Economic indivisibility entails that in certain periods some ... [capital goods] used in production may be unused.' He gives the example of a lorry that is not used at weekends. 'On the other hand, the technical indivisibility [of capital goods] means that in operation they may run below their full productive capacity (for instance, a lorry that travels half-empty or below its optimal speed' (Morroni 1992, p.27).

11. Robinson identifies the division of labour as an example of indivisibility, 'since the units of the factors are indivisible, the most specialized method of production will involve the largest outlay, and it is not profitable to make use of the full equipment of highly specialized factors for a very small output. As output increases a method higher in the hierarchy of specialization can be adopted, and for this reason cost falls as the output of a commodity increases' (Robinson 1933, pp.335–336).

12. Along with learning by doing, Kaldor (1972) emphasizes this source in his account of increasing returns. Some industry economists express considerable scepticism about the benefits of increases in the physical dimensions of plant (Gold 1981, pp.11–13).

13. The neoclassical definition of scale economies arising from equi-proportional increases in factor inputs sometimes conflicts with examples of sources of scale economies in production provided by neoclassical writers. In his famous textbook, Paul Samuelson cites changes in the organization of production arising from increased specialization, and the use of more capital-intensive production methods as sources of 'economies of scale' (Samuelson 1973, pp.48–49). This is despite the fact that such modifications to the technique of production 'are changes which may alter the proportions among inputs (if not the inputs themselves)' (Morroni 1992, p.142n). Samuelson also confuses the benefits obtained from increases in a firm's capacity utilization rate with scale economies. He describes improvements in capacity utilization rates as 'genuine reversible economies of large-scale production by a firm' (Samuelson 1973, p.536). It is interesting to note that Young explicitly warned against confusing the benefits of increased capacity utilization rates with increasing returns (Kaldor 1990, p.54).

14. The 'two...basic weaknesses of the "rigorous" or restrictive theory of scale' are firstly, 'its requirement of fixed-factor proportions is seldom encountered in actual cases...[and] it is especially anomalous to impose such a constraint within the long-run context, which is defined as permitting changes in all input factors.' Secondly, 'its correlative requirement of unchanged technology is likewise contrary to most experience' (Gold 1981, p.14).

15. Another example of diagreement in the literature over definitions is the contention that 'dynamic economies' encompass productivity gains from 'the division and specialisation of labour as output expands over time' (Whiteman 1990, p.38). For Pratten (1971) such specialization is a static scale economy.

16. Pasinetti's 'vertically integrated' model of dynamic growth has many striking similarities with the CC approach. One of these is the central place of learning, on the part of producers and consumers in the explanation of growth (Pasinetti 1981, p.3).

17. Nathan Rosenberg has identified another source of increasing returns resulting from what he terms 'learning by using'. Learning by doing 'takes place at the manufacturing stage' of the production process, but 'there are essential aspects of the learning process that are a function not of the experience involved in producing the product but of its *utilisation* by the final user. This is particularly important in the case of capital goods' (Rosenberg 1982, pp.121–122). Learning by using entails the flow of information from users to producers, which enables the producer to gradually improve the quality of their product. Learning by using, like learning by doing, should be classified as a dynamic scale economy since it arises from cumulative increases in the volume of production. In many industries learning by using is institutionalized, as in the computer software industry where early versions of software (alpha and beta versions) are provided to users who identify 'bugs' that are removed in subsequent versions. Rosenberg notes that learning by using is a positive externality since the information provided to manufacturers to improve the quality of their output is provided free of charge (Rosenberg 1982, p.121). Prior to Rosenberg, Leontief made a similar argument to explain the vertical integration of industries and geographic agglomeration of industries. '[A] growing economy derives a considerable, although less measurable advantage from developing whole families of structurally related industries rather than isolated industries that depend on foreign trade for supplies and markets. The incessant process of technological change derives strong stimulus from intimate contact between sellers and buyers, between the maker and the potential user of a new process or product' (Leontief 1963, p.185).

18. Papandreou (1994) provides an excellent summary of the evolution of the externality concept from Marshall through to developments in the 1980s.

19. It is interesting to note that Scitovsky does not accept as a valid example of technological externality 'inventions that facilitate production and become available to producers without charge'. This is because 'patent laws have eliminated...this form of direct interdependence, and transformed it into a case of interdependence through the market mechanism' (Scitovsky 1954, pp.297–98). In contrast, the general failure of intellectual property law to exclude the free flow of productive knowledge is one of the foundations of 'new growth theory' associated with Romer, and Helpman and Grossman, etc. The 'new growth theory' is examined in Chapter 7.

20. Viner (1931) is the source for the terms 'technological and pecuniary' externality. Viner defines technological externalities as 'reductions of the

technological coefficients of production' (Viner 1931, p.213) for a firm arising from increases in the output of the industry as a whole (where the increase in output is met by an increase in the number of firms in the industry). Examples include, 'better organization of the labour and raw materials markets' as well as 'exchange of ideas among the different producers'. Pecuniary external economies occur when 'reductions in the prices of services and materials result from the increase in the amounts of services and materials purchased by the industry' (Viner 1931, pp.217–218). In contrast to Scitovsky, Viner argues (like Marshall before him) that 'net external economies of large scale production' are consistent with competitive equilibrium conditions. For Viner, 'irrespective of whether these economies are technological, or pecuniary or both', an increase in the demand for an industry's output produces in the long-run a new competitive equilibrium where firms belonging to the industry benefit from reduced costs (Viner 1931, pp.218–219). For Scitovsky, 'technological external economies are the only external economies that can arise...within the framework of general equilibrium theory' (Scitovsky 1954, p.298). This difference is due to their opposed conception of the origins of pecuniary externalities. For Scitovsky, pecuniary externalities arise from a variety of market failures, such as existence of indivisibilities, and imperfect information.

21. E.J. Mishan (1965, 1971) has been a sustained critic of the concept of pecuniary externalities. For Mishan, given equilibrium conditions, pecuniary externalities cannot arise. The achievement of a Pareto optimum requires two conditions; perfect competition and the absence of externalities. If externalities are present, output and or price adjustments are required in order to re-establish an equilibrium of private and social costs and benefits. Mishan argues that the pricing of an externality 'internalizes' the benefits/losses of the previously unrecompensed/uncompensated outcomes. The internalizing or pricing of an externality means that the economic value of the externality 'is now determined by the market along with the prices of all other goods and factors; to the extent that the levels of outputs and utility are dependent on [this externality]...they are, for everyone, now affected only "indirectly" by price changes'(Mishan 1971, p.4). The market internalization of an externality given 'universal perfect competition would tend to a general equilibrium that would, indeed, be Pareto-optimal' (Mishan 1971, p.4). Given these assumptions, the notion of a 'pecuniary' externality operating through the price mechanism is simply a non sequitur. As a point of clarification, external economies in orthodoxy are traditionally analysed in a partial equilibrium framework, though it is understood that perfect competition obtains in all other industries. '[U]nless the rest of the economy remains organized in conformity with optimum conditions, one runs smack into second-best problems' (Mishan 1965, p.8). In a detailed analytical account of external economies, Bohm (1967) confirms Scitovsky's claim that 'price effects' arising from imperfect information and indivisibilities prevent the attainment of 'a Pareto-optimal level of production' (Bohm 1967, p.58).

22. The term vertical and horizontal externality was introduced by J. Marcus Fleming (1955).

23. 'complementarity and income effects are the two chief impediments to sharp results in microeconomic theory' (Newman 1987, p.545).

24. Subject to the condition that 'economies due to technological progress must, of course, be reckoned net of (internal or external) diseconomies of obsolescence' (Arndt 1955, p.208n).

25. The famous economist of technological innovation, Nathan Rosenberg, has highlighted another area of complementarity in production. 'The growing

productivity of industrial economies is the complex outcome of large numbers of interlocking, mutually reinforcing technologies, the individual components of which are of very limited economic consequence by themselves... In each case a central innovation, or some small number of innovations, provided the bases around which a larger number of further cumulative improvements and complementary inventions were eventually positioned' (Rosenberg 1982, p.58). He concludes that the 'need for further innovations in *complementary* activities is an important reason why even spectacular breakthroughs eventually have only a gradually rising productivity curve flowing from them' (Rosenberg 1982, p.58, my italics).

26. 'The most important complementarities... arise in the process of rising consumption... Progress consists in the discovery and generation of new wants clustering on each other, and of new technological gaps, as much as, or even more than, in meeting existing wants and filling existing technological gaps' (Streeten 1959, p.173).

27. R-R adapted Young's notion of complementarity in consumption to underdeveloped regions. R-R considered that at very low per capita income levels, demand is concentrated on a narrow range or cluster of basic wage goods. These commodities are essential for subsistence, and would consume all of a workers' income.

2 ALLYN YOUNG: INCREASING RETURNS AND ECONOMIC PROGRESS

1. Indeed, the only book-length biographical account of Young is Charles Blitch (1995).

2. Even during the cost controversy Young's contribution was largely ignored. In the Symposium on 'Increasing Returns and the Representative Firm' in the *Economic Journal* of 1930, posthumous reference to Young is very limited. It is restricted to Shove's acceptance of Young's argument that Marshall's neat distinction between internal and external economies is problematic (Shove 1930, p.115–116).

3. The quotations in this section are taken from Marshall 1920, 8th edition.

4. Arndt (1955, pp.193–194), provides a very useful compilation of the numerous sources of external economies used by Marshall.

5. Elsewhere Marshall was less circumspect. 'Those *internal* economies which each establishment has to arrange for itself are frequently very small as compared with those *external* economies which result from the general progress of the individual environment' (Marshall 1920, p.365).

6. The Statical method required the production technology be reversible, so that a lowering of demand would result in the contraction of supply along a fixed curve to a previous equilibrium position (Marshall 1920, pp.287–288). However, in increasing returns industries 'a great increase in the production of any commodity' results in 'the introduction of extensive economies, [and] these economies are not readily lost' (Marshall 1920, p.666n).

7. Clapham notes that in over two thousand pages of Marshall's *Principles* and Pigou's *Economics of Welfare* extensive reference is routinely made to increasing and decreasing return industries and commodities, but no concrete example of such an industry or commodity is furnished (Clapham 1922[a], p.305). In a number of subsequent entertaining and enlightening exchanges between

Clapham and Pigou, the latter defended the foundation of economics in the *a priori* and deductive method. This method is the basis for 'the intellectual machinery by which the main part of modern Economic thought functions' (Pigou 1922, p.461). His solution to the problem of 'empty boxes' was to 'endeavour to train up more men of the calibre of Jevons, who are equally at home' in the 'fields' of 'economic analysis and modern statistical technique' (Pigou 1922, p.465). Dissatisfied with Pigou's response, Clapham wittily noted, 'I am paid with a cheque drawn on the bank of an unborn Jevons' (Clapham 1922[b], p.562).

8. Marshall was of course aware of these profound measurement difficulties. 'The quantities' of inputs and outputs 'cannot be taken out exactly, because changing methods of production call for machinery, and for unskilled and skilled labour of new kinds and in new proportions' (Marshall 1920, p.266).

9. The subsequent manifold dilemmas confronting applied economists in the measurement of increasing returns (Pratten 1971, Gold 1981) have been founded largely on those problems identified by Clapham.

10. Pigou's solution to reconciling competition and increasing returns was to have each firm working under increasing cost, with the industry working under conditions of decreasing cost (Pigou 1924, p.192). Young rejected this solution, with the comment, 'I cannot imagine "external economies" adequate to bring about this result' (Young 1913, p.678n). Young (1928) emphasizes the role of both internal and external economies in increasing returns.

11. There are passages where Marshall comes close to identifying the way in which the division of labour and growth in the size of the market mutually reinforce each other to promote ongoing growth. Marshall notes 'how every increase of wealth tends in many ways to make a greater increase more easy than before' (Marshall 1920, p.262).

12. As noted earlier, with the device of external economies Marshall was able to account for significant endogenous productivity growth whilst maintaining a competitive industry structure. By identifying a primary source of increasing returns in external economies, 'Marshall could now reconcile pure competition – where the individual firm operates under conditions of increasing marginal cost – with decreasing average cost for the industry' (Bohm 1967, p.10). This approach was later formalized by Viner (1931) in his classic treatment of external economies for an industry under competitive conditions. Some writers are critical of this widely held interpretation of Marshall's 'reconciliation problem'. Hart for example, argues that Marshall 'did not intend his supply schedule to be confined to the analysis of "competitive" markets' (Hart N. 1992, p.235). Marshall's biological life cycle analogy of the individual firm was an attempt to introduce dynamic elements into economics and overcome the necessary limitations of the Statical method (Hart N. 1992, p.241). For Hart, Marshall's reconciliation problem was not so much concerned with increasing returns and perfect competition but rather the 'coming to terms with dynamic processes proceeding in historical time' (Hart N.1992, p.241). Hart is undoubtedly correct in demanding a more subtle interpretation of Marshall, though it is arguable Marshall's biological analogy was incapable of such a reconciliation. Only by abandoning equilibrium notions altogether, as Young advocated, is it possible to come to terms with dynamic processes.

13. 'The determinants of technical change, of the growth of output per worker, were the classical economists' fundamental concerns, for these are the major determinants of the wealth of a nation' (Eatwell 1982, p.57).

14. 'The nature of agriculture, indeed, does not admit of so many subdivisions of labour, nor of so complete a separation of one business from another, as

manufactures. This...is perhaps the reason that the improvement in the productive powers of labour in this art, does not always keep pace with their improvement in manufactures' (Smith 1776, p.16).

15.   Smith explained that the 'great increase of the quantity of work, which, in consequence of the division of labour, the same number of people are capable of performing, is owing to three different circumstances; first, to the increase of dexterity in every particular workman; secondly, to the saving of the time which is commonly lost in passing from one species of work to another; and lastly, to the invention of a great number of machines which facilitate and abridge labour, and enable one man to do the work of many'. Like Young, Smith also argued that '[t]he productive powers of the same number of labourers cannot be increased, but in consequence of some addition and improvements to those machines and instruments which facilitate and abridge labour: or of a more proper division or distribution of employment'. (Smith 1776, p.17, p.343).

16.   Young does not use the term 'capital – labour ratio', but it is employed here as a short-hand expression for roundabout production methods. Other writers on Young such as Kaldor (1972[c], 1975) also adopt this term. Whilst Young did not detail the precise benefits of increases in the capital – labour ratio or increased specialization of production, he does assume that more recent capital goods embody technological improvements. Technological change is endogenous in Young's system, in that Young assumes a circular relation between the rate of growth of output and the rate of growth of scientific knowledge. This is examined in Section 2.5.

17.   Kaldor regarded this as a devastating argument against general equilibrium. '[I]f at any actual level of output the "best" available technique for that output is less than that available for a somewhat larger output – if, in other words, there is a whole hierarchy of activities not all of which are feasible or attainable at any point of time – the choice among "activities" becomes primarily not a matter of prices but of the scale of production. With every enlargement of production new "activities" become profitable which would not have been employed earlier, whilst the introduction of such new "activities" leads to the invention of further "activities" which have not been "known" earlier' (Kaldor 1972[c], p.1255).

18.   Stigler's (1951) classic article in which he sought to rehabilitate the notion of the division of labour as a 'fundamental principle of economic organization' and in 'the theory of the firm and the competition of industry' is an investigation into and elaboration of the work of Marshall and Young. Increasing returns are achieved primarily through the division of labour and specialization of production across industries. As the size of the market increases it becomes economic for firms to 'abandon' various 'functions' subject to increasing returns, in effect by buying these inputs or 'functions' in from specialist firms. '[W]ith the expansion of industry, the magnitude of the [firm's] function subject to increasing returns may become sufficient to permit a firm to specialise in performing it.' As with Young, this model of increasing returns and specialization is consistent with a form of competition. Although a newly established specialized firm is a monopoly supplier, it is confronted with 'an elastic demand schedule. This new firm cannot...charge a price for the process higher than the average cost of the process to the firms which are abandoning it.' Further, with the continued expansion of industry, the number of firms supplying the specialized product or process increases 'so that the new industry becomes competitive and the new industry may, in turn, abandon parts of [its production]...to a new set of specialists' (Stigler 1951, p.188).

19.   This proposition, which is arguably the central proposition of CC theory, has
        been highlighted by the leading figures in the CC tradition. 'Young saw clearly
        that... [s]omething more is needed linking the effects of changes in production
        to demand: something that would ensure that an increase in supply... has a
        stimulating effect, and not a depressing effect... Given that factor, the process
        of economic development can be looked upon as the resultant of a continued
        process of interaction – one could almost say, of a chain reaction – between
        demand increases which have been induced by increases in supply, and
        increases in supply which have been evoked by increases in demand' (Kaldor
        1972[c], p.1246). Lauchlin Currie argued that 'Adam Smith's statement that the
        division of labour is limited by the size of the market was not developed by him
        into a theory of growth. For Smith the size of the market was a restraint on the
        division of labour. Once the division of labour is fully adapted to a particular
        market size, growth ceases... Young developed Smith's insight into a theory of
        self-sustaining growth based on the endogenous creation of opportunities to
        adopt new and known technologies to increase productivity (increasing returns)
        as the size of the market expanded. With the extension of the division of labour
        the market was further expanded' (Sandilands 1990, p.304).
20.   Baumol (1977) provides an excellent analysis of Say's development of his Law of
        Markets from its early formulation as an 'identity' or tautology, to the identifi-
        cation of adjustment mechanisms that ensure an 'equality' of supply and
        demand.
21.   Young adapted Marshall and Edgeworth's concept of 'reciprocal demand' for
        commodities based on 'offer curves' (Young 1928, p.533). The offer curve
        simultaneously expresses supply and demand relations by showing the quantity
        of one commodity which can be directly exchanged or bartered for a given
        quantity of another commodity. 'Along such a curve goods exchange for
        goods. It shows the quantity of one good, say steel, which steel producers
        would supply to producers of another good, say textiles, for different amounts
        of textiles... Thus the steel producers' offer curve is simultaneously their supply
        curve for steel as well as their demand curve (of a kind) for textiles. The curve
        subsumes demand and supply conditions within each industry. In this pure
        barter situation demand and supply are interdependent, as the supply of steel
        represents demand for textiles just as the supply of textiles represents demand
        for steel' (Blitch 1983, p.368). Young used various formulations of the notion of
        reciprocal demand in the 1928 article. The following formulation is the most
        rigorous he employed, and also the most difficult and cryptic. 'If the circum-
        stance that commodity a is produced under conditions of increasing returns is
        taken into account as a factor in the elasticity of demand for b in terms of a,
        elasticity of demand and elasticity of supply may be looked upon as different
        ways of expressing a single functional relation' (Young 1928, p.534n). However,
        one must add that only insofar as the demand for commodity a is elastic, will an
        increase in its supply (at constant or declining unit price) result in an increased
        demand for other commodities. 'Only so far as the demand for a particular
        commodity is elastic is it true in any significant sense that an increase of its
        supply is an effective increase of demand for other commodities' (Young
        1929[a], p.580).
22.   Young wrote very little on competition and income distribution, and these
        comments are mostly limited to a criticism of neoclassical and Marxist positions
        on this subject rather than an exposition of his own views. Young, for example,
        argues that owing to increasing returns it 'cannot be assumed, therefore, that an
        increase of the aggregate supply of labour will normally have the effect of

reducing wages...Little or nothing is to be gained by looking to the general formula of supply and demand for an explanation of the determination of wages' (Kaldor 1990, p.138). Young also criticizes marginal productivity theories, by highlighting the non-homogeneity of factors, as well as the difficulty of differentiating the relative contribution to output within and between factors (Kaldor 1990, p.142).

23.   Pasinetti similarly argues that as 'productivity increases, per capita incomes rise: the increments of demand will cluster in succession around different goods. This means that the rate of change of demand for each commodity will be continually changing over time and will normally be different from the rate of change for another commodity. The actual production of each sector will follow a growth path of its own, at a *non-steady* rate of change' (Pasinetti 1981, p.223).

24.   The view that all capital investment (and new products) are complements is surely an overstatement. Young notes that with the 'enlarging of the market' and consequent changes in production methods and consumption patterns, 'the initial displacement may be considerable and the repercussions upon particular industries unfavourable' (Young 1928, p.537).

25.   Young's ambivalence to the role of technological change in growth is in part a legacy of Marshall's explicit rejection of technological change from the study of the equilibrium conditions of the firm or industry. 'We exclude from view any economies that may result from substantive new inventions; but we include those which may be expected to arise naturally out of adaptations of existing ideas' (Marshall 1920, p.281). Young's difficulties reflect the onerous task of breaking from equilibrium modes of thinking. Arndt's (1955) claim that Young treated technological change in exactly the same way as Marshall understates the degree to which Young attempted to incorporate technological change in the growth process.

26.   W. W. Rostow has a similar interpretation, regarding Young's 1928 article 'as much in the spirit of Leontief' (Rostow 1990, p.470). Young's inchoate input – output conception is reinforced by the overwhelming emphasis Young gives in his account of production to intermediate and capital goods inputs. In his account of the 'increasingly intricate nexus of specialized undertakings' in the printing industry Young describes not only industries directly supplying the printing industry, but also those indirectly supplying this industry. He describes how the 'list could be extended, both by enumerating other industries which are directly ancillary to the present printing trades and by going back to industries which, while supplying the industries which supply the printing trades, also supply other industries, concerned with preliminary stages in the making of final products other than printed books and newspapers' (Young 1928, p.528).

27.   Young also formulated an approach to the study of increasing returns arising from inter-industry specialization by studying the chain of production of a particular commodity. 'To appreciate the nature and significance of these [external] economies, one must fix one's eyes, not upon the activities of a particular firm, but upon the operation of an entire industry or, better yet, upon the operations of the whole group of related industries which contribute to the making of a single product. Producers of raw materials, of fuel, of auxiliary supplies, of machines, together with railways, and other transport agencies are all in the picture'. Young provides a concrete example of this approach to the study of increasing returns by reference to the printing industry. 'The average printing establishment is not, even today, a very large affair. Back of it, however, and, as one might say, reaching the final consumer only through it and by means of it, are the type-founders, the makers of linotypes and

monotypes, of printing presses and of other specialized machines, of inks, of wood pulp, and of paper, together with the industries which, in turn, supply the equipment and materials to those which are immediately auxiliary to that of printing. Thus the books, magazines, the newspapers, and the multitude of printed forms... are seen to be the products, not necessarily of large printing establishments, but of an intricately organized system of industries, operating, as an aggregate, on an exceedingly large scale' (Young 1929[c] p.163).

28. Elsewhere Young reflected on the type and causes of concentrated industries. Two factors are identified as favourable to the growth of 'big plant'. The first is infrastructure and 'public utilities' which require 'a considerable initial investment of capital' and normally operate as a 'monopoly'. Secondly, '[u]nified management and large-scale undertakings succeed best when the product itself can be standardized (so that any one unit is like any other unit) and when the processes of production, however complex, can be reduced to an ordered succession of routine operation'. Examples in the latter category include the United States Steel Corporation and the Ford Motor works. (Young 1929[c], pp.163–4).

29. A good example of other sources of indivisibility and sunk costs not explicitly considered by Young, R-R, or Hirschman, is the enormous expenditure required for research and development in areas such as pharmaceuticals and information technology. The Prices Surveillance Authority Inquiry Into the Prices of Farm Chemicals (which the author co-wrote) found that the cost of researching and developing a new agricultural or veterinary chemical was in the order of $120–150 million (PSA 1993, 107–110). The high cost of entry created by these R&D expenditures (and patents on discoveries) contribute to the creation of an oligopolistic industry structure in agricultural chemicals and pharmaceuticals (Prices Surveillance Authority 1993, Ch.5). These expenditures may also generate considerable externalities, sufficient in some cases to justify government support for these activities (Whiteman 1990 p.45).

30. The view of Romer (1986) and others, that the difficulty of mathematically formalizing Young's vision explains its neglect by mainstream economics, is disingenuous. ('[T]he chief technical problems being those of non-convex technologies and the introduction of new intermediate technologies' Newman 1987, p.939).

3   PAUL N. ROSENSTEIN-RODAN: FROM CIRCULAR CAUSATION TO BALANCED GROWTH

1. R-R does not cite Young's famous 1928 article, but refers to an unsourced argument of Young's relating to external economies. The lineage of R-R to Young is, however, not in dispute. This lineage is, for example, explicitly argued for by Arndt (1955), Fleming (1995), Bohm (1987) and Stern (1989).

2. R-R believes he made another important innovation in the 1943 article – that is, the notion of 'agrarian underemployment' in underdeveloped regions. This arises where marginal units of labour employed in agriculture have very low or zero marginal physical productivity. A programme of industrialization is necessary to absorb this labour pool and generally raise per capita income. Surplus labour also implies that the supply of labour for manufacturing is highly elastic (R-R 1943, p.245;1984, p.208). This notion of agrarian underemployment and its implications for modernization predates by a decade Lewis's (1954)

classic article. In Kaldor's (1970, 1975) two sector-two stage model of development, surplus labour supply in agriculture is essential to initiate industrialization.

3.　'The inducement to invest is limited by the size of the market. That is essentially what Allyn Young brought out in his reinterpretation of Adam Smith's famous thesis. What determines the size of the market? ... reductions in any cost of production tend to have that effect. So the size of the market is determined by the general level of productivity. Capacity to buy means capacity to produce. In its turn, the level of productivity depends – not entirely by any means, but largely – on the use of capital in production. But the use of capital is inhibited, to start with, by the small size of the market. Where is the way out of this circle?' (Nurkse 1952, p.256)

　　In what is otherwise a brilliant article, Arndt (1955) is mistaken in his analysis of differences between Young and R-R in their treatment of increasing returns. Allyn Young's 'interest' in increasing returns and external economies claims Arndt 'is confined to the effect of an increase in the market in reducing costs (thus increasing productivity and output and widening the market further) ... the stimulus given to investment by a widening of the market *is not his primary concern*' (Arndt 1955, p.196, my italics). To this it must be objected that Young's theory of increasing returns is a unity: increases in the size of the market induce investment and such investment reduces costs and prices and thereby widens the market. To emphasize, as Arndt does, only the second element is to ignore the mechanism of cumulative growth Young introduced to the Smith–Marshall notion of increasing returns. Conversely, Arndt claims R-R introduced 'a change of context and emphasis so drastic as virtually to give the concept [of increasing returns and external economies] a new meaning' (Arndt 1955, p.196). In particular, the 'important change lies in the new emphasis on the significance of external economies for the inducement to invest. In place of increasing returns, in the sense of falling costs with increasing output, we are now concerned with mutual support between acts of investment in different fields' (Arndt 1955, p.197). It is true that R-R did place particular emphasis on this effect of external economies, though he also retained Young's view of the circular and cumulative relation between increasing returns and growth in the size of the market. R-R identified the benefits of introducing large-scale production units and gaining the advantages of increasing returns precisely in the 'falling costs' of consumer goods and widening of the market to which such capital-intensive techniques give rise.

4.　'Frequently the objection is made: But why use machinery? Why adopt capital-using methods in areas where labour is cheap and plentiful? Why not accordingly employ techniques that are labour intensive instead of capital intensive? The answer is obvious. As an adaptation to existing circumstances, including the existing factor proportions, the pursuit of labour-intensive methods with a view to economizing capital may be perfectly correct. But the study of economic development must concern itself with changing these circumstances, not accepting them as they are' (Nurkse 1958, p.641).

5.　'It is usually ... assumed that the divergence between the "private and social marginal net product" is not very considerable. This assumption may be too optimistic even in the case of a crystallized competitive economy. It is certainly not true in the case of fundamental structural changes in the international depressed areas. External economies may there be of the same order of magnitude as profits which appear on the profit and loss account for the enterprise' (R-R 1943, p.250).

6. 'I have tried to explain how the balanced growth idea is related to the classical law of markets. Supply creates its own demand, provided that supply is properly distributed among different commodities in accordance with consumers' wants... Each industry must advance along an expansion path determined by the income elasticity of consumer demand for its product... It is hardly necessary to add that the pattern of consumable demand cannot be expected to remain the same in successive stages of development' (Nurkse 1958, p.642).

7. The analysis of demand provided by Young and R-R is closely related to that in Pasinetti's (1981) 'vertical integration' model, though the latter has provided a far more analytical account of the subject than the former. Firstly, Pasinetti notes the very large body of evidence supporting Engel's Law, which he generalizes to an 'empirical law, stating that the proportion of income spent *on any type of good* changes as per capita incomes increases' (Pasinetti 1981, p.70). From this he draws 'the conclusion that the hypothesis of a uniform expansion of per capita demand, which has been put so far as the basis of almost all theories of economic growth with technical progress [except CC], is incompatible with one of the most fundamental empirical "laws" of economics' (Pasinetti 1981, p.70). Secondly, in an argument similar to the very early work of R-R (1934) on consumer demand, Pasinetti argues: 'there exists a very definite *order of priority* in consumers' wants, and therefore among groups of goods and services, which manifests itself as real incomes increase. This order of priority is particularly clear-cut at low levels of income... But the order persists at higher levels as well' (Pasinetti 1981, p.75). From the empirical law and the assumption of a definite priority in consumer wants at different per capita income levels, Pasinetti argues that income levels and not relative prices are the critical factor in the formation of consumer preferences. '[I]n the long run, it is the level of real income – not the price structure – that becomes the relevant and crucial variable... For, at any given level of personal income, some goods – or partial quantities of some goods – may be substituted for others if their prices increase. But the magnitude of these effects of price changes will always depend on the level of real income. This is so much so that, in general, it is always possible to find a level of real income that will make the effects of price changes disappear' (Pasinetti 1981, pp.73–74).

8. The advantages arising from learning by doing may, in the first instance at least, be a benefit accruing to the firm and not, as suggested by R-R, an external economy benefiting all firms. For example, Lieberman (1984, 1987) indicates that firms are able to prevent to varying degrees, and for varying periods of time, the 'spillover' of learning by doing to competitors (Vassilakis 1987[a], p.151).

9. Chenery provides a convenient summary of the major market imperfections identified by R-R and Nurkse in underdeveloped regions: '(a) factor prices do not necessarily reflect opportunity costs with any accuracy; (b) the quantity and quality of factors may change substantially over time, in part as a result of the production process itself; (c) economies of scale relative to the size of the market are important in a number of sectors of production; (d) complementarity among commodities is dominant in both producer and consumer demand' (Chenery 1961, p.275). Rao's (1952) famous article is a useful supplement to the analysis of market imperfection in underdeveloped regions. Rao details the major structural differences between developed and underdeveloped regions which account for the failure of the Keynesian income multiplier and investment accelerator to work in these regions.

10. 'The proper co-ordination of investment decisions, therefore, would require a signalling device to transmit information about present plans and future conditions as they are determined by present plans; and the pricing system fails to provide this. Hence the belief that there is the need for centralized investment planning or for some additional communication system to supplement the pricing system as a signalling device' (Scitovsky 1954, p.306).

11. The vertical and horizontal integration amongst Japanese *keiretsu* is a good example of this private co-operation. However, it was also official Japanese Government policy to promote this form of private synergy (Johnson 1982). In addition, there has been very considerable recent academic interest in the use of consortia, 'networks', and other forms of inter-firm co-operation (Whiteman 1990). Studies of Australian engineering industry, for example, indicate that the ability of several firms to form consortia or pool expertise and resources has been critical to the success of leading engineering companies (BIE 1987).

12. It is interesting to compare Nurkse's formulation of over-consumption in poor regions with the long-run tendency towards under-consumption, argued by Keynes, in the *General Theory*. In developed economies under-consumption results from a declining propensity to consume as income increases (Keynes 1936, pp.104–105).

13. Gunnar Myrdal, was of course, the one who systematically examined the role of these elements in creating and sustaining virtuous and vicious cycles of regional, and national growth or decline. In his key work, *Economic Theory and Under-developed Regions* (1957), Myrdal approvingly cited Nurkse, and stated that the 'application' of the theory of circular and cumulative causation 'moves any realistic study of underdevelopment and development in a country...far outside the boundaries of traditional economic theory' (Myrdal 1957, p.190).

14. The argument that a co-ordinated programme of investment gives rise to a qualitatively different industrial structure compared to that subject to market forces alone seems to have escaped even one of the more perceptive commentators on these growth models. Nath states that the 'recommendation of balanced growth' rests simply 'on the assertion that...growth is *faster* than unco-ordinated growth' (Nath 1962, p.300).

15. The title-page to the *Principles* has Marshall's famous aphorism '*natura non facit saltum*' (nature does not move in jumps).

16. It is interesting to note that the dependence of economic outcomes on joint decision making between economic agents is a central theme of games theory. The seminal work on this subject is von Neumann and Morgenstern, *The Theory of Games and Economic Behaviour* (1944) first published one year after R-R's article.

17. Kurt Mandelbaum's *The Industrialization of Backward Areas*, (1945) provided a detailed quantitative development plan for south-eastern Europe employing the key ideas of R-R.

18. Dagnino-Pastore (1963) provides an excellent survey of the development of balanced growth and its critics.

19. The subject of the failure of balanced growth to utilize vertical integration is somewhat clouded as some famous commentators, such as Scitovsky, argued that balanced growth did advocate this pattern of investment. Scitovsky interprets R-R as suggesting the optimal means of reconciling private and public benefit is 'the complete integration of all industries', including 'vertical integration' (Scitovsky 1954 p.305). Scitovsky seems to be imposing his own logical extension of the theory onto its original proponents, rather than giving a fair rendering of the latter. Chenery clarified the distinction between vertical and

horizontal integration as used in CC theory: 'Market interrelations can be classified in various ways, but the most important distinction is between interdependence in production (supplier–user, users of a common inputs, and so forth) and interdependence through increased consumer incomes' (Chenery 1959, p.178n).

20. Whilst the originators of balanced growth, R-R and Nurkse, focused only on horizontal integration, applied economists such as Chenery gave equal attention to vertical integration. A good example of this is his classic, 'The Interdependence of Investment Decisions' (Chenery, 1959). One can speculate that for applied economists, especially those with an expert knowledge of input–output techniques, the issue of input supplies and the elasticity of those supplies is a central concern.

21. 'Traditional analysis does not provide an established home for the proposition that a low level of real income acts to inhibit investment on the demand side. It suggests the opposite: in so far as low income is associated with a low ratio of capital to co-operating factors of production, the marginal product of capital should be higher than in capital-rich countries, and investment should pay rather well... But Nurkse's point cuts deeper analytically; is it possible, even given a climate of rational calculation by competent enterpreneurs... that the process of capital accumulation will be systematically thwarted because individual investment projects cannot pay? If so, if investment must proceed in a balanced pattern meeting all directions of demand simultaneously, then a number of basic arguments from factor proportions, and traditional ideas of specialization and trade need serious revision' (Sheahan 1958, pp.183–184).

22. Sheahan (1959) is highly critical of Ronald Findlay's (1959) formalization of balanced growth in general equilibrium terms and assumption of fixed-factor supply and constant returns. Indeed, Sheahan argues that Findlay's model, which denied the benefits of balanced growth, ironically shows that 'balanced growth *is* possibly consistent with an optimum pattern of output' (Sheahan 1959, p.347).

23. As a point of clarification, the term 'specialization' as used here has two distinct meanings. Firstly, in Kaldor and Sheahan's prescription for national development strategies, it means restricting the number of industries to be established. Secondly, specialization is an essential element of increasing returns arising from 'roundabout production methods'. Specialization in the second usage results from the progressive division of labour within firms and across industries as the size of the market increases.

24. Streeten does not amplify the point, but 'distortion of demand' means that unbalanced growth will not adopt the procedure of balanced growth, which is to balance the composition of output and rate of change in the composition with consumers' changing income elasticity of demand.

4 ALBERT O. HIRSCHMAN: FROM BALANCED TO UNBALANCED GROWTH

1. Streeten wrote of *The Strategy*: 'the most important plea for unbalanced growth has been made by Albert O. Hirschman' (Streeten 1959, p.169n).

2. There are some similarities in Hirschman's formulation of contradictions in the role of the state and that proposed by James O'Connor. The latter argued that 'the capitalist state must try to fulfil two basic and often mutually contradictory functions – *accumulation* and *legitimization*. This means the state must try to

     maintain or create the conditions in which profitable capital accumulation is possible. However, the state must also try to maintain or create the conditions of social harmony' (O'Connor 1973, p.6).

3.   '[T]he complementary effect will lose importance as the economy reaches higher levels of development. New investments no longer lead necessarily to a chain of related new investments once the economy is well rounded out' (Hirschman 1958, p.43).

4.   In addition to linkage effects, Hirschman finds other reasons for the commencement of import replacing manufacturing. Firstly, 'importing-requires special skills and therefore reduces the number of potential entrants'. Secondly, 'importing is subject to special balance of payments uncertainties, and production largely based on imports is therefore particularly risky'. Thirdly, 'and perhaps most importantly, the fact that a certain product is produced domestically is likely to result in efforts on the part of producers to propagate its further uses...The domestic availability of a product thus brings into being active forces to that make for its utilisation as input in new economic activities' (Hirschman 1958, pp.99–100). The first explanation is improbable, since the skills requirements for importing surely do not exceed those required to organize domestic production of the imported commodity. The second explanation is plausible, if not sufficient, to account for the rise of import-substitution activity. The third explanation is clearly inadequate, as Hirschman assumes that domestic producers are either more active or more efficient than importers in propagating the 'further uses' of their products.

5.   The particular technique used to identify these linkages is 'triangulation' of the transaction table (See Miernyk 1965, pp.92–99 for an explanation of this technique).

6.   Hirschman's argument is supported by a key stylized fact of advanced industrial economies, in that these economies have a remarkably similar input–output structure (Leontief 1963, pp.170–171). Advanced economies have a diversified and interdependent national economy, which is consistent with the claim of Young, R-R and Hirschman that rising per capita income in an industrial economy is causally linked to increases in the density of national inter-industry and intra-industry transactions. Hirschman was at the forefront of development thinkers who used input–output techniques to locate the *differentia specifica* between developed and underdeveloped economies. A few years after Hirschman's *Strategy*, the eminent Wassily Leontief used the same ideas in his explanation of underdevelopment. 'The larger and more advanced an economy is, the more complete and articulated is its structure...In a sense the input–output coefficient matrix derived from the U.S.-European input-output table represents a complete cookbook of modern technology. It constitutes, without doubt, the structure of a fully developed economy insofar as development has proceeded anywhere today. *An underdeveloped economy can now be defined as underdeveloped to the extent that it lacks the working parts of this system*' (Leontief 1963, pp.169–170, my italics). From this analysis Leontief drew the same policy inferences as Hirschman. 'The process of development consists essentially in the installation and building of an approximation of the system embodied in advanced economies of the U.S. and Western Europe and, more recently, of the Soviet Union – with due allowance for the limitations imposed by the local mix of resources and the availability of technology to exploit them' (Leontief 1963, p.172).

7.   The idea that a vertically integrated industrial structure is a sound measure of development is now used widely in writing on development. Wade, for example,

uses the 'ratio of intermediate demand to total manufacturing output' as a 'measure of industrial "depth" or "roundaboutness" in production' (Wade 1990, p.44; see also Syrquin 1988).

8. The focus on getting the 'correct' industrial structure, emphasized by development economists such as Hirschman, Chenery, and Leontief in the 1950s, has a remarkable resonance with the architects of post-war Japanese industry policy. This is examined in more detail in the Conclusion.

9. Hirschman noted the similarity of his model, where investment in period t^1 is largely determined by the industrial structure and investment in period t, to the Feldman growth model. In particular, he interpreted the Feldman model as 'an attempt to build a sequence where investment of one period is directly related to the investments of prior periods, without the intermediary of the savings ratio' (Hirschman 1958, p.73). The central place of the machine-tools sector in Feldman's growth model (Jones 1982, pp.114–122) has resonances in Hirschman's focus on the capital and intermediate goods sector. Making the growth of investment a direct function of output growth also has obvious links to the Keynesian accelerator principle, though Hirschman does not make this association.

10. These other factors include, for example, volatility in currency movements, which may considerably increase the risk of borrowing overseas capital or importing capital/intermediate goods; large movements in interest rates (especially as they affect cash flow); and, the fact that production of many manufactured commodities is subject to patents on processes and equipment, or other impediments to the international transfer of technology (BIE 1988[b]). In addition, in the case of multinational corporations, the decision as to the location of investments may be part of a global strategy in which local (national) demand conditions are only one factor (Crough and Wheelwright 1982, Chapter 2).

11. Pasinetti's 'vertically integrated' model of development emphasizes the interdependence between growth in the size of the market and cumulative learning. The interaction of these two influences creates a definite pattern or 'priority' in the introduction of new technologies and products within a given nation. Pasinetti gives the example of two nations A and U, with A having a per capita income some five times greater than U. '[A]'s time and economic growth go on, country U will be able to enlarge the variety of its production. But this process will have to follow a very strict order. At any given point of time, producers in U are not free to pick up any type of commodity they like from among the 4/5th's of all types which are not produced. They will have to start production only of those commodities for which demand is expanding... But a fixed order in which the production process can be enlarged also represents a fixed order in which the various methods of production can be learnt. Thus, however big the stock of accumulated technical knowledge may be in A, country U can take advantage only of that small part of it which refers to the few products for which demand is expanding and for those commodities... which are produced already' (Pasinetti 1981, pp.251-252).

12. Throughout the 1960s and 1970s there was a very considerable effort to construct and use input–output tables along these lines, especially for Latin American nations. See Tibor Barna (ed.), *Structural Interdependence and Economic Development*, St.Martins Press, New York 1963, and 'Symposium on Measurement of Linkages', *Quarterly Journal of Economics*, May 1976.

13. It is possible to create dynamic input–output tables which have a non-linear production technology (Miernyk W., 1965, Ch.6). It is also possible to use estimates of training rates and R&D expenditures for each industry, which could then be entered as a column vector and inverted to show the direct and

indirect effect on these variables from a given expansion in final demand (see Phibbs and Toner, 1994). Pasinetti is critical of these attempts to create dynamic input–output models, and claims that the analysis of technical change through time is one of the principal virtues of his 'vertically integrated' model (Pasinetti 1981, pp.114–123).

14.   A developing economy could, of course, employ input–output information from a comparable country at a slightly higher stage of development to identify such possible changes. For example, Chenery (1986) details the changes in the income elasticity of demand for broad industrial categories at various levels of per capita income.

15.   The BIE (1990) for example, employed a case study methodology in their analysis of the causes and effects of inter-firm alliances in high-technology industries. This study provided a detailed analysis of the causes and effects of externalities arising from various forms of inter-firm co-operation or 'strategic alliances'. An outstanding example of historical scholarship using the concepts of externality and complementarity is Alfred Chandler's (1990) monumental work, *Scale and Scope: The Dynamics of Industrial Capitalism*. This work charts the growth from the mid-nineteenth century of key industries in textiles, metals, chemicals and electrical goods. These industries were very capital-intensive and economies of scale and scope were, and are, very important in their development. Chandler highlights the complementary or interdependent nature of these investments. For example, expansion of metals and electrical industries required development of transport and communications, railway and telegraph. Transport and communications provided a direct benefit by expanding the geographic size of the market for the products of metal and electrical industries. Metal and electrical industries also benefited by expansion of transport (notably rail) and communications, since the former were major inputs into the latter.

16.   Nathan Rosenberg strongly endorses the utility of input–output techniques for providing insights into the changing structure of the economy. '[T]he great virtue of input–output is that it helps us to understand the structural interdependence of the economic system, and the change over time in this structural interdependence' (Rosenberg 1982, p.72).

17.   The arguments of Young and Hirschman have been strongly confirmed by Chenery's empirical work on systematic patterns of transformation in the composition of demand, production and inter-industry structure in the process of industrialization. For example, on the specific matter of the rise in intermediate inputs Chenery found that '[a]s countries industrialize, their productive structures become more "roundabout" in the sense that a higher proportion of output is sold to other producers rather than to final users … [This is attributed to] a shift in output toward manufacturing and other sectors that use more intermediate inputs, and, technological changes within the sector that lead to a greater use of intermediate inputs' (Chenery 1986, p.57).

5   GUNNAR MYRDAL: CIRCULAR AND CUMULATIVE CAUSATION AS THE METHODOLOGY OF THE SOCIAL SCIENCES

1.   It is generally accepted that Myrdal developed the concept from Wicksell's monetary theory, and especially the notion that the deviation of the 'market' rate of interest from the 'natural' rate of interest tends to become cumulatively

larger, until an eventual equilibrium is achieved. (Gruchy 1972, p.180.) For a detailed account of Myrdal's monetary theory, and the influence of Wicksell under whom Myrdal studied, see G.L.S. Shackle, *The Years of High Theory*, CUP 1972, Chs.9–11.) Myrdal's anti-equilibrium approach was evident from the beginning of his published work. His famous *Monetary Equilibrium* (1931, translated into English in 1939), anticipated much of Keynes's *General Theory*, and was especially important in formulating the role of uncertainty in terms of *ex ante* expectations and *ex post* outcomes. 'By introducing expectations into the analysis of economic processes, he [Myrdal] made a major contribution to liberating economics from static theory' (Streeten 1984, p.581).

2. This of course is not to imply that Myrdal's methodology remained static over these four decades. His early methodological writings reflect the view of many 'social scientists' of his era, that his discipline was on an evolutionary, asymptotic path towards a genuinely scientific status. 'Ideally, the scientific solution... should thus be given in the form of an interconnected series of quantitative equations, describing the movement of the actual system under various influences. That this complete, quantitative and truly scientific solution is far beyond the horizon does not need to be pointed out. But in principle it is possible to execute, and remains as the scientific ideal steering our endeavours' (Myrdal 1944, p.1069). This positivism is largely absent in his later works (Argyrous and Sethi 1996, p.488). Angresano (1997) finds three overlapping but distinct periods in Myrdal's intellectual development. The first – from 1915 to the early 1930s – covers Myrdal's contributions to economics within a 'neoclassical-Wicksellian' approach. The second is Myrdal's conversion to a 'political economist' over the 1930s. As a result of his work on poverty and population decline in Sweden during the early 1930s, Myrdal expanded the circular and cumulative mechanism to include social and institutional elements. The time from the late 1930s marked his emergence as an Institutional economist, to which he remained committed till his death.

3. Hirschman was critical of Myrdal's emphasis on largely unconstrained vicious or virtuous circles: 'Myrdal's analysis strikes me as excessively dismal' (Hirschman 1958, p.187n). Hirschman has greater belief in the self-correcting efficacy of the market mechanism than that possessed by R-R, Myrdal or Kaldor (Hirschman 1984, p.89 and p.91).

4. Thirlwall's account of Myrdal is unsatisfactory and highly selective. For example, Thirlwall ignores Myrdal's emphasis on the problems of specialization in commodities and their low price and income elasticity of demand (Thirlwall 1994, p.134). These arguments regarding the problems of specialization in commodity production were later taken up by Kaldor in support of national plans for industrialisation. This reflects the general failure of contemporary CC theorists to adequately acknowledge the contributions of writers in the CC tradition prior to Kaldor.

5. Writing of the Third World, Myrdal commented that 'What the poor do need are radical institutional reforms on a scale far outside the field enclosed by reasoning about growth and distribution accounted for in terms of money' (Myrdal 1978, p.782). Aside from Myrdal, the only other major writer in the CC tradition to focus on social influences was Ragnar Nurkse. Current leading proponents of CC, such as Eatwell (1982), also give institutional effects some prominence. For example, the effect of the City of London and the ideology of Free Trade are central to Eatwell's explanation of Britain's industrial decline. Nevertheless, in general, contemporary CC theorists do not give non-economic factors the central role that Myrdal allocated them.

6. Trevor Swan (1962) provided a novel diagrammatic account of the circular and cumulative interaction of 'Negro' living standards and 'White Prejudice'.
7. Geoff Hodgson (1989) grafts an Institutionalist approach on to Kaldor's economics. Kapp (1976) and Argyrous and Sethi (1996) highlight the use of circular and cumulative reasoning amongst Institutionalist economists. The inclusion of historical, institutional, and cultural factors in 'economic' explanations is intuitively appealing. Unfortunately, in unsophisticated hands such tools are employed to shape crude tautological explanations, of the type represented by the statement: 'poor people exist because they have a "culture of poverty"' (Hewison, Robison, and Rodan 1993, pp.14–15). In the hands of more skilled artisans, such as Marx, Weber, Veblen, Galbraith, Myrdal and Chalmers Johnson, plausible and complex models of interaction are fashioned.

6   NICHOLAS KALDOR: 'THE MARRIAGE OF YOUNG AND KEYNES'

1. Thirlwall (1987) has a nine-page bibliography. Since 1987 several important works of Kaldor have been published. Kaldor's Mattioli Lectures, *Causes of Growth and Stagnation in the World Economy*, delivered in 1984 and published in 1996 are the closest to an integrated magnum opus. They reached me too late to be properly incorporated into this book.
2. The following summary is based on Wood (1987) and Thirlwall (1987, 1991) and Targetti (1991).
3. Thirlwall (1987) argues that Kaldor expressed a well-developed form of these CC ideas in the 1950s during a lecture tour of South America.
4. Kaldor's intellectual autobiography 'Recollections of an Economist' (1986) also provides no hint of the extent of these and other debts to earlier CC theorists.
5. Lawson (1989) provides a detailed philosophical analysis of Kaldor's notion of 'stylized facts'. This notion has considerable similarity to Myrdal's 'bold simplifications', as outlined in chapter 5, though Myrdal did not develop the idea to the same extent as Kaldor.
6. This is a generally accepted view of Kaldor's oeuvre. Kaldor's work in the 1950s and early 1960s was 'a theoretical whole in which the theories of distribution, growth and technological progress are admirably combined in a single model'. The post-1966 work did not attain 'that level of synthesis' evident in his earlier writings (Targetti 1991, p.411).
7. Kaldor cited Marshall at length against the over-use of mathematics in economic reasoning (Kaldor 1985). Given Kaldor's clear methodological pronouncements on this subject, the criticisms that Kaldor's Growth Laws are econometrically 'under-specified' (Boyer and Petit 1991, p.492) or require detailed 'macro-economic modelling', (Gordon 1991, p.519) are somewhat disingenuous. Whatever the merits of these large-scale modelling approaches, it should be acknowledged by such critics that Kaldor questioned the efficacy of these methods.
8. The exception to this would be Myrdal, who took a very catholic view of the sources of increasing returns – though, as argued previously, Myrdal did not provide a detailed analysis of these sources of increasing returns.
9. In the appendix to his (1972[c]) article, Kaldor recanted his earlier position (Kaldor, 1934) that identified increasing returns solely with the overcoming of indivisibilities. The 'existence of a non-linear relationship between costs and capacity is inherent in the nature of *space*, and there is nothing "indivisible"

about space as such' (Kaldor 1972, p.1253). He also admitted the crucial role of dynamic scale economies such as learning by doing.

10. As the surface area of a cylinder increases by the square, the volume increases by the cube.

11. Kaldor's assessment is over-enthusiastic, since there are inherent engineering or cost constraints on continuously increasing the size of cylinders etc., be they boilers, ships or aeroplanes (Pratten 1971).

12. An important caveat to this, of course, is the supply of materials from 'land-based' activities which Kaldor assumes are subject to diminishing returns. Within an 'open' economy, this supply constraint is not significant, but within a 'closed' economy it is the elasticity of materials supply, governed by the rate of technical progress in this sector, which is the ultimate determinant of the rate of growth. This is discussed in Section 6.3.

13. McCombie and Thirlwall (1994) provide a comprehensive discussion of demand (CC) and supply-side (neoclassical) approaches to economic growth.

14. Heinz Arndt has perceptively commented on the relation between Young and Keynes. 'Writing in 1928, Allyn Young was able to take his stand on Say's Law of Markets without any of the inhibitions which would naturally afflict an economist writing after 1936. We have learned to qualify Allyn Young's proposition: supply creates its own demand only if investment offsets savings. At the same time, without being conscious of this aspect, Allyn Young, with his insistence on the manifold ways in which increases in aggregate income give rise to new opportunities, not merely of widening investment, but also of deepening and especially innovatory investment . . . stressed the very factors on which optimists about economic progress in a private enterprise economy must rely to lay the Keynesian spectre of stagnation' (Arndt 1955, p.206).

15. 'The principle of effective demand, which is the core of his [Keynes's] theory, was in fact a refinement, or a development, of Say's Law rather than a simple rejection of it. Keynes did not deny that incomes are derived from productive activities, or that "incomes" are merely different aspect of costs incurred, and therefore are both a measure of the value of things produced and the source of purchasing power – the source of demand for goods. What he denied was that there was a necessary equivalence between the costs incurred and the demand generated by the costs incurred' (Kaldor 1982, p.2).

16. Kaldor's interpretation of Young is highly suspect, as Young never expressed the view that elasticity of demand and elasticity of substitution were equivalent. Rather, the burden of his argument was that the rate of growth of a particular commodity was a function of its elasticity of supply (the extent to which it was subject to increasing returns in production) and its elasticity of demand. Growth in sales of commodity A did not have to occur at the expense of commodity B. The rate of growth of a particular commodity was primarily a function of the rate of growth of all other commodities. Kaldor attempts to establish a logical flaw in Young's growth model that would prevent the absorption of increased output. To account for the absorption of increased output, as explained above, Kaldor argued that it was necessary to introduce a number of Keynesian elements. (Kaldor's interpretation of this aspect of Young's model is examined in more detail in Section 6.7.1).

17. Kaldor's critique of Young's failure to provide a model of income generation and induced investment also applies to Hirschman, who, it will be recalled, had a very mechanistic view of the relationship between demand and investment. Hirschman's notion of 'induced investment' largely reflects Young's view that the volume of capital investment was determined by the size of the market.

18. Kaldor (1982) indicated the key role of merchants' inventory holding activities was taken from Kornai (1971) pp.178–180.
19. Spraos 1989, provides a detailed account of Kaldor's views on commodities.
20. In Section 6.7.3 it is argued that in his Cambridge Inaugural Lecture Kaldor employed a different model of CC development which assumes growth in the industrial sector is largely self-sustaining, and as such is much closer to the approach of earlier CC theorists.
21. Kaldor argued that Ricardo, Mill, Adam Smith, and Marx were aware of the fact that 'the food-value of wages tend to be very rigid downward in all communities at some *attained* level ... but they had not thought out its consequences in terms of Say's Law' (Kaldor 1975, p.352).
22. Kaldor undertook simple regression analysis of these laws for the period 1953–4 to 1963–64 for nine European nations, Japan, Canada and the U.S. (Kaldor 1966[a], p.5). Kaldor regressed the logarithm of annual rates of change in labour productivity and employment for a variety of industries against rates of change of output in these industries. The expression 'Kaldor's Growth Laws' is derived from Thirlwall (1983). The following is drawn largely from Kaldor (1966;1967) and Thirlwall (1983;1987).
23. The leading Kaldorian scholar, Professor John Cornwall, has stressed the role of manufacturing in the diffusion of technology. The capital goods, electronics and chemical industries especially 'have been the main purveyors of technological and technical progress throughout much of the economy ... Hence, growth in manufacturing output in these areas gives rise, in effect, to important forward linkages in the extended view of the interdependence of productive activities' (Cornwall 1977, p.135, see also Ch.7, 'The Manufacturing Sector as the Engine of Growth').
24. In the 1966[a] article, Kaldor argued that it 'is the existence of an elastic supply curve of labour to the secondary and tertiary sectors which is the main pre-condition of a fast rate of development ... Britain, having started the process of industrialization earlier than any other country, has reached "maturity" much earlier – in the sense that ... industry can no longer attract the labour it needs by drawing on the labour reserves of other sectors.' Kaldor concludes that the slow rate of growth of Britain is to be accounted for by the fact 'that manpower shortage is the main handicap from which we are suffering'. Kaldor even advocated imposing barriers to 'the absorption of labour into those sectors in which – if I may use a Pigovian phrase – the marginal social product is likely to be appreciably below the marginal private product' (Kaldor 1966[a] pp.30–31). As chief economic adviser to Labour Governments, Kaldor was instrumental in the development of the Selective Employment Tax during the late 1960s, which operated as an impost on the employment of labour in decreasing returns industries (service sector) and a subsidy to increasing returns industries (manufacturing) (Thirlwall 1987, pp.240–245). Kaldor later recanted the view that inelastic labour supply was the major obstacle to increasing the rate of growth in Britain.
25. Regressing the log of labour productivity growth against the log of manufacturing output growth for several European countries over several years, 'it was found that the average value of the elasticity of productivity with respect to output is approximately 0.45' (Verdoorn 1949, p.1). Verdoorn attributed this positive relation to the increased scope for the division of labour following an increase in output, 'one could have expected *a priori* to find a correlation between labour productivity and output, given that the division of labour only comes about through increases in the volume of production' (Verdoorn 1949, p.3).

26. Thirlwall argues that 'the Verdoorn Law ... is *not* an indispensable element of the complete Kaldor model ... Even in the absence of increasing returns in manufacturing the growth of industry would still be the governing factor determining overall output growth as long as resources used by industry represent a *net* addition to the use of resources' (Thirlwall 1987, p.192). Thirlwall's claim, which relates mainly to Kaldor's First Growth Law, cannot be accepted. If increasing returns (i.e. Verdoorn's Law) do not hold for manufacturing industry, there would be no net benefit in the transfer of [net additional] resources to manufacturing compared to the employment of these resources by other industries.

27. The Australian Bureau of Industry Economics estimated the Verdoorn relation for Australian manufacturing over the period 1952–53/1981–82. They found that the long-run elasticity of productivity growth with respect to growth of value added was just over 1 (BIE 1985, p.43). The report does not explain why this elasticity is substantially higher than either the original Verdoorn estimate or Kaldor's regression coefficient (BIE 1985, p.38).

28. As noted in the introduction, Kaldor's Growth Laws generated considerable theoretical and empirical controversy. Firstly, it was objected that the Laws suffered from a variety of estimation and specification errors. A 'spurious' Verdoorn relation may arise when a positive relation between productivity and output growth in a cross-country sample may be due simply to the diffusion of advanced technology to developing nations, rather than the key mechanisms of endogenous productivity such as scale economies and learning by doing, etc. This 'spurious' relation, it is argued, may have affected Kaldor's original sample estimates, which included data on Japan for the 1950s and 1960s (McCombie 1983, p.419). Secondly, time series data can conflate the short-run relations between changes in output and productivity arising from changes in capacity utilisation, and long-run effects of scale and technological change, etc. (Boyer and Petit 1991, p.500). This is especially the case when economies emerge from recessions as they experience a strong pro-cyclical increase in productivity. In this case a statistically significant relation between increasing productivity and output growth could be found which would not be due to increasing returns. Thirdly, specification of the Second Law ignores the effect of productivity growth in stimulating the growth of output. The recognition of such interdependence is certainly more in the spirit of a circular and cumulative growth model. A proper specification of the model requires a simultaneous equation approach, where productivity and output interact and reinforce one another (Parikh 1978). Kaldor subsequently agreed that this method was preferable to his single equation model (Thirlwall 1987, p.190). Fourthly, as originally formulated, Kaldor (1966[a]) expressed his Growth Laws ambiguously such that the growth of manufacturing output in some regression equations appeared to be a dependent variable of the growth of manufacturing employment. This followed from his view that the growth of manufacturing output could be constrained in the U.K. by the small size of the agricultural sector, and thus the limited scope for transference of labour from low- to high-productivity sectors. Kaldor soon recanted this position, emphasizing demand and not labour supply as the principal constraint to manufacturing output (Kaldor 1972[c]; 1975; Thirlwall 1983, p.353). Fifthly, some recent studies have found that the Verdoorn Law breaks down after 1973. From this date for OECD nations, change in national 'productivity is independent from any conventional factor', with the exception of per capita R&D expenditures (Boyer and Petit 1991, p.508).

29. This is the so-called 'dynamic' Harrod formula (Thirlwall 1979).

30. Kaldor provided a simple arithmetical example of this principle. 'Suppose that exports correspond to 20 per cent of "full employment" output, but 30 per cent of (marginal and average) income is spent on imports. In that case actual output will settle at two-thirds of "full employment" output, since at that level both imports and exports will be equal to each other' (Kaldor 1982, p.11).

31. The use of a divergent cobweb to represent the dis-equilibrium growth process within the CC School has a considerable history. The term 'cobweb' theorem was invented by Kaldor in 1934 (Thirlwall 1987, p.40). As an early contributor to the 'cobweb' theorem, R-R argued that concepts such as indivisibilities, complementarities in demand, hierarchies of wants and expectations, could generate 'cumulative effects' resulting in perpetual movements away from equilibrium (R-R 1934, pp.95–96). Albert Hirschman proposed the following dynamic view of development. 'If the economy is to be kept moving ahead, the task of development policy is to maintain tensions, disproportions, and dis-equilibria. That nightmare of equilibrium economics, the endlessly spinning cobweb, is the *kind* of mechanism we must assiduously look for as an invaluable help in the development process '(Hirschman 1958, p.66).

32. 'Even with a stationary population and in the absence of new discoveries in pure and applied science there are no limits to the process of expansion except the limits beyond which demand is not elastic and returns do not increase' (Young 1928, p.534).

33. The policy of concentrating resources in a limited number of industries (through the international division of labour) was not restricted to developing nations. Even a 'mature economy could continue to reap the benefits of economies of scale, not through a fast growth of manufacturing industry as a whole, but through greater international specialisation. If the main hypothesis advanced in this lecture is correct, and economies of scale in industry are the main engine of fast growth, at least some of its benefits could continue to be secured by concentrating our resources in fewer fields and abandoning others – in other words, by increasing the degree of interdependence of British industry with the industries of other countries' (Kaldor 1966[a], p.32).

34. Stigler's (1951) classic article, which explicitly drew much of its inspiration from Marshall and Young, identified joint production between small firms as an important source of the division of labour and increasing returns. Agglomeration or 'Localization is one method of increasing the economic size of an industry and achieving the gains of specialization. The auxiliary and complementary industries that must operate in intimate co-operation can seldom do so efficiently at a distance' (Stigler 1951, p.192). In particular, Stigler emphasized the complex transfer of intermediate goods between many small specialized firms, each undertaking some processing of the good or supplying and fitting some component to the good. In a similar vein, Jane Jacobs' work on the growth and decline of cities provides marvellous descriptions of 'the symbiotic nests of suppliers and producers that are all-important to a city's economy' (Jacobs 1984, p.119).

35. Stuart Holland (1976) *Capital versus the Regions*, makes extensive use of Myrdal and Kaldor's broad concept of increasing returns and external economies in his famous study of regional economics.

36. Singh (1989) provides a detailed theoretical account and supportive empirical test of Kaldor's de-industrialization thesis. He concludes that the de-industrialisation of Britain was due more to trade with First World nations than to the loss of its domestic market to newly industrialising countries.

37. 'comparing the United States with India, we see that the capital–labour ratio is in the order of 30:1, while the capital-output ratio is around 1:1' (Kaldor 1975, p.356).

38. Pasinetti provides an alternative explanation of these trends in capital–labour and capital–output ratios in his 'vertically integrated' model (Pasinetti 1981, pp.183–184).

39. Kaldor seems to have borrowed this idea of risk associated with external funds from Kalecki (Sawyer 1985, pp.101–106).

40. Real price reductions for a particular commodity can, of course, occur through price reductions with constant money wages, nominal prices increasing at a slower rate than wages, or an improvement in the 'quality' of manufactures which is not matched by an equivalent price increase. Kaldor regards such quality improvements as an essential aspect of real price reductions, and a very important form of competition (Kaldor 1981, pp.603–604). The apparently clear distinction between price and non-price competition in the economics literature is blurred in the case where quality improvements are only partially reflected in price increases. McCombie and Thirlwall (1994) have identified quality differences as a key element in the CC explanation for the existence of international trade and the comparative success of some nations in this trade.

41. Kaldor, of course, produced several famous papers in the 1950s relating investment to his own distribution theory. Following his adoption of CC theory in the late 1960s, Kaldor wrote almost nothing on income distribution, and certainly did not propose any grand synthesis of growth and distribution. Other CC writers such as Lauchlin Currie and Roger Sandilands consider that the 'overall product is divided between owners [of capital] and labour in accordance with quite definite and continuing market forces, especially competition of capital. The residue after compensating capital is divided among labour sectors' (Currie 1997, p.12). New investment is funded primarily from retained earnings with 'additional output providing depreciation allowances and retained profits sufficient to meet the cost of new equipment' (Currie 1997 p.11; Sandilands 1997, p.21).

42. Sandilands cites Young's statement in the famous textbook *Outlines in Economics* [New York: Macmillan 5th ed., 1930 p.417] which he co-authored with Richard T. Ely and others, that the law of diminishing returns 'operates in an exceedingly elastic manner' and it would be 'absurd to make the fundamental tendency towards diminishing returns in agriculture a basis for pessimistic views regarding the possibility of economic progress' (Sandilands 1990, p.310).

43. The literature on commodity price movements and the net barter terms of trade between commodities and manufactures is vast, and whilst there is considerable debate it would seem there is general consensus on this point (MacBean and Nguyen 1987, Ch. 3).

44. Referring to the 'closed' model, Thirlwall writes, 'In the long-run equilibrium of the model it can be shown formally how variations in the pace of industrial growth depend fundamentally on the rate of land-saving innovations, and that technical progress in industry affects only the equilibrium terms of trade [between manufacturing and agriculture]...but not the long-run equilibrium growth rate' (Thirlwall 1987, pp.217–218).

45. There are passages, however, where these scholars adopt a more open position. Thirlwall and McCombie (1994) note that much of the supply of labour in post-war Europe employed in the expanding manufacturing sector came from agriculture. In 'many of the advanced countries...agriculture was based on small family-owned spatially fragmented farms. The process of consolidation of these farms that occurred in many countries after the war...allowed substantial

economies of scale to be achieved, together with a widespread increase in the degree of mechanization. This resulted in a rapid growth of agricultural productivity' (Thirlwall and McCombie 1994, p.158, my italics).

46. Kaldor's regression equations for Public utilities $P_{(u)}$, and Construction $P_{(c)}$ respectively are,

$$P_{(u)} = 2.707 + 0.419\,X, r^2 = 0.451$$
$$(0.155)$$
$$P_{(c)} = -.543 + 0.572X, r^2 = 0.810$$
$$(0.153)$$

47. Within the *Australian and New Zealand Standard Industrial Classification* (1993), Property and Business Services (Sub-Division 78) includes Scientific Research (Four Digit 7810) biological, natural, engineering, industrial and medical research (excluding universities), Consultant Engineering Services (Four Digit 7823) and Computer Consultancy Services (Four Digit 7834). The services provided by firms in this industry are very diverse and include scientific and industrial research and development, writing software applications for computer-controlled manufacturing processes, assisting firms to select, install and operate major new capital investments, or certifying firms under various quality assurance programmes, etc. According to the latest estimates of research and development expenditure by industry, 20 per cent and 57 per cent of national expenditure was in the business services and manufacturing industries respectively (Research and *Experimental Development. Business Enterprises 1994–95.* ABS 8104.0)

48. In the 1966 Inaugural Lecture Kaldor formulated his model of growth using virtually the same language as Young, and without many of the Keynesian qualifications which marked his later work. 'Economic growth is the result of a complex process of interaction between increases of demand induced by increases in supply and of increases in supply generated in response to increases in demand. Since in the market as a whole commodities are exchanged against commodities, the increase in demand for any commodity, or group of commodities, reflects the increase in supply of other commodities, and vice versa. The nature of this chain reaction will be conditioned by both demand elasticities and supply constraints; by individual preferences or attitudes and by technological factors. The chain reaction is likely to be the more rapid the more the demand increases are focussed on commodities which have a *large supply* response and the larger the demand response induced by increases in production – the latter is not just a matter of the marginal propensities in consumption but also of induced investment'(Kaldor 1966[a], p.19).

49. 'Import duties are efficacious in promoting industrialization so long as there is scope for creating an internal demand for home-manufactured produced goods through the replacement of the pre-existing imports of such goods. But once the limits of "easy" import substitution have been reached, the momentum for further industrialization is virtually exhausted – particularly where this development was only brought about by slowing down the growth of agricultural production. For as soon as import substitution is accomplished, the further growth of domestic industry becomes dependent either on the development of industrial exports or on the growth of production in the complementary sector of the economy, that is, in agriculture' (Kaldor 1972[b], p.145).

50. The role of import-substitution and growth of the home market in industrialization in the economcs literature is of course controversial, and for every case
study supporting one position another can be found to deny it. Nevertheless, a
number of prominent scholars emphasize the contribution of growth in domestic demand and import-substitution in the explanation of rapid Japanese growth
from the early 1950s to the first oil price crisis in 1974. Komiya and Itoh (1988)
bluntly state that 'it is not correct to characterize Japan's economic growth as
export-led' (p.186). Yoshikawa (1993) argues that 'economic growth in this
period [1950–1970] was basically led by domestic demand' (p.19). 'Over the
long-run, developmental policies that promoted exports and discouraged
imports in Japan contributed to domestic expansion that fuelled both savings
and investment . . . *Japan's performance is consistent with the cumulative effects of
the import-substitution strategy*' (Johnson, Tyson, Zysman 1991, p.107, my italics).
'From the very beginning of Japan's modern development,' writes Jane Jacobs,
'trade in new products (new to Japan) among Japanese cities has been far more
intensively pursued than foreign trade. This still remains true. Thus, in 1980,
Japan was exceeded only by the United States in the proportion of its total trade
that is domestic, a Japanese achievement more remarkable than America's
considering the fact that so many American resource goods are produced
domestically while Japan must import most raw materials' (Jacobs 1984,
p.147). Exports were promoted to gain scale economies by reducing fixed unit
costs (Yamamura 1990, p.43) and to overcome the chronic balance of payments
constraint to growth.

51. By the mid-1970s Japan had an advanced and highly productive industrial base,
though policies of strict import-substitution were used to develop the computer
industry in this period (Johnson, Tyson and Zysman, 1991). Robert Wade's
study of Taiwan demonstrates that high rates of protection and import substitution were, and are, an essential element in industrialization and export success.
The apparent paradox of high levels of simultaneous import protection and high
levels of exports in the same industry is resolved when it is recognized that
'Taiwan's openness and outward orientation have not been based on free trade'
(Wade 1990, p.113). It is 'misleading . . . to present import substitution and
export promotion as mutually exclusive strategies . . . at the individual industry
level, import substitution and export promotion can be complementary '(Wade
1990, p.363). A key cause preventing 'x-inefficiency' in protected industries due
to an absence of international competition was that assistance was generally
temporary and/or tied to the achievement of specific export targets (Wade 1990,
p.359). Most industry assistance was 'performance-tested', and this was the
principal means of evaluating the progress of firms receiving assistance and/or
the effectiveness of policy instruments themselves (Wade 1990, p.189). Alice
Amsden's classic study of the development of Taiwan's machine tool industry
found that even after it became a major exporter of such equipment, significant
non-tariff barriers were still imposed. Whilst the tariff on machine tools similar
to those manufactured in Taiwan is only fifteen per cent, such equipment cannot
be imported by 'machinery distributors' and imports are totally banned 'from a
handful of countries which just happen to be those which pose a genuine
competitive threat (for example, Japan, South Korea, and Hong Kong)' (Amsden 1985, p.282).

52. As a point of clarification, the term 'specialization' as used here has two distinct
meanings. Firstly, in Kaldor's and Sheahan's prescription for national development strategies, it means restricting the number of industries to be established.
Secondly, specialization is an essential element of increasing returns arising

from 'roundabout production methods'. Specialization in the second usage results from the progressive division of labour within firms and across industries as the size of the market increases.

53.   Writing in the CC or 'structuralist' tradition, Argyrous makes a similar argument against advocates of industry policy who argue that the growth of specialized or 'niche' industries and firms can occur independently of a large diversified national market. Large diversified national markets are a source of demand for the products of specialized firms, as well as a source of high quality inputs. 'From a structuralist perspective, issues of general assistance to manufacturing become paramount. Without a domestic base that is significantly diverse and contains within it large mass production and heavy engineering industries, the kinds of processes out of which SMEs [small and medium-sized establishments] emerge lose a vital component. The existence of such a base is the most critical factor in determining whether the 90 per cent of SMEs who are not exporting actually make the transition [to exporting]... [A]s Australia's manufacturing base is eroded by policies which cause its heavy industries to contract under the weight of foreign competition, the learning processes and financial supports which also give rise to exports will become weaker' (Argyrous 1993, p.123). Interestingly, Argyrous cites Kaldor's (1966[a]) four-stage model to support his argument about the necessity for a large-scale and integrated domestic industrial base.

54.   Whilst Lauchlin Currie disagreed with much of Kaldor's interpretation of Young, they shared a similar difficulty in formulating a detailed and systematic theory of distribution within the CC framework. Like Kaldor, Currie rejected the marginal productivity theory of income distribution. Currie regarded the wages share as a 'residue' after capital is compensated, with this residue 'divided amongst labour sectors... according to the strength of market forces, particularly labour mobility. With perfect mobility, earnings would differ only by the agreeableness of the work. The less the mobility, the greater the difference in earnings' (Currie, 1997, forthcoming).

7   CONCLUSION

1.   CC theorists have either explicitly or implicitly focused their analyses of growth on the region or the nation state. Development is causally related to the creation of an interdependent and integrated industrial base within national boundaries. A crucial assumption was the link between growth in the size of the market and increased investment. It is arguable, however, that with the increased globalization of production, and especially the international division of labour, the spatial concentration of an integrated or coherent industrial base may be breaking down (Cowling and Sugden 1996). The implications of this for growth are uncertain.

2.   Romer (1994), provides a summary of the various models and mathematical techniques used in endogenous growth theory since 1983. BIE (1992) also provides a useful summary of the evolution of endogenous growth models since 1986.

3.   There are four principal channels in the diffusion of knowledge between firms. 'Positive disclosure' of information occurs when a firm makes an innovation readily available to competitors. This may occur when an innovating firm wants to establish a new industry standard based on its new product or process. The

patent system also provides valuable information to competitors via patent searches. Secondly, interpersonal networks involve information flows between common customers, suppliers or professional associations. Thirdly, mobility of skilled trade, technical, or professional personnel between firms can disseminate knowledge. Finally, 'reverse engineering' of a product, embodying a new product or process technology, can be undertaken by competitors to copy or improve the innovation (BIE 1994, pp.20–23).

4. Knowledge also has another unique economic property – 'knowledge is cumulative, with each idea building on the last, whereas machines deteriorate and must be replaced. In that sense, every knowledge-oriented dollar makes a productivity contribution on the margin, while perhaps three-quarters of private investment in machinery and equipment is simply to replace depreciation' (Grossman and Helpman 1994, p.31). This view seems to ignore the possibility that some research projects, for example, might be 'dead-ends'.

5. Knight regarded external economies as inimical to competitive conditions, since continuously increasing returns must lead to monopoly. 'Until a plausible example is brought forward, the category of decreasing costs under stable competitive conditions remains an "empty economic box"' (Knight 1925, pp.333). Professor Allyn Young was Knight's doctoral supervisor, and Knight refused to accept Young's contention that increasing returns took their most important form not in the growth of the individual enterprise but in the development of new specialized firms and industries (Blitch 1983, p.363). Knight's claim that no empirical example of Marshallian-type external economies has been furnished, and Romer's acceptance of this claim, must be rejected. The classic examples are creation of a local skilled labour market due to the concentration of firms in a locality, and the lowering in the supply price of capital goods to a growing industry as capital goods producers realize increasing returns (Arndt 1955, has a detailed list of Marshall's examples of external economies).

6. It will be recalled that pecuniary externalities operate through the market mechanism. Because the price mechanism itself generates the divergence between private and social benefits, 'pecuniary externalities have no place in equilibrium theory' (Scitovsky 1954, pp.298–299).

7. Within equilibrium theory R&D activities are 'sunk costs', and as such they 'do not contribute to the marginal costs of producing the new goods that result...If the equilibrium price of a good must be equal to its marginal cost of production, then firms that spend resources on invention or research and development will not break even' (Romer 1991, p.90).

8. Bardhan is also critical of modern growth theory because 'it tends to overlook (and thus fails to learn from) the earlier development literature which abounds with many examples of (and sophisticated debates on) these effects through learning by doing, skill formation, user–supplier interaction, networks of technology diffusion, and so on'. In addition, he notes that: 'Development economists of the 1940s and 1950s made an especially impressive contribution in the case of "pecuniary" external economies, in particular, the case of what may be called economics of market co-ordination...The Rosenstein-Rodan idea must be one of the early examples of the general literature on co-ordination failures in economics' (Bardhan 1993, pp.133–34).

9. These neoclassical accounts include, for example, the World Bank (1993).

10. In addition to these economic histories of East Asia, a small number of writers have employed the notion of pecuniary external economies to develop a variety of mathematical models of growth based on 'demand spillovers between sectors' (Murphy, Schleifer, and Vishny 1989, p.1004). Drawing explicitly on the work of

Rosenstein-Rodan, Nurkse, Fleming and Scitovsky, they argue: 'Countries such as South Korea that have implemented a co-ordinated investment programme can achieve industrialization of each sector at a lower explicit cost in terms of temporary tariffs and subsidies than a country that industrializes piecemeal. The reason is that potentially large implicit subsidies flow across sectors under a programme of simultaneous industrialization' (Murphy, Schleifer, and Vishny 1989, p.1004). In many respects, these recent modelling exercises add nothing new to the earlier work of Chenery (1959, 1961). Indeed, Chenery's work has the distinct advantage of using actual production cost data from under-developed regions to examine the potential benefits of co-ordinated development. The results of Murphy et al. (1989), simply depend on the assumptions in their deductive mathematical model.

11. The concentration by economic orthodoxy within the Anglo-American tradition and economic bureaucracy on macro-economics and the failure to either integrate this approach with industrial structure policy or acknowledge the profound industry-specific effects of particular macropolicies is examined in Jones (1993).

12. The Ministry of International Trade and Industry played a major role in the formation of keiretsu. Thus, in addition to Johnson's emphasis on 'micro' and 'macro' aspects of Japanese industry policy, this policy also operated at a 'meso' level, concerned with clusters of industries, and linkages between industries.

13. There has been very considerable recent interest in inter-firm co-operation through the study of 'networks' (BIE 1991) and 'strategic alliances' (BIE 1990).

14. Examples of such approaches include Head (1983) and Hewison, Robison, and Rodan (1993).

15. It is worth noting the very hostile reception given by the Federal bureaucracy (BIE 1984, IAC 1985) to the Metal Trades' Union (1984) CC based development plan for Australian heavy engineering industry.

16. There are of course exceptions. Eatwell (1982) and Bowles and Eatwell (1983) provide an Institutionalist approach to the long-term decline of British industry. In particular, they focus on the effect of the ideology of Free Trade, which up until the latter nineteenth century had been of assistance to British industry, but subsequently became an impediment as other nations such as Germany and the U.S. developed their own manufacturing industries – often behind high tariff walls – and rapidly reduced British manufacturing's share of foreign markets. The maintenance of Free Trade policies is itself explained by the strength of the City of London and its commitment to free financial flows.

17. Thirlwall and McCombie's (1994) exhaustive analysis of the 'balance of payments constraint to growth' highlights the key role of differences in industry structure, investment rates, diffusion of technology, product innovation and so forth in explaining differences between national growth rates. They also emphasize the central place of the state in influencing these variables. Their analysis of state action is limited largely to an updating of Kaldor's views on the causes and implications of the decline of Britain's manufacturing industries.

18. Some work has been done on the evaluation of Australian industry policy programmes from an explicitly Kaldorian perspective (Argyrous 1993; Sheehan, Pappas, Cheng 1994). Earlier detailed proposals for industry policy include the MTFU (1984).

19. On numerous occasions Kaldor emphasized the importance of 'history', though he used this in the special sense that factors of production, consumer preferences, etc. are endogenously created and not exogenously given as general equilibrium theory assumes (Kaldor 1985, p.61). It might be objected that

Kaldor did in fact have a very strong sense of history, and one could cite his important and insightful reflections on the particular conditions giving rise to the Industrial Revolution in Britain. Kaldor emphasized the particular form that the modernization of agriculture took in Britain (enclosures leading to the concentration of production) compared to Continental Europe, and especially France, where the French Revolution resulted in ownership of land being dispersed in relatively small landholdings amongst the peasantry. Kaldor explained that the greater concentration of land in Britain facilitated both the Agricultural Revolution and the Industrial Revolution by the creation of large labour-force and capital for industrial enterprises (Kaldor 1972[a]). Nevertheless, in the context of Kaldor's oeuvre such historical insights are atypical. Setterfield (1997) is also critical of Kaldor and the cumulative causation doctrine more generally for ignoring the role of history and institutional factors in growth and decline. He is critical of 'deterministic' Kaldorian models in which growth is simply a function of initial conditions.

20. In this context it is interesting to note the very high regard in which Young held the Institutionalist and early advocate of the notion of cumulative causation, Thorstein Veblen (Blitch 1995, p.26). Indeed, Young was instrumental in Veblen's initial appointment to Stanford in 1906 (Blitch 1995, p.22). The 'Kaldor–Young version of cumulative causation' has been argued to be 'not as complete as that put forward by Veblen. This lacuna derives from the lack of any explicit treatment of the norms, habits, and institutions which affect human behaviour' (Argyrous and Sethi, 1996, 487–88).

21. There is, in fact, a vital and considerable current research effort based largely on the early 'structuralist' work of Leontief, Hirschman and Chenery. Examples include Chenery's recent work in which he examined long-run patterns of industrialization within a 'disequilibrium growth' model (Chenery, Robinson, Syrquin 1986, pp.14–16). One of the conclusions to the *Proceedings of the Seventh International Conference on Input-Output Techniques* (1979) was that '[e]conomic growth is always a process of structural change, and I/O analysis, which puts such strong emphasis on inter-industry flows, is a most useful tool for its investigation' (p.3). Reference should also be made to the Japanese Institute of Developing Economies, which, over the past thirty years, has undertaken detailed studies of the input–output structure of Asian nations and the evolving linkages between these nations and the economies of Japan and the United States (IDE Occasional Papers). Within Australia, Jensen, West and Hewings (1987, 1988) have examined the relation between the size of regional economies (as measured by gross output and value-added) and their corresponding input–output structures. They found very strong correlations across Australian regions between various sizes of regional economies and their disaggregated input–output structures. The consistency of these results has led them to suggest the existence of 'fundamental economic structures' which relate the size of the market to particular industrial structures.

22. One of the advantages of the Verdoorn Law is that it is calculated at an aggregate industry level and thereby avoids those manifold difficulties faced by industry economists working at an plant or firm level. The Law conforms with Young's entreaty that 'the mechanism of increasing returns is not to be discerned adequately by observing the effects of variations in the size of an individual firm or of a particular industry, for the progressive division and specialization of industries is an essential part of the process by which increasing returns are realized. What is required is that industrial operations be seen as an interrelated whole' (Young 1928, pp.538–39). However, econometric estimates

of aggregate increasing returns such as the Verdoorn Law provide no information on the sources of such returns or their extent in particular manufacturing industries. Amongst current leading theorists McCombie's (1985) empirical work on the measurement of increasing returns in manufacturing industries highlighted the extreme sensitivity of the results to specifications chosen.

23. One area where considerable empirical effort has been made is the role of income elasticity of demand, which has been central to CC theory since Young originally employed the notion in his account of reciprocal demand. Contemporary theorists have studied income elasticity of demand to explain international growth rate differentials and the balance of payments constraint to growth. They highlight the way 'in which some economies produce goods which are expanding fast while other economies produce goods which are in sluggish demand, it is the difference between the income elasticity of exports and imports which is the essence of...Kaldor's view that the opening up of trade between economies may create growth rate differences which are sustained or even widened by the process of trade' (McCombie and Thirlwall 1994, p.431). Differences in the income elasticity of countries' manufactured goods is primarily the result of differences in non-price competitiveness (McCombie and Thirlwall 1994, Ch.4).

24. Rosenberg refers to 'the prevalence, in modern industrial economies of a special kind of external economy. Specifically, many of the benefits of increased productivity flowing from an innovation are captured in industries *other* than the one in which the innovation was made...it is impossible to compartmentalize the consequences of technological innovation even within conventional Marshallian industrial boundaries'. Moreover, historical studies of innovation highlight the role of the capital goods sector. 'One component of changing patterns of industrial specialization is the emergence of specialized firms and industries that produce no final product at all – capital goods. In fact, much of the technological change of the last two centuries or so has been generated by these specialist firms' (Rosenberg 1982, p.71).

25. A good summary of these ideas is provided by Rosenberg (1994, Chapter 1, 'Path-Dependent Aspects of Technological Change').

26. The expression 'big push', meaning a large-scale expansion of demand and supply capacity across several related industries, is taken from Rosenstein-Rodan's (1957) 'Notes on the Theory of the Big Push'.

27. This form of sequential externality was identified by Hirschman (1958) as a 'forward linkage', where for example, the establishment of a steel mill encourages the creation of metalworking firms. In addition, Wade makes extensive use of Hirschman's notion that development is strongly associated with expanding linkages between industrial sectors. Wade in fact employs a measure, the ratio of intermediate to total manufacturing output, as an index of relative industrial development (Wade 1990, pp.44–46). Hirschman has been rightly criticized for being excessively vague about the way externalities 'induce' further investment. In Wade's account and other studies of post-war Japanese development to be noted shortly, the volume and industrial composition of investment are the result, to a very large extent, of state direction.

Bibliography

Agarwala A.N. and Singh S.P (eds), *The Economics of Underdevelopment*, Oxford University Press, New Delhi, 1973.

Amsden A., 'The Division of Labour is Limited by the Rate of Growth of the Market: The Taiwan Machine Tool Industry in the 1970's', *Cambridge Journal of Economics*, Vol.9, 1985, pp.271–284.

Angresano J., *The Political Economy of Gunnar Myrdal. An Institutional Basis for the Transformation Problem*, Edward Elgar, Cheltenham, UK and Lyme US, 1997.

Aoki M., 'The Japanese Firm in Transition' in Inoguchi and Okimoto (eds 1988), pp.263–288.

Argy V. and Stein L., *The Japanese Economy*, Macmillan Press Ltd. 1997.

Argyrous G., 'McKinsey and Co./Australian Manufacturing Council, *Emerging Exporters*', *Journal of Australian Political Economy*, No. 32, December, 1993, pp.106–126.

and Sethi R., 'The Theory of Evolution and the Evolution of Theory', *Cambridge Journal of Economics*, Vol.20, 1996, pp.475–495.

Arndt H.W., 'External Economies in Economic Growth', *The Economic Record*, Vol.31 November 1955, pp.192–214.

Arthur W. B., 'Positive Feedbacks in the Economy', *Scientific American*, February 1990, pp.92–99.

Asimakopulos A., *An Introduction to Economic Theory: Microeconomics*, Oxford University Press, Toronto, 1978.

Australian Bureau of Statistics, *Australian and New Zealand Standard Industrial Classification*, AGPS Canberra (1993).

Research and Experimental Development. Business Enterprises 1994–95. ABS Cat. No. 8104.0.

Australian National Accounts. National Income, Expenditure and Product. ABS Cat. No. 5204.0.

Balogh T., *The Irrelevance of Conventional Economics*, Weidenfeld and Nicolson, London, 1982.

Bardan P., 'Economics of Development and the Development of Economics', *Journal of Economic Perspectives*, Vol.7 No.2, Spring 1993, pp.129–142.

Barna T. (ed.), *Structural Interdependence and Economic Development*, St.Martins Press, New York, 1963.

Barnett W.A., Cornet B., D'Aspremont C., Gabszewicz J., Mas-Colell A. (eds), *Equilibrium Theory and Applications, Proceedings of the Sixth International Symposium in Economic Theory and Econometrics*, Cambridge University Press, 1991.

Baumol W. J., 'Say's (at Least) Eight Laws, or What Say and James Mill May Really Have Meant', *Economica*,Vol.44, May 1977, pp.145–161.

Blair J., *Economic Concentration, Structure, Behaviour, and Public Policy*, Harcourt, Brace, Jovanovich, New York, 1972.

Brain P., *The Microeconomic Structure of the Australian Economy*, Longman Cheshire, Melbourne, 1986.

Bureau of Industry Economics, *A Review of the Report By the Metal Trades Unions, 'Policy for Industry Development and More Jobs'*, Background Paper, 1984.

Flexible Manufacturing Systems: Some Implications for the Theory of Production, Working Paper No. 44, 1988[a].

Importing Technology. Research Report No. 25. 1988[b].

Strategic Alliances in the Internationalisation of Australian Industry, AGPS 1990.
Networks: A Third Form of Organisation, Discussion Paper No. 14, AGPS 1991.
Recent Developments in the Theory of Economic Growth: Policy Implications, Occasional Paper No. 11, AGPS 1992.
Beyond the Innovator: Spillovers From Australian R&D, Occasional Paper No. 16, AGPS 1994.
Blitch C., 'Allyn Young on Increasing Returns', *Journal of Post-Keynesian Economics*, Vol.V. No.3, Spring 1983, pp.350–372.
Allyn Young: The Peripatetic Economist, Macmillan, London and Basingstoke, 1995.
Bohm P., *External Economies in Production*, Almqvist and Wiksell, Stockholm, 1967.
'External Economies' in Eatwell J. et al., 1987, Vol.1., 261–263.
Bowles S. and Eatwell J., 'Between Two Worlds: Interest Groups, Class Structure, and Capitalist Growth' in Mueller D.C. (ed.), *The Political Economy of Growth*, Yale University Press, New Haven, 1983.
Boyer R. and Petit P., 'Kaldor's Growth Theories: Past, Present and Future' in Nell E.J. and Semmler W. (eds), *Nicholas Kaldor and Mainstream Economics: Confrontation or Convergence*, St Martin's Press, New York, 1991.
Chakravarty S., 'Paul Rosenstein-Rodan: An Appreciation', *World Development*, Vol.11 No.1, 1983, pp.73–75.
Chandler A., *Scale and Scope. The Dynamics of Industrial Capitalism*, The Belknap Press, Harvard University, Cambridge Mass. 1994.
Chenery H., 'Comparative Advantage and Development Policy', *American Economic Review*, Vol.51 No.1, March 1961, in Chenery 1979, pp.272–308.
'The Interdependence of Investment Decisions', *The Allocation of Economic Resources*, Abramovitz M. (ed.), Stanford University Press, 1959, in Chenery (1979), pp.173–216.
'The Structuralist Approach to Economic Development' *American Economic Review*, Vol.65, May 1975, pp.310–316.
Structural Change and Development Policy, Oxford University Press, A World Bank Publication, Washington, 1979.
and Watanabe T., 'International Comparisons of the Structure of Production' *Econometrica*, Vol.26, October 1958, pp.487–521.
with Robinson S. and Syrquin M., *Industrialisation and Growth. A Comparative Study*, Oxford University Press, London 1986.
and Srinivasan T.N., *Handbook of Development Economics*, North Holland, 1988.
Clapham J.H., 'Of Empty Economic Boxes', *Economic Journal*, Vol.XXXII No.127, September 1922[a], pp.305–314.
'The Economic Boxes. A Rejoinder', *Economic Journal*, Vol.XXXII No.128, December 1922[b], pp.560–563.
Clark C., *The Conditions of Economic Progress*, Macmillan, London, 1957.
Cornwall J., *Modern Capitalism. Its Growth and Transformation*, Martin Robertson, Oxford 1977.
W. Cornwall, 'Growth Theory and Economic Structure', *Economica*, Vol.61, 1994, pp.237–251.
Cowling K. and Sugden R., 'Capacity, Transnationals, and Industrial Strategy' in Michie J. and Grieve Smith J. (eds) *Creating Industrial Capacity. Towards Full Employment*, Oxford University Press, Oxford 1996.
Crough G. and Wheelwright E., *Australia: A Client State*, Penguin Australia, 1982.
Currie L., 'Allyn Young and the Development of Growth Theory', *Journal of Economic Studies*, Vol 8 No.1, 1981, pp.52–60.

'Implications of an Endogenous Theory of Growth in Allyn Young's Macroeconomic Concept of Increasng Returns', *History of Political Economy* (forthcoming, 1997)

Dagnino-Pastore J.M. 'Balanced Growth: An Interpretation', *Oxford Economic Papers*, Vol.15 No.2, 1963, pp.164–176.

Devine P.J., Jones R.M., Lee N., and Tyson W.J., *An Introduction to Industrial Economics* (Second Edition), George Allen & Unwin, London, 1976.

Dixon R. and Thirlwall A.P., 'A Model of Regional Growth Rate Differences Along Kaldorian Lines', *Oxford Economic Papers*, Vol.27 No.2, July 1975, pp.201–214.

Dorfman R., *The Price System*, Prentice-Hall, New Jersey, 1964.

Dosi G., *Technical Change and Industrial Transformation*, Macmillan, London, 1984.

> Dosi G., Tyson L.., Zysman J., 'Trade, Technologies and Development. A Framework for Discussing Japan' in Johnson C., Tyson L., and Zysman J. (eds), 1991, pp.3–38.

> Pavitt K., and Soete L., *The Economics of Technical Change and International Trade*, Harvester Wheatsheaf, Hemel Hempstead, 1990.

Eatwell J., *Whatever Happened to Britain? The Economics of Decline*, Duckworth, London, 1982.

> 'Import substitution and export-led growth', in Eatwell et al. (eds) 1987, Vol.2, pp.737–738.

> Eatwell J., Milgate M., and Newman P. (eds), *The New Palgrave*, 4 Volumes, Macmillan Press Ltd. London, 1987.

Ellis H.S. and Wallich H.C. (eds), *Economic Development in Latin America*, Macmillan, London, 1963.

Findlay R., 'International Specialisation and the Concept of Balanced Growth: Comment', *Quarterly Journal Of Economics*, Vol.LXXIII, May 1959, pp.339–346.

Fleming J.M., 'External Economies and the Doctrine of Balanced Growth', *Economic Journal*, Vol.LXV June 1955, in Agarwala and Singh (eds) 1973, pp.272–293.

Frank C.R., *Production Theory and Indivisible Commodities*, Princeton University Press, Princeton, 1969.

Gerlach M., 'Keiretsu Organisation in the Japanese Economy' in Inoguchi and Okimoto, (eds) 1988, pp.141–165.

Gold B., 'Changing Perspectives on Size, Scale, and Returns: An Interpretive Essay' *Journal of Economic Literature*, Vol.XIX, March 1981, pp.5–33.

Grossman G.M. and Helpmann E. (1994), 'Endogenous Innovation in the Theory of Growth', *Journal of Economic Perspectives*, Vol.8 No.1 Winter, 1994, 23–44.

Gruchy A., *Contemporary Economic Thought: The Contributions of Neo-Institutionalist Economics*, Augustus Kelly, Clifton, New Jersey, 1972.

Haddad L., 'List Revisited: Dynamic Consideration of Trade and Protection', *The Hetsa Bulletin*, No. 11, Winter 1989.

Hahn F.H., 'Neoclassical Growth Theory' in Eatwell et al. (eds) 1987, Vol.3, pp.625–634.

Hamada K. and Horiuchi A., 'The Political Economy of the Financial Market', in Inoguchi and Okimoto (eds) 1988, pp.223–256.

Hart J.A., *Rival Capitalists. International Competitiveness in the United States, Japan, and Western Europe*, Cornell University Press, 1992.

Hart N., 'Increasing Returns and Marshall's Theory of Value', *Australian Economic Papers*, December 1992, pp.234–244.

Head B., *State and Economy in Australia*, Oxford University Press, Melbourne, 1983.

Hewison K., Robison R., and Rodan G., *Southeast Asia in the 1990's*, Allen and Unwin, Sydney, 1993.

Hennings J.H., 'Roundabout Methods of Production', in Eatwell et al. (eds) 1987, Vol.4, pp.224–225.

Hirschman A. O., *The Strategy of Economic Development*, Yale University Press, New Haven and London, 1958.

'A Dissenter's Confession: "The Strategy of Economic Development" Revisited', in Meier and Seers (eds) (1984), pp.85–115.

'Linkages', in Eatwell et al. (eds) 1987, Vol.3, pp.206–211.

Hodgson G., 'Institutional Rigidities and Economic Growth', in Lawson et al. (1989), pp. 79–102.

Holland S., *Capital versus the Regions*, Macmillan Press, London, 1976.

Industries Assistance Commission, *Issues Arising From the Metal Trades Unions' Proposal for the Selective Development of Manufacturing Industries*, Discussion Paper, 1985.

Inoguchi T. and Okimoto D. (eds), *The Political Economy of Japan*, Stanford University Press, Stanford 1988.

Institute of Developing Economies, *Occasional Papers Series* (various issues) Tokyo, Japan.

Jacobs J., *Cities and the Wealth of Nations*, Penguin Books, Harmondsworth 1984.

Jacquemin A.P. and de Jong H W., *European Industrial Organisation*, John Wiley and Sons, New York and Toronto, 1977.

Jensen R.C., West G.R., and Hewings G.J.D., 'On a Taxonomy of Economies', *Australian Journal of Regional Studies*, No.2, December, 1987, pp.3–24.

'The Study of Regional Economic Structure Using Input-Output Tables' *Regional Studies,* Volume 22, 1988, pp.209–220.

Johnson C., *MITI and the Japanese Miracle*, Stanford University Press, Stanford, 1982.

Tyson L., and Zysman J. (eds), *Politics and Productivity. The Real Story of Why Japan Works,* Harper Business, New York 1991.

Jones E., 'The Macroeconomic Fetish in Anglo-American Economies', *1993 Conference of Economists*, Economic Society of Australia.

Kaldor N., 'The Equilibrium of the Firm', *Economic Journal*, Vol.XLIV, March 1934, pp.60–76.

'Market Imperfection and Excess Capacity', *Economica New Series*, Vol.II, 1935 pp.33–50, reprinted in American Economic Association, *Readings in Price Theory*, George Allen and Unwin 1953, pp.384–403.

'A Model of Economic Growth', *Economic Journal*, Vol.LXVII, 1957, pp.591–624.

with Mirlees J.A., 'A New Model of Economic Growth', *The Review of Economic Studies*, Vol.XXIX, 1962, pp.174–92.

Causes of the Slow Rate of Economic Growth of the United Kingdom, Cambridge University Press, 1966[a].

'Marginal Productivity and the Macro-Economic Theories of Distribution: Comment on Samuelson and Modigliani', *Review of Economic Studies*, Vol.XXXIII, No. 4, 1966[b].

Strategic Factors in Economic Development. The Frank W. Pierce Memorial Lecture, Cornell University, Ithaca New York, 1967.

'The Case for Regional Policies', *Scottish Journal of Political Economy*, Vol.17 November 1970, pp.337–348.

'Conflicts in National Economic Objectives', *Economic Journal*, Vol.LXXXI March 1971, pp.1–16.

'Capitalism and Industrial Development: Some Lessons From Britain's Experience' (first published in Spanish 1972 [a]), in Kaldor 1978, pp.154–172.

'Advanced Technology in a Strategy of Development' (first published by the ILO 1972 [b]), in Kaldor 1978, pp.138–153.

'The Irrelevance of Equilibrium Economics', *Economic Journal*, Vol.LXXXII, December 1972 [c], pp.1237–1255.

'What is Wrong With Economic Theory', *Quarterly Journal of Economics*, Vol.LXXXIX No.3, August 1975, pp.347–357.

Further Essays on Applied Economics, Duckworth, London, 1978.

'The role of increasing returns, technical progress and cumulative causation in the theory of international trade and economic growth', *Economie Appliquée*, Tome XXXIV 1981, pp.593–617.

Limitations of the General Theory, Keynes Lecture in Economics 1982. From the Proceedings of the British Academy, London, Vol.LXVIII Oxford University Press.

'Keynesian Economics After Fifty Years', in Trevithick J. and Worswick G. (eds) *Keynes and the Modern World*, Cambridge University Press 1983, in Kaldor 1989, pp.41–73.

Economics Without Equilibrium, ME Sharpe Inc. New York, 1985.

'Recollections of an Economist', *Banca nazionale del Lavoro Quarterly Review*, March 1986, in Kaldor 1989, pp.13–37.

Further Essays on Economic Theory and Policy, (eds) Targetti F. and Thirlwall A.P., Duckworth, London 1989.

'Nicholas Kaldor's Notes on Allyn Young's LSE Lectures, 1927–29' ed. R.J. Sandilands, *Journal of Economic Studies* (Special Issue), Vol.17 No. 3/4, 1990, pp.18–114.

Causes of Growth and Stagnation in the World Economy Cambridge University Press, Cambridge, 1996.

Kapp K.W., 'The Nature and Significance of Institutionalist Economics', *Kyklos*, Vol.29 No.2, 1976, pp.209–232.

Keynes J.M., *The General Theory of Employment, Interest and Money*, Macmillan, London and Basingstoke, 1983.

Knight F.H., 'Some Fallacies in the Interpretation of Social Cost', *Quarterly Journal of Economics*, Vol.38, August 1924, pp.582–606.

'Decreasing Cost and Comparative Cost: A Rejoinder', *Quarterly Journal of Economics*, Vol.39, February 1925, pp.332–333.

Kornai J., *Anti-Equilibrium. On Economic Systems Theory and the Tasks of Research*, North-Holland Publishing Company, London, 1971.

Landes D., *The Unbound Prometheus*, Cambridge University Press, 1969.

Lawson T., Palma G.T., and Sender S. (eds.), *Kaldor's Political Economy*, Academic Press Ltd. London, 1989.

Lawrence R.J., 'Japan's Different Trade Regime: An Analysis with Particular Reference to Keiretsu', *Journal Of Economic Perspectives*, Vol.7 No.3, Summer 1993, pp.3–20.

Leontief W., 'The Structure of Development', *Scientific American*, Vol.CCIX No.3, September 1963, pp.148–166 in Leontief W., *Input-Output Economics*, Second Edition, Oxford University Press, 1986.

Lewis W.A., 'Economic Development With Unlimited Supplies of Labour', *Manchester School*, May 1954, in Argwala and Singh, pp.400–449.

The Theory of Economic Growth, Allen and Unwin, 1955.

Lieberman M.B., 'The Learning Curve and Pricing in the Chemical Processing Industries', *Rand Journal of Economics*, Vol.15. No.2, Summer 1984, pp.213–228.

'Patents, Learning by Doing, and Market Structure in the Chemical Processing Industries', *International Journal of Industrial Organisation*, Vol.5, 1987, pp.257–276.

Livingstone I. (ed.), *Economic Policy for Development*, Penguin, Harmondsworth 1971.

MacBean A.I. and Nguyen D.T., *Commodity Policies: Problems and Prospects*, Croom Helm, 1987.

Mandelbaum K., *The Industrialisation of Backward Areas*, Oxford University Institute of Statistics, 1945.

Marshall A., *The Principles of Economics*, Eighth Edition, Macmillan and Co. Ltd., 1920.

McCombie J.S.L., 'Kaldor's Laws in Retrospect', *Journal of Post-Keynesian Economics*, Vol.V. No. 3, Spring 1983, pp.414–429.

'Increasing Returns and the Manufacturing Industries: Some Empirical Issues', *The Manchester School*, March 1985, pp.55–75.

and Thirlwall A.P., *Economic Growth and the Balance-of-Payments Constraint*, St Martin's Press, London and New York 1994.

Meade J.E., 'External Economies and Diseconomies in a Competitive Situation', *Economic Journal*, Vol.LXII, March 1952, pp.54–57.

Meier G.M. (ed.), *Leading Issues in Economic Development*, Third Edition, Oxford University Press, 1976.

'The Formative Years', in Meier and Seers (eds) 1984, pp.3–24.

and Seers D.(eds), *Pioneers in Development*, A World Bank Publication, Oxford University Press, 1984.

Metal Trades Unions, *Policy for Industry Development and More Jobs*, August 1984.

Mishan E.J., 'Reflections on Recent Developments in the Concept of External Effects', *The Canadian Journal of Economics and Political Science*, Vol.31, 1965, pp.3–34.

'The Postwar Literature on Externalities', *Journal of Economic Literature*, Vol.9, March 1971, pp.1–28.

Morroni M., *Production Process and Technical Change*, Cambridge University Press, 1992.

Murakami Y., 'The Japanese Model of Political Economy', in Inoguchi and Okimoto (eds) 1988, pp.33–90.

Murphy K.M., Schleifer A., and Vishny R., 'Industrialisation and the Big Push', *Journal of Political Economy*, Vol.97, 1989, pp.1003–1026.

Myrdal G., *An American Dilemma. The Negro Problem and Modern Democracy*, 2 Volumes, Harper and Row, 1944.

The Political Element in the Development of Economic Theory, (First Published 1929, Translated by Paul Streeten), Routledge & Kegan Paul Ltd. London, 1953.

Economic Theory and Underdeveloped Regions, Methuen and Company, London, 1958.

Asian Drama: An Inquiry Into the Poverty of Nations, Twentieth Century Fund, New York, 1968.

Against the Stream: Critical Essays on Economics, Pantheon, New York, 1972.

'Institutional Economics' *Journal of Economic Issues*, Vol.12, No.4, 1978, pp.771–783.

Nath S.K., 'The Theory of Balanced Growth', *Oxford Economic Papers*, Vol.14, 1962, in Livingstone (ed.), 1971, pp.290–310.

Nell E.J. and Semmler W. (eds), *Nicholas Kaldor and Mainstream Economics: Confrontation or Convergence*, St Martin's Press, New York, 1991.

Newman P., 'Young, Allyn Abbott (1876–1929)' in Eatwell et al. (eds) 1987, Vol.4, pp.937–939.

Nurkse R., 'Some International Aspects of the Problem of Economic Development', *American Economic Review*, May 1952, in Agarwala and Singh (1973), pp.256–271.

'Balanced Growth on Static Assumptions', *Economic Journal*, Vol.LXVI, June 1956, pp.365–367.

'The Conflict Between 'Balanced Growth' and International Specialisation', *Lectures on Economic Development*, Faculty of Economics (Istanbul University) and Faculty of Political Science (Ankara University) Istanbul 1958, in Meier 1976 pp.640–643.

'International Trade Theory and Development Policy', in Ellis and Wallich (eds) 1963, pp.234–274.

O'Connor J., *The Fiscal Crisis of the State*, St. Martin's Press, New York, 1973.

Papandreou A., *Externality and Institutions*, Oxford University Press, 1994

Parikh A., 'Differences in Growth Rates and Kaldor's Laws', *Economica*, Vol.45 February 1978, pp.83–91.

Pasinetti L., *Structural Change and Economic Growth. A Theoretical Essay on the Dynamics of the Wealth of Nations*, Cambridge University Press, 1981.

Phibbs P. and Toner P., 'A Note on the Use of Australian Input–Output for Occupational Analysis', *Australian Journal of Regional Studies*, Vol.7, October 1994, pp.1–5.

Pigou A. C., *The Economics of Welfare*, Second Edition, Macmillan and Co. Ltd., London, 1924.

'Empty Economic Boxes: A Reply', *Economic Journal*, Vol.XXXII, December 1922, pp.458–465.

'The Laws of Diminishing and Increasing Cost', *Economic Journal*, Vol.XXXVII, June 1927, pp.188–197.

Pratten C.R., *Economies of Scale in Manufacturing Industry*, Cambridge University Press, U.K., 1971.

Prebisch R., *The Economic Development of Latin America and Its Principal Problems*, U.N. Commission for Latin America, New York, 1950.

Prices Surveillance Authority, *Inquiry Into the Prices of Farm Chemicals*, Report No. 49, 1993.

Proceedings of the Seventh International Conference on Input-Output Techniques (1979), United Nations Industrial Development Organisation, New York 1984.

Ricoy C.J. (1987), 'Cumulative Causation' in Eatwell J. et al. Vol.1, 730–736.

Robertson D.H., 'Those Empty Boxes', *Economic Journal*, Vol.XXXIV, 1924, pp.16–34.

Romer P., *Increasing Returns, Specialisation, and External Economies: Growth as Described by Allyn Young*, Rochester Centre for Economic Research, Working Paper No. 64, December 1986.

'Increasing Returns and New Developments in the Theory of Growth', in Barnett et al. (eds) 1991, pp.83–110.

'The Origins of Endogenous Growth', *Journal of Economic Perspectives*, Vol.8. No.1, Winter 1994, pp.3–22.

Rosenberg N., *Perspectives on Technology*, Cambridge University Press, 1976.

Inside the Black Box: Technology and Economics, Cambridge University Press, 1982.

Exploring the Black Box. Technology, Economics and History, Cambridge University Press, 1994.

Rosenstein-Rodan P.N., 'The Role of Time in Economc Theory', *Economica* (New Series) February, 1934, pp.77–97.

'Problems of Industrialisation in Eastern and South Eastern Europe', *Economic Journal*, Vol.LVIII, June–September 1943, in Agarwala and Singh (1973), pp.245–255.

'Programming in Theory and Italian Practice', *MIT Centre for International Studies*, 1955.

'Notes on the Theory of the "Big Push",' *MIT Centre for International Studies*, 1957, in Ellis and Wallich, (eds) 1963, pp.57–73.

'Natura Facit Saltum: Analysis of the Disequilibrium Growth Process', in Meier and Seers, (eds) 1984, pp.207–221.

Rostow W.W., *Theorists of Economic Growth from David Hume to the Present*, Oxford University Press, 1990

Samuelson P., Hancock K., Wallace R., *Economics*, Second Australian Edition, McGraw-Hill Book Company, Sydney 1975.

Sandilands R.J., *The Life and Political Economy of Lauchlin Currie*, Duke University Press, Durham and London, 1990.

'Allyn Young, Lauchlin Currie and Modern Endogenous Growth Theory', 1997, (unpublished)

Sawyer M.C., *The Economics of Michal Kalecki*, Macmillan, London, 1985.

Scitovsky T., 'Two Concepts of External Economies', *Journal of Political Economy*, Vol.62, April, 1954, in Agarwala and Singh (eds) 1973, pp.295–308.

Setterfield M., 'History versus equilibrium' and the theory of economic growth, *Cambridge Journal of Economics*, Vol 21, 1997, pp.365–378.

Shackle G.L.S., *The Years of High Theory*, Cambridge University Press, 1982.

Sheahan J., 'International Specialisation and the Concept of Balanced Growth', *Quarterly Journal of Economics*, Vol.LXXII, May 1958, pp.183–197.

'Reply', *Quarterly Journal Of Economics*,Vol.LXXIII, May 1959, pp.346–347.

Sheehan P.J., Pappas N., Cheng E., *The Rebirth of Australian Industry*, Centre for Strategic Economic Studies, Victoria University, 1994.

Singh A., 'Third World Competition and De-Industrialisation in Advanced Countries', in Lawson et al. (eds) 1989, pp.103–120.

Smith A., *An Inquiry Into the Nature and Causes of the Wealth of Nations*, (1776), ed. Campbell R.H., Skinner A.S., and Todd W.B., Oxford, Clarendon Press 1976.

Solow R., 'A Contribution to the Theory of Economic Growth', *Quarterly Journal of Economics*, Vol.LXX, February, 1956, pp.65–94.

'Perspectives on Growth Theory', *Journal of Economic Perspectives*, Vol.8. No.1, Winter 1994, pp.45–54.

Spraos J., 'The Statistical Debate on the Net Barter Terms of Trade Between Primary Commodities and Manufactures: A Comment and Some Additional Evidence', *Economic Journal*, Vol.XC, 1980, pp.107–128.

'Kaldor on Commodities' in Lawson et al. (eds) 1989, pp.201–222.

Sraffa P., 'The Laws of Returns Under Competitive Conditions', *Economic Journal*, Vol.XXXVI, December 1926, pp.535–550.

Stein. L., *Japanese Industrial Policy*, Centre for Japanese Economic Studies Macquarie University, July 1993, Working Paper no.93–7.

Stern. N. 'The Economics of Development: A Survey', *Economic Journal*, Vol.99, 1989, pp. 597–685.

Stigler J., 'The Division of Labour is Limited by the Extent of the Market', *Journal of Political Economy*, Vol 59, 1951, pp.185–193.

Streeten P., 'Unbalanced Growth', *Oxford Economic Papers*, New Series Vol.2, No.2, June 1959, pp.167–190.

'Comment on Hirschman', in Meier and Seers (eds) 1984, pp.115–118.

'Myrdal, Gunnar (1898–1987)', in Eatwell et al. (eds) 1987, Vol.3, pp.581–583.

Svennilson I., *Growth and Stagnation in the European Economy*, UN Economic Commission for Europe, Geneva 1954.

Swan T., 'Circular Causation', *The Economic Record*, Vol.38, No. 84, December, 1962. pp.421–426.

Syrquin M. 'Patterns of Structural Change' in Chenery and Srinivasan (eds) 1988, Vol.1. pp.202–273.

Targetti F. 'Change and Continuity in Kaldor's Thought on Growth and Distribution', in Nell and Semmler (eds) 1991, pp.13–47.

Thirlwall A.P., 'The Balance of Payments Constraint as an Explanation of International Growth Rate Differences', *Banca Nazionale Del Lavoro Quarterly Review*, Vol 128, 1979, pp.45–53.

'A Plain Man's Guide to Kaldor's Growth Laws', *Journal of Post-Keynesian Economics*, Vol.4 No.3, Spring 1983, pp.345–358.

Nicholas Kaldor, Wheatsheaf Books, Brighton, 1987.

'Nicholas Kaldor 1908–86' in Nell and Semmler (eds) 1991, pp.13–47.

Growth and Development, Fifth Edition, MacMillan, 1994.

Toner P.A., 'The Crisis of Equipment Investment in Australia', *Journal of Australian Political Economy*, No. 22, February 1988, pp.39–56.

Vassilakis S., 'Learning By Doing', in Eatwell et al. (eds) 1987, Vol.3, pp.151–152.

'Increasing Returns to Scale', in Eatwell et al. (eds) 1987, Vol.2, pp.761–765.

Verdoorn P.J., 'Factors that Determine the Growth of Labour Productivity', *L'industria,* 1949 (Translated by G. and A.P. Thirlwall. Privately circulated).

Viner J., 'Cost Curves and Supply Curves', *Zeitschrift fur Nationalokonomie*, III (1931) pp.23–46 in American Economic Association, Stigler J. and Boulding K. (eds) *Readings in Price Theory*, George Allen & Unwin London, 1953, pp.198–232.

Wade R., *Governing the Market: Economic Theory and the Role of Government in East Asian Industrialisation*, Princeton University Press, 1990.

Whiteman J., 'Globalisation and Strategic Trade Policy: Some Implications for the Australian Information Technology Industry', *Prometheus*, Vol.8, No. 1, June 1990 pp.35–49.

World Bank, *The East Asian Miracle. Economic Growth and Public Policy*, Oxford University Press, New York, 1993.

Yamamura K., *Japan's Economic Structure: Should it Change,* Society for Japanese Studies, Seattle, 1990.

Yoshikawa H., 'High Economic Growth of the Japanese Economy and Its End: an Explanation by a Model of Demand-Led Growth', *Conference on the Contemporary Japanese Economy*, August, Macquarie University 1993.

Young A., 'Pigou's Wealth and Welfare', *Quarterly Journal of Economics*, Vol.XXVII, 1913, pp.672–686.

'Increasing Returns and Economic Progress', *Economic Journal*, Vol.XXXVIII, December 1928, pp.527–542.

'Supply and Demand' entry in *The Encyclopaedia Britannica*, Fourteenth Edition, Vol.21. pp.579–580 New York 1929[a].

'Economics' entry in *The Encyclopaedia Britannica*, Fourteenth Edition, Vol.7, pp.925–932 New York 1929[b].

'Big Business: How the Economic System Grows and Evolves Like a Living Organism', *The Book of Popular Science*, Vol.15, New York 1929[c] in Kaldor 1990, pp.161–170.

Index